such Manner as shall be judged most conducive to the public Weal.

4. That no Man, or Set of Men, are entitled to exclusive or separate Emoluments or privileges from the Community, but in consideration of public Services; which not being descendible, neither ought the Offices of Magistrate, Legislator, or Judge to be hereditary.

5. That the Legislative & executive powers of the State should be separate & distinct from the judicial; and that the Members of the two first may be restrained from Oppression by feeling & participating the Burthens of the People, they should at fixed periods, be reduced to a private Station, & return into that Body from which they were originally taken; and the Vacancys be supplied by frequent, certain & regular Elections.

6. That Elections of Members, to serve as Representatives of the People in the Legislature, ought to be free; and that all Men having sufficient Evidence of permanent common Interest with, & Attachment to the Community, have the Right of Suffrage; and can not be taxed, or deprived of their property for public Uses, without their own Consent, or that of their Representatives so elected, nor bound by any Law to which they have not, in like Manner, assented for the Common Good.

7. That all power of suspending Laws, or the Execution of Laws, by any Authority, without Consent of the Representatives of the People, is injurious to their Rights, and ought not to be exercised.

That

THE CASE FOR LIBERTY

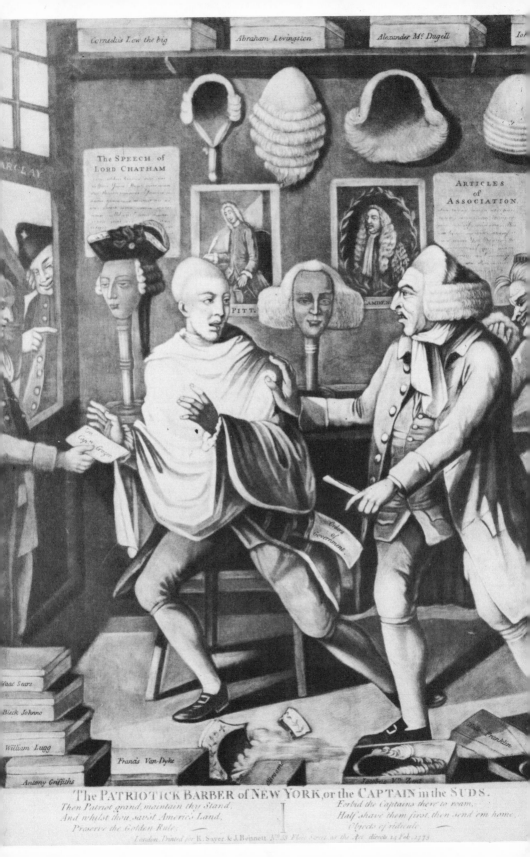

The PATRIOTICK BARBER of NEW YORK, or the CAPTAIN in the SUDS.

Then Patriot grand, maintain thy Stand,　　　　Forbid the Captains there to roam,
And whilst thou sav'st Americ's Land,　　　　Half shave them first, then send em home,
Preserve the Golden Rule;　　　　　　　　　　Objects of ridicule.

London, Printed for R. Sayer & J. Bennett, No 53 Fleet Street, as the Act directs, 14 Feb. 1775.

THE CASE

FOR

LIBERTY

By HELEN HILL MILLER

THE UNIVERSITY OF NORTH CAROLINA PRESS

CHAPEL HILL

CONTENTS

		Page
List of Illustrations		vii
Introduction		xi

I. FREEDOM OF RELIGION
*Virginia, jailings of Baptist preachers, especially
Waller, Webber, et al., in Middlesex County, 1771*   1

II. FREEDOM OF THE PRESS
*Philadelphia, the Bradford case, 1692; New York,
the Zenger case, 1735*   29

III. THE RIGHT TO BEAR ARMS
*Virginia, courts-martial following Bacon's Rebel-
lion, 1676*   67

IV. QUARTERING OF TROOPS
*New York, indictment of Alexander MacDougall
for seditious libel, 1771*   101

V. SEARCH AND SEIZURE
*Massachusetts, Superior Court hearings on writs
of assistance, 1761*   121

VI. DUE PROCESS OF LAW
*South Carolina, imprisonment of Thomas Powell
for contempt of the Council, 1773*   145

VII. TRIAL IN THE VICINAGE
Rhode Island, investigation of the Gaspee *burning by a special tribunal, 1773*   163

VIII. THE RIGHT TO A JURY
New York, Forsey v. Cunningham, 1764   185

IX. FREEDOM FROM EXTORTION
*North Carolina, mock trials by the Regulators at
Hillsborough, 1770*   203

Note on Sources	227
Index	251

LIST OF ILLUSTRATIONS

Page

THE PATRIOTIC BARBER OF NEW YORK, OR THE CAPTAIN
IN THE SUDS   *Frontispiece*

*Mezzotint, 1773. Courtesy, the I. N. Phelps Stokes
Collection of American Historical Prints, Prints
Division, The New York Public Library.*

GEORGE WHITEFIELD   6

*Oil painting by John Wollaston. Courtesy, National
Portrait Gallery, London.*

AN ATTEMPT TO LAND A BISHOP IN AMERICA   23

*Engraving, 1768. Courtesy, Prints and Photographs
Division, Library of Congress.*

PRINTERS AT WORK   49

Detail from Centennial Mirror 1776-1876, *lithograph
by the American Oleograph Co., 1876.*

ANDREW HAMILTON   59

*Oil painting, copy of a lost original, by A. Wertmüller,
1808. Courtesy, The Historical Society of Pennsylvania.*

THE HABEAS CORPUS, OR THE WILD GEESE FLYING AWAY WITH FOX
TO AMERICA   65

*Engraving, 1782. Courtesy, Prints and Photographs
Division, Library of Congress.*

AN INDIAN OF VIRGINIA   72

*Etching by Wenceslaus Hollar, 1645. Courtesy, Prints
Division, The New York Public Library.*

SIR WILLIAM BERKELEY   79

*Portrait by Sir Peter Lely. By kind permission of the
Trustees of the late Randal Thomas Mowbray
8th Earl of Berkeley.*

List of Illustrations

CARTOUCHE FROM THE HERRMAN MAP OF VIRGINIA AND
MARYLAND, 1673   98
Courtesy, Map Division, Library of Congress.

JOHN WILKES, ESQ.   113
*Engraving after William Hogarth, 1763. Courtesy,
Prints Division, The New York Public Library.*

THE NEW YORK COMMON   116
*Drawing by Pierre Eugène de Simitière, 1770. Courtesy,
Ridgway Branch, Library Company of Philadelphia.*

JAMES OTIS   132
*Oil painting by Joseph Blackburn, 1755. Courtesy,
Mr. and Mrs. Carlos Happ and Hirschl-Adler Galleries,
New York.*

BRITISH SHIPS LANDING TROOPS, BOSTON HARBOR   139
*Engraving by Paul Revere, 1768. Courtesy, Museum
of Fine Arts, Boston.*

THE CURIOUS ZEBRA   143
*Engraving, 1776. Courtesy, Prints and Photographs
Division, Library of Congress.*

MR. AND MRS. RALPH IZARD   151
*Oil painting by John Singleton Copley in Rome, 1775.
Courtesy, Museum of Fine Arts, Boston.*

MR. PETER MANIGAULT AND HIS FRIENDS   153
*Copy by Louis Manigault from a drawing by George
Roupell, 1754. Courtesy, Joseph E. Jenkins and
American Heritage Publishing Co., Inc.*

A POLITICAL CONCERT: THE VOCAL PARTS BY (1) MISS AMERICA,   161
(2) FRANKLIN, (3) F-X, (4) KEPP-LL, (5) MRS. BRITTANIA,
(6) SHELB—N, (7) DUN-I-G, (8) BENEDICK RATTLE SNAKE
*Engraving, 1783. Courtesy, Prints and Photographs
Division, Library of Congress.*

CAPTAIN ABRAHAM WHIPPLE   170
  *Oil painting by Edward Savage. Courtesy, U.S. Naval
  Academy.*

THE ABLE DOCTOR, OR AMERICA SWALLOWING THE BITTER DRAUGHT 181
  Engraving from the London Magazine, *May 1, 1774.
  Courtesy, Prints and Photographs Division, Library of
  Congress.*

CADWALLADER COLDEN WITH WARREN DELANCEY   191
  *Oil painting by Matthew Pratt. Courtesy of Peter DeL.
  Swords and the Museum of the City of New York.*

WILLIAM SMITH, JR.   195
  *Miniature by Henry Stubble. Courtesy, The New-York
  Historical Society, New York City.*

THE RECONCILIATION BETWEEN BRITANIA AND HER DAUGHTER
AMERICA   201
  *Engraving, 1782. Courtesy, Prints and Photographs
  Division, Library of Congress.*

EDMUND FANNING   208
  *Engraving. Courtesy, North Carolina Department of
  Archives and History, Raleigh.*

HUSBAND TOSSING THE "TAXES" ON THE TABLE BEFORE THE
GOVERNOR   211
  Reproduced in Some Neglected History of North Caro-
  lina, *by William Edwards Fitch, M.D., 1905.*

TO BE SOLD TO THE BEST BIDDER   212
  *Engraving, 1773. Courtesy, Prints and Photographs
  Division, Library of Congress.*

HILLSBOROUGH DISTRICT COURT—TRIAL, REFERENCE, AND
APPEARANCE DOCKETS (1768-73)   218
  *Facsimile showing Regulator defacings in right column.
  Courtesy, North Carolina Department of Archives and
  History, Raleigh.*

List of Illustrations

MAP OF THE HILLSBOROUGH-ALAMANCE AREA   222

*Detail from Mouzon's "Accurate Map of North and South
Carolina," 1775. Courtesy, Map Division, Library of
Congress.*

THE VIRGINIA DECLARATION OF RIGHTS   *End Papers*

*Facsimile of the first draft in the handwriting of George
Mason, 1776. Courtesy, Board of Regents, Gunston
Hall, Lorton, Virginia.*

INTRODUCTION

A New York lawyer, in Washington after an excursion through tidewater Virginia, asked me a question that resulted in this book.

At Gunston Hall, a few miles down the Potomac from Mount Vernon, he had seen a facsimile of the first declaration of rights to be drawn up in America, written by George Mason and adopted when Virginia turned from colonial status to statehood at Williamsburg in 1776.

We discussed why, in colony after colony as the Revolution necessitated new governmental structure, members of the constitutional conventions of the new states had placed first importance on setting down in black and white and formally adopting general declarations of the rights of man and of citizens; and why, in spite of the fact that these safeguards already existed on the state level, willingness to ratify the federal Constitution in such key states as Massachusetts, Virginia, and New York had turned on the immediate addition of amendments comprising a bill of rights.

We spoke of the English ancestors of the American documents: Magna Carta and the Bill of Rights of the Glorious Revolution of 1689. He noted that even some of the exact wording of the federal Bill of Rights repeats earlier English affirmations: both Article 10 of the English Bill of Rights and the Eighth Amendment to the Constitution declare that excessive bail shall not be required, nor excessive fines imposed, nor cruel and unusual punishments inflicted.

I pointed to a difference that goes beyond wording. The third of the trio of fundamental rights that the English bill adopted from John Locke's philosophy, the rights to life, liberty, and property, was not accepted here without change. The phrase by which George Mason replaced it was an early example of the classical American emphasis on opportunity rather than on property: "Life and liberty, with the means of acquiring and possessing property, and pursuing and obtaining happiness and safety."

In addition to the ancestors of the American bills, we spoke of their descendents, especially the *Déclaration des droits de l'homme* of the French revolutionaries of 1789.

But the lawyer did not allow generalities of political philosophy to distract him from his professional predilections. "Nobody can tell me," he suddenly insisted, "that when the first copies of the declaration of rights were lifted off the press in a given colony, the citizens who stood around the printer's shop and read them were thinking in abstractions. What jumped to their minds were the names of well-remembered legal tests, trials in their vicinity in which these rights were at issue before a court in particular form, cases with a real plaintiff and a real defendent, ending in the upholding or denial of a particular assertion of right.

"Unless I'm very much mistaken," he went on, "when Citizen John Doe finished reading his colony's declaration of rights, he turned to Citizen Richard Roe and said with satisfaction, 'Well, Article X certainly takes care of the so-and-so case.' And Richard Roe agreed."

The eyes behind the legal glasses then widened with intensity; looking straight at me, in his best cross-examining manner, he directed his question: "Now tell me, *what were those cases?*"

At that time, beyond mumbling something about freedom of the press and the Zenger case, I had no ready answer.

Yet in our own day, it is not hard to make a list of court cases in which a clash of principles has made the contest broadly—and emotionally—familiar to citizens who ordinarily have little interest in matters before the courts. The trust-busting indictments of the Theodore Roosevelt era; the Brandeis briefs on wages and hours; the Schecter case that buried the NRA with the carcass of one sick chicken in the New Deal years; the still unresolved Sacco-Vanzetti case; the Hiss case; the ten-month trial of strength between Judge Medina and the eleven Communists accused of conspiracy to overthrow the United States government by force in 1949; the school desegregation cases beginning with the Supreme Court's ruling in 1954; the legislative reapportionment cases and the school prayer cases of the 1960's—all have had effects on economic practices, political structures, or social institutions far beyond the scope of the usual legal encounter.

The decision in each of these cases, when announced, caused the side whose contention was upheld to swell with the righteousness of the vindicated. The side whose contention was denied often choked with the disappointed anger of those who feel that justice has done them wrong. And they swelled or choked, not solely as individuals, but as individuals holding themselves to be representative of a social order in which they deeply believed.

To some observers, a judgment represented legalized injustice and the end of an era; to others, substantiation of inherent rights and justification of the coming society. The only point on which both sides could agree was that the decision would have an aftermath.

What were the colonial counterparts of these decisions?

Over the years since the lawyer asked his question, as opportunity offered, I have taken my reporter's notebook and set out to find an answer. In ranging up and down the eastern seaboard, I have come upon many cases. Those I describe come from more than half the colonies. But the list is by no means exhaustive; other cases, in other places, stirred popular feeling quite as much as these.

As a framework, I have used the eventual greatest common denominator of the various bills of rights adopted in the several colonies at the time of the Revolution—the Bill of Rights incorporated into the federal Constitution in 1791.

Drawing on their own respective bills, the state conventions that ratified the Constitution proposed a vast number of articles for inclusion in the federal document. From these, Madison drafted twelve amendments, which the first Congress approved and proposed to the states. Ten of the twelve were adopted; the first eight were substantive affirmations of the rights of man.

In describing a case illustrative of part or all of each of these articles, I begin the account by citing the wording of the federal bill and end it with its counterpart as phrased in the colony in which the case occurred. As program notes for nine dramas of colonial courtrooms, I have supplied today's audience with an account of the dramatis personae—bench, bar, litigants, spectators. I have also called attention to the larger setting, popular and governmental, in which the actors presented a particular trial of strength and will. Occasionally, I have added a brief epilogue—for instance, the story of the passage of the legislation required to make effective Virginia's affirmation of religious freedom.

Cases such as these are never tried in obscurity—they are tried in the floodlight of social conflict. In order that a rule of law may exist, an area of common consent must underlie the body politic; beyond that area, decisions are made by force and violence. All of the cases I report are borderline cases. Force and violence, on or off stage, was a component of most of them. Contemporary upholders of the status quo condemned that force and violence as ungoverned. Those who resorted to it, from dissenters to rebels, justified their action as an exercise of natural rights transcending the prerogative of the sovereign or the sovereignty of the statute book.

Some of the instances I cite are hearings or attempts to obtain evidence rather than court cases. No trial was in process when the Massachusetts Superior Court heard argument on the validity of issuing general search warrants. The special tribunal of colonial chief justices that sat at Newport, Rhode Island, as a commission of inquiry—parallel, in its way, to the commission under Chief Justice Warren that probed the facts of President Kennedy's assassination—was set up in an effort to discern who burned His Brittanic Majesty's schooner *Gaspee*. One chapter recounts the action of a mock court. One case was a court martial.

Frequently, the trial of an individual was part of an elaborate choreography, a test of strength between an appointed governor in council and an elected assembly, or between citizenry and officialdom, that eventually brought more and more people on stage until the larger contest absorbed the smaller. Sometimes a suit was brought for its shock value and later withdrawn for foreseeable lack of evidence.

The circumstances of these colonial trials transpose readily into contemporary circumstances. In the development of freedom of religion in Virginia, court trials witnessed the slow erosion of a social attitude over half a century until, after violence and ridicule had run their course, a tolerance that was unthinkable at the beginning of the transition became unnoticed at its close. Perhaps a likeness will some day be drawn between the development of toleration in the eighteenth century with regard to religion and in the twentieth century with regard to race.

The cases in which utterance of seditious libel was charged by a government unwilling to permit criticism—the press cases in Philadelphia and New York—sound very familiar to a generation that has witnessed suppression of the *Berliner Tageblatt* and *La Prensa*, observed confiscations of *Le Monde* and *L'Express* in Algeria, and read the party press of Moscow and Peiping.

The story of the resort to arms at the time of Bacon's Rebellion is the story of the American counterpart of the Cromwellian period, ending, as did its English predecessor, in the death of a dynamic leader who left behind an insufficient structure of government. The contemporary revolutions in the developing countries afford many parallels.

Among citizens' safeguards enumerated in the Bill of Rights, the right to be free from the quartering of troops in peacetime appears as quaint anachronism. Yet the fundamental objection to it as a highly inequitable means of securing military supplies has a current counterpart: the peacetime draft requires some households to contribute manpower to the armed forces, but not others.

The issue over the use of general search warrants by eighteenth-century customs officers looking for contraband is very similar to today's controversy over the use of the wiretap and the bug by enforcement officers of various specialized agencies and the FBI.

Unauthorized publication of material prepared for executive sessions of the legislature, which caused the imprisonment of South Carolina's printer in Charleston in 1773, is in general taken less seriously now than in the eighteenth century. In our time, the leaking and receiving of classified government information rarely brings people to court. Most of the persons recently jailed for contempt of Congress have made use of the self-incrimination clause of the Fifth Amendment before going in, rather than the due process clause in order to get out.

While many revolutionary documents, including the Declaration of Independence, used the past tense in ranking transportation for trial overseas high among the crimes of George III, this furor was an instance of the political potency of viewing the nonexistent with alarm. The possibility of transportation was indeed a clear and present danger during the inquiry into the burning of *Gaspee,* and parliamentary authority for it had been specifically reaffirmed with America in view. But actual instances are elusive. Yet twentieth-century objections have been politically successful with far less basis. In each country where publicly operated insurance systems for payment of medical bills have been brought forward, the organized medical profession has protested against government control of their professional skill. Such control was not proposed, and where such systems have been adopted has not occurred, but this has in no way detracted from the political potency of the protest.

Deftness in deflecting cases from a regular court with a jury into the hands of administrative agencies whose top staff includes reliable friends pays the expense accounts of many a legal lobbyist in Washington. Uninformed but obstinate office-holders whose pride can be played upon as in the attempted appeal of *Forsey* v. *Cunningham* in the 1760's did not die out with New York's aging acting governor, Cadwallader Colden.

The contrast in the South between the mighty and the lowly, between the grandees of the tidewater capitals and the people of the foothills, has been softened by the coming of literacy and industry and by wider exercise of the vote. The University of North Carolina has risen in the very county where the eighteenth-century Regulators held mock court in Hillsborough and fought the Battle of Alamance. But in pockets of the South, in large areas of the Southwest, and in the big cities from New York to Los Angeles, petty extortion goes on, practiced by local officials on poor people who are either illiterate or not literate in English, and now, unlike the Regulators at Alamance, the exploited know in advance which side has the bigger artillery.

I am a reporter. I have relied on the reporter's technique of direct quotes—from letters, memoirs, eyewitness accounts, official texts—to convey what was felt and what was thought as well as what happened. A *cause célèbre* is not contained in the hard facts of the court record: one must know why the case acquired enhanced proportions; why the spotlight of a whole society was turned in its direction; why the issue was magnified until the plaintiff and the defendant took on theatrical proportions as protagonists of human destiny.

Around any courtroom, official documents set forth the facts established, the arguments presented, the judgments given. Comments by witnesses, press stories, reactions of spectators supply the color, suggest the motives, estimate the results of the litigation. With regard to a rather surprising number of eighteenth-century cases, both types of source material exist.

So from these public records and private accounts, here is my answer to the lawyer's question. The evidence illumines critical hours in the nation's past. It also makes more intelligible some of the events and forces in our own time and lives.

CHAPTER I

FREEDOM OF RELIGION

The Bill of Rights: Congress shall make no law respecting an establishment of religion, or prohibiting the free exercise thereof. . . .

BACKGROUND

U p and down the American coast, in the mid-eighteenth century, vast missionary journeys traversed the wilderness. In 1735, the Wesley brothers crossed the ocean to evangelize in the South. Over the next two decades, seven transatlantic preaching missions by their colleague, George Whitefield, took him from Savannah, Georgia, to York, Maine, before his body was laid to rest in Newburyport, Massachusetts. In New England and later from Princeton, the reverberating voice of Jonathan Edwards summoned Christians to a more fervid and personal religion; many of his followers became itinerant evangelists and settled in the South.

Especially among those whom the rich and well-born referred to as the lower orders, religious awakening engendered new confidence. By contrast to the ritual of the Established Church, revivalist worship disregarded traditional form, evoked faith and feeling. New converts gathered in groups that became new denominations, competitors of the state church.

The focal point of the new denominations was Philadelphia, where the speaker of the assembly, Andrew Hamilton, declared in 1739: "By many years' Experience, we find that an Equality among Religious Societies, without distinguishing any one Sect with greater Privileges than another, is the most effectual Method to discourage Hypocrisy, promote the Practice of Moral Virtues, and prevent the Plagues and Mischiefs that always attend religious squabbling." The Philadelphia Baptist Association was freely formed in 1707. A Presbyterian church was founded in 1701, then a presbytery, and in 1717 a synod.

Philadelphia had a special place in Presbyterian developments for a further reason: it was a major port of entry to the New World at a time when bad crop-years in Ireland redoubled Scotch-Irish emigration. Much of the Calvinist influx into America funneled through Philadelphia harbor before it fanned out into the back country.

As the wagons moved west and south down the long fertile valleys—past Lancaster, York, Hagerstown to Winchester, Virginia, along the Shenandoah, all the way to the Waxhaws of the

Carolinas—these settlers kept in touch with their co-religionists in Philadelphia. They looked to them for spiritual support, for theological instruction, and upon occasion for ministers. They sent their ablest youth back for training, first at the Tennants' Log College, then Princeton. At times, the Philadelphia synod represented them in an almost political capacity; in 1738, it initiated an agreement with Governor Gooch of Virginia to assure enjoyment of the Toleration Act of 1689 by incoming Presbyterians in the empty areas beyond the Blue Ridge.

By the end of the 1760's the degree of toleration to be granted dissenters in the settled parts of the country, the relation of their churches to the Established Church, and the relation of both to the state had become major political issues. In tidewater Virginia, jailings of Baptists determined to worship as they chose insistently and repeatedly dramatized a demand for fundamental reconsideration of the conditions of religious liberty, to which decisive strength was added by the growth of Presbyterianism in the counties above the fall lines.

When the Virginia Declaration of Rights of 1776 was drafted, George Mason affirmed that religious expression "can be directed only by reason and conviction, not by force or violence," and James Madison clarified the difference between a doctrine of toleration which merely demands that the state treat all denominations alike, and a doctrine of religious liberty which regards freedom of worship as an inalienable natural right over which the state can properly exercise no jurisdiction whatsoever.

The Virginia constitutional convention adopted the declaration of rights, including the Mason-Madison article, but left to subsequent legislation the difficult decision as to how organized religion should receive its support: whether, at least in part, from public taxation, with continuance of the assessment of compulsory tithes such as had sustained the Church of England; or exclusively from private voluntary offerings. The statute of religious liberty drafted by Jefferson in 1779 proposed the latter alternative, with complete separation of church and state, but many were attracted by the competing general assessment bill, a measure to continue compulsory tithing, with pro rata division of the proceeds among recognized denominations.

It was only after ten years of incessant discussion, and by the narrowest of political margins, that Jefferson's view, newly ex-

3

pounded in Madison's *Memorial and Remonstrance,* prevailed against the general assessment bill, and complete separation of church and state became law in Virginia.

The debate underlined the contrast in philosophic background between American developments and the parallel struggle for religious freedom in the Old World. In revolutionary France, the dancer dressed as Liberty who performed on the high altar of Notre Dame dramatized an anticlericalism bent on elimination of organized religion from the national life. In the American colonies, on the contrary, the change in relationship between church and state was the result of a new access of religious fervor.

The eclipse of the Church of England and the neglect of its buildings in the years just after the Revolution were temporary and political, due to the statutory ties of the Establishment with the sovereign from which the colonies were breaking away. After reorganization as the Protestant Episcopal church, its congregations gradually reassembled. And to the growing number of expanding denominations now no longer stigmatized as dissenters, the new freedom was a very positive liberty. The absence of any form of state control released their voluntary initiative for public expression of their devotion through orders of service and ministers of their own choosing, in buildings erected through their own sacrifice.

THE CASE

"I would give a hundred guineas," declaimed London's theater idol David Garrick, "if I could only say 'OH!' like Mr. Whitefield." What manner of man was this new-styled evangelist, whose missionary journeys left his mark on the whole Atlantic seaboard?

Just as William Penn, at the age of twelve, had been "suddenly surprised with an inward comfort," Whitefield while a student at Oxford had undergone a "new birth." Yet the start of his ministry was orthodox enough. He was ordained deacon and offered a promising curacy in London—but he declined it when the Wesleys urged him to follow them to Georgia. On his return, he was ordained a Church of England priest—but the personal fervor of his preaching and the size and enthusiasm of his audiences shortly caused the more conventional divines to denounce him as a "spiritual pickpocket." On his second trip to America, the bishop of London's representative in Charleston preached from the text: "Those who have turned the world upside down have come hither also."

As church doors closed against him, he took to exhorting all who would listen from a portable pulpit outside in the open fields. These open-air assemblies gave full force to his exceptional physical asset—his penetrating, impelling, theatrical voice. As to its volume, when he reached Philadelphia Benjamin Franklin made a characteristically precise measurement:

He preached one evening from the top of the courthouse steps, which are in the middle of Market Street, and on the west side of Second-Street, which crosses it at right angles. Both streets were filled with hearers to a considerable distance. Being among the hindmost in Market-street, I had the curiosity to learn how far he could be heard, by retiring backward down the street toward the river; and I found his voice distinct till I came near Front-street, when some noises in the street obscured it.

Imagining then a semi-circle, of which my distance should be the radius, and that it was filled with auditors, to each of whom I allowed two square feet, I computed he might well be heard by more than thirty thousand. This reconciled me to the newspaper accounts of his having preached to twenty-five thousand people.

5

Ruefully, Franklin also cites an instance of the persuasiveness of what he said. Whitefield was soliciting funds up and down the coast for erection of an orphanage in Georgia. Interviewed on its behalf, Franklin refused to contribute "as Georgia was then destitute of materials and workmen. . . . I thought it would have been better to have built the house at Philadelphia, and brought the children to it." But that was not the last of the matter: "I happened soon after to attend one of his sermons, in the course of which I perceived he intended to finish with a collection, and I silently resolved that he should get nothing from me. I had in my pocket a handful of copper money, three or four silver dollars, and five pistoles in gold. As he proceeded I began to soften, and concluded to give the copper. Another stroke of his oratory made me ashamed of this and determined me to give the silver; and he finished so admirably, that I emptied my pockets wholly into the collector's dish, gold and all."

Whitefield himself was quite aware of his magnetism. Describing one preaching session, he wrote: "After singing, I gave a word of exhortation; with what power none can fully express but those who saw it. Oh, how the word did fall like a hammer and like a fire. What weeping was there!"

His rounded sentences on drunkards included the awful assurance: "Indeed you shall drink, but it shall be a cup of God's fury, for in the hand of the Lord there will be a cup of fury; it will be full-mixed; and as for the dregs thereof, all the drunkards of the land shall suck them out."

The "almost Christian" was one of his favorite themes. Castigating the semifaithful, he demanded, "Good God! how will you be able to stand at the bar of an angry, sin-avenging judge, and see so many discourses you have dispised, so many ministers, who once longed and labour'd for the salvation of your precious and immortal souls, brought out as so many swift witnesses against you?"

But at the same time, he assured the child of God that when received into glory he would be made to know "why he met with such a trial, and from such a quarter—why the whip sometimes was turned into a scorpion and the furnace heated seven times hotter; then the believer sees the need of it." Apocalyptic preaching of this type was unheard and unheard of in the churches of the Establishment.

The somnolence of the Church of England in a colony such as Virginia had a double cause. Well satisfied with things as they

7

were, the upper orders of society, from whom vestrymen were chosen, were content of a Sunday to have their sociable churchyard gatherings sanctified by an ordered ritual; but in general they desired little more. And though local vestries sometimes took initiative in presenting candidates, many of the rectors assigned to Virginia parishes by the bishop of London were not rated too highly even by the bishop: "A great part are the Scotch or Irish, who can get no employment at home, and enter into the service more out of necessity than choice."

On his first trip south, Whitefield made numerous observations on the society of which the Established Church was a part: "At Annapolis, I preached twice and spoke home to some ladies concerning the vanity of their false politeness. But Alas, they are wedded to their Quadrille and Ombre. The minister of the place . . . will not frighten people . . . with harsh doctrine—he loves to prophesy smooth things."

In upper-class company, the evangelist felt little understood: "If I talk of the Spirit, I am a Quaker, if I say grace at Breakfast, and behave seriously, I am Presbyterian. Alas! What must I do to be accounted a Member of the Church of England?"

From Williamsburg he wrote, "In these parts, satan seems to lead people captive at his will. The distance of the plantations prevents people's assembling themselves together. Here are no great towns, as in other provinces, and the commonality is made up of Negroes and convicts, and if they pretend to serve God, their masters, Pharoah-like, cry out, 'Ye are idle, ye are idle.' "

Yet a wide, if secular, welcome awaited him at the Virginia capital: he dined with the governor and when he paid his respects to Mr. Commissary Blair at William and Mary College, he found Blair the most worthy clergyman with whom he had so far conversed in America. He was invited to preach at Bruton Parish Church, where *The Virginia Gazette* reported "there was a numerous Congregation, and 'tis thought there would have been many more, if timely Notice had been given. . . . His extraordinary Manner of Preaching, gains him the Admiration and Applause of most of his Hearers."

But while the great awakening owed much of its initial impetus to the commonalty's response to evangelists like Whitefield, it was only as dissent acquired a local habitation that it became a power in the community strong enough to challenge the Establishment.

Such strength developed in the 1740's as two streams of White-field's influence flowed into the Virginia counties between the Rappahannock and the James. In Hanover, Presbyterianism took its start with the importation from Glasgow of a book of his sermons. A decade and a half later, in Spotsylvania and adjacent counties, Baptist churches were formed through missionary efforts by some of his New England converts.

Viewing these developments, the Virginia commissary wrote the bishop of London: "I cannot forbear expressing my own concern to see Schism spreading itself through a Colony which has been *Famous for Uniformity of Religion.*" Whitefield commented: "There is a sweet stirring among the dry bones."

The growth of dissent in Hanover can be watched through two sets of eyes: the eyes of those who fostered it as a sweet stirring and the eyes of those who saw it as a schism to be firmly suppressed.

Having obtained a collection of religious books, a bricklayer named Samuel Morris desired to read them with friends and neighbors. Before doing so, they had to regularize their situation under the colony's laws governing the practice of religion.

The Charter of 1606 had provided that all inhabitants, including "the salvage people," should have the faith preached them "according to the doctrine, rites and religion established within the realm of England." Five years later, the Code of Sir Thomas Dale required colonists to "repair unto the minister" for instruction. Should they refuse, the governor was to have a first offender whipped once, a second offender whipped twice and on the Sabbath made to acknowledge his offense before the congregation. A third offender was to be whipped every day until he asked forgiveness.

Every settlement, under the Act of 1623, was to set aside a house or room for worship. Attendance was compulsory; absentees without good excuses were fined. Compulsory tithes were levied to pay the minister and provide the church budget—over the century the statutory county quota for salary mounted to sixteen thousand pounds of tobacco.

At midcentury, the assembly declared that all ministers in Virginia should be in conformity with the Church of England—a few Quakers, Congregationalists, and Baptists were sent packing. In the 1660's, a fine of two thousand pounds of tobacco, to be divided between the informer and the public purse, was laid on schismatical persons, who "out of their averseness to the orthodox established

9

religion, or out of new fangled conceits of their owne hereticall inventions refuse to have their children baptized."

But in 1689, under William and Mary, the Act of Toleration brought benefits to subjects overseas as well as in England. Dissenters still had to subscribe to the Articles of Religion and attend and pay tithes in support of the Established Church, but they could apply to the General Court at Williamsburg for permission to hold services of their own persuasion. Licenses were required not only for the preacher but also for the place where he would preach.

In 1711, Parliament liberalized the Act of Toleration to permit licensed dissenting ministers to preach in licensed places elsewhere than in their own counties in England, but legal opinion held the act to be without force overseas and therefore not to countenance evangelistic journeys in America.

Under these restrictions, Samuel Morris and his friends obtained licenses for a series of reading houses. At first they merely read their books aloud. They were laity of the laity—Morris said, "having never been used to social prayer, none of us durst attempt it." When first called on to name their denomination, they were at a loss for an answer, but in 1743 a representative of the New Side Presbyterians from Philadelphia, the most aggressive of the Presbyterian bodies, made them its affiliate and thereafter supplied them with ministers.

The preaching of the first of these, John Roan, became the subject of litigation when an informer charged that he had inveighed against the Establishment and assured his hearers that their rectors preached false doctrine and all who followed them were going to hell. Governor Gooch presented Roan to the grand jury as a threat to peace and order, saying a stop must be put to "the devices and intrigues of these associated fanatics." But the case faded out: the New Side synod sent two able conciliators to Williamsburg; the witness who laid the information against Roan vanished; Roan returned north before the case came up; and the jury found that while the people did assemble as stated, they did not do so "in a riotous manner," and that while John Roan did preach, he did not speak "against the canons of the Church of England."

But the existence of a growing body of dissenters, even if they were well behaved, was disruptive in any community. How disruptive the Hanover Reading House, rival minister, and congregation with divided loyalties looked from the study window of the

Church of England glebe can be seen in the correspondence of the Rev. Patrick Henry, rector of St. Paul's, Hanover.

With querulous frequency during the 1740's, Henry took pen in hand to complain to the bishop's commissary about the doings of the dissenters. He said that the new doctrines these schismatics were at great pains to propagate included the belief that "a true Christian may know whether a Minister be converted or not by hearing him preach or pray. This wild notion prevails among our Enthusiasts here, and I have been condemn'd by some of them as a stranger to true religion."

In his next letter, he begged leave "to add a few sentences relating to their practice . . . scolding, calling the old people, Grey headed Devils and . . . double damn'd whose souls are in hell, though they are alive on earth, Lumps of hellfire, incarnate Devils . . . and all the while the Preacher exhalts his voice puts himself into a violent agitation stamping & beating his Desk unmercifully until the weaker sort of his hearers being scar'd, cry out, fall down & work like people in convulsive fits to the amazement of the Spectators. . . . You may probably think, Sir, I am a little hyperbolical in this last relation, but . . . I have unquestionable authority for the truth of it."

Then Whitefield himself came to Hanover.

His host sent a note to Henry saying that Whitefield wanted to preach on Sunday in Henry's church. Henry replied, "if he will come to my house that I may have some conversation with him I shall be able to determine whether or not it will be proper for me to allow him the use of my Pulpit tomorrow." When Whitefield did not respond, Henry "set out for the Church and was told by the way that he [Whitefield] was to preach either in the Church or Churchyard, I found a great multitude waiting for him at the Church, and after consulting some of my Friends, I thought it adviseable to give him leave to preach in the Church . . . If I had refused him access . . . he would have preached in the Church yard . . . and then the whole congregation would have gone over to him . . . for tho the number of his followers there were but few, yet all the people to a man had a great desire to hear the famous Whitefield."

Two years later, when Samuel Davies, later president of Princeton, arrived to begin an eleven-year ministry in Hanover, Henry made an issue of the range of his activities, writing the commissary:

"I persuaded my self that the Govinor & Council never intended to encourage Itinerant Preachers, and therefore think it my duty to acquaint you with this Man's behavior."

By 1750, dissenters were affiliating with Davies' churches at a rate that caused alarmed supporters of the Establishment to petition the House of Burgesses, saying these Presbyterians were "strolling pretended ministers," seeking to "inveigle ignorant and unwary people with their sophistry." Five years later, the first Virginia presbytery was formed in Hanover.

Schism penetrated the Henry family circle. The Reverend Patrick's brother John was a Church of England adherent. But his wife, a self-possessed widow when he married her, was one of Davies' parishioners. Sunday after Sunday, she took her son, Patrick's namesake, to Forks Presbyterian Church and, according to legend, provided early training in dramatic oratory by making young Patrick reproduce the sermon on the way home in the gig. When a cleavage between vestries and clergy in the Church of England added a new dimension to the turmoil in Hanover, the young Patrick's capacity to move an audience was discovered in the lawsuit known as the Parson's Cause. The issue in this case was economic and political rather than religious, but its result was to discredit the rectors in the eyes of the generality of citizens and set a mood favorable to disestablishment.

For decades the statutory salaries of the Church of England clergy had been payable either in tobacco—sixteen thousand pounds of it—or in currency at the going rate of exchange, tuppence a pound. It had frequently been observed that "thouse counties where the Presbyterian meetings are, produced very mean tobacco, and for that reason can't get an orthodox minister to stay among them," but by the 1750's, soil exhaustion due to one-crop farming had reduced yields in formerly prosperous areas.

In 1755, a near crop failure occurred. The sudden acute scarcity inflated the market price of tobacco from tuppence to six or seven pence per pound. The legislature, coming to the aid of the planters, legalized payment of clergy salaries for this year in currency rather than tobacco, with the price calculated at the old tuppenny rate. The clergy felt short-changed.

When the legislation was renewed in 1758, the bishop's commissary denounced it in a pamphlet, *The Two Penny Act*. Two gentlemen of substance published a rebuttal; the battle was joined.

By petitioning the King in council, the clergy secured a royal disallowance of the act. The Rev. James Maury and a number of other rectors then brought suit against their vestries to recover either tobacco or its cash equivalent at the going market price. At the November 1763 term of court, Maury, as chief plaintiff, contended that the 1758 act had not received royal assent in the first place and that the King in council since then had specifically disallowed it. The court sustained him. Regretfully, the attorney for the vestry informed his clients that their case was lost.

But they determined to make one more effort. Young Patrick Henry, after failing twice in business and once at farming, had been put to law. Examined in Williamsburg after a few months of desultory reading, he showed a lamentable deficiency in knowledge of how to draw the most ordinary legal instruments, but his capacity to sustain a broad argument impressed the attorney general. He was granted a license. The vestry thought he might be just the right man to re-argue their case.

The new trial was bountifully attended by both clergy and laity. It took place in Hanover Courthouse, just across from the tavern belonging to young Patrick's father-in-law. Among the rectors to arrive was Uncle Patrick. Young Patrick implored him to leave, saying that this was his first big case and to do his duty by his clients he was going to have to say some harsh things about the clergy. Grumbling that his nephew would harm himself more than those of whom he spoke, Uncle Patrick withdrew.

Lacking any shred of legislation to sustain him, Henry based his argument on fundamental constitutional principles: specifically, on the reciprocal duties of king and subjects. Government was a mutual compact. Violation by one party discharged the other from responsibility. In disallowing the Tuppenny Act, the King had been indifferent to the distress of the colony and had thereby dissolved the political compact between him and the people. The Act of 1758 was their effort to take care of their own safety. Notwithstanding its disallowance, it should therefore be considered the law of the land and the only legitimate measure of the claims of the clergy.

The effect of Henry's words must have been similar to that of a Whitefield preaching. The crowd listened transfixed, then burst into violent applause. Patrick's amazed father, who was presiding justice, exclaimed: "Patrick spoke in this cause near an hour! and

13

in a manner, that surprised me! and showed himself well-informed on a subject of which I did not think he had any knowledge!"

The jury found that the Rev. James Maury had sustained damage to the extent of one penny; the court ruled against a motion for a new trial; the clergy departed in disorder. The secular elements in the crowd carried Patrick Henry shoulder-high around the courthouse green in a mood of electioneering enthusiasm. In the county where dissent was best organized, the rectors of the Established Church had been convicted of an attempt to profiteer.

Meanwhile, in the counties west and north of Hanover, a series of specifically religious court cases had begun to force the pace toward toleration.

For a decade, the Separate Baptists had been gaining converts. Shubal Stearns of Boston had established a center of evangelization at Sandy Creek, Guilford County, North Carolina; in 1765, one of his missionaries toured Virginia's central counties and in 1767 organized Upper Spotsylvania, the first Separate Baptist church between the Rappahannock and the James, with 25 members and Lewis Craig as pastor. Two years later, Lower Spotsylvania was formed, with John Waller as pastor and 154 members.

These two men became highly controversial figures. John Waller, in particular, had a turbulent history. In his twenties, he had swaggered about as "Swearing Jack," a self-declared hell-of-a-fellow who had trained his horse to rear and strike at a man—and had thus killed a drunken butcher.

His conversion occurred on jury duty in Fredericksburg. Lewis Craig was brought in charged with unlicensed preaching; afterwards, Craig invited the jurymen to the tavern for a mug of grog, and startled them by saying, "I thank you gentlemen of the grandjury, for the honour you have done me. While I was wicked and injurious, you took no notice of me; but since I have altered my course of life, and endeavored to reform my neighbors, you concern yourselves much about me, I have gotten this mug of grog, to treat you with; and shall take the spoiling of my goods joyfully."

To Waller, this particular grog was sobering stuff; he "ate no pleasant bread and drank no pleasant water, for seven or eight months, during which time he was almost in despair." Baptised in 1767, he became one of the most active Baptist preachers.

These were plain people, and their preaching was to the commonalty. If they met a group of drovers in a tavern, a religious discussion was likely to start. Sometimes it ended in a brawl. On one occasion when Waller preached in Hanover, "a huge fellow (in the habit of a waggoner) pulled him down and dragged him about by (the hair of his head); a second as stout as he ran to rescue Waller; upon which one took hold of one hand and the other of the other, that between friend and foe poor Waller was like to lost both arms (the hurt stuck to him for many weeks)." In Caroline County the established clergyman ran the butt end of a horse-whip into Waller's mouth as he preached. As he prayed he was jerked off the stage and out through a gate, where he was flogged and denounced; picking himself up, he shook off the dust and returned to complete the service.

At wayside taverns, baiting Baptist preachers was not only relished in the downstairs bars where brick or flagstone flooring made easy the sweeping out of red clay mud from drovers' boots; in more genteel form, it was a gentleman's diversion in the upper rooms where arrack punch was served in Lowestoft bowls before carved overmantels. *The Virginia Gazette* of October 31, 1771, instanced the more delicate forms of indignity in its "Recipe to Make an Annabaptist Preacher in 2 days time: Take the Herbs of Hypocrisy and Ambition, of each an Handful, of the Spirit of Pride 2 Drams, of the Seed of Dissention and Discord one Ounce, of the Flower of Formality 3 Scruples, of the Roots of Stubbornness and Obstinacy 4 pounds; and bruise them altogether in the Mortar of Vain Glory, with the Pestle of Contradiction, putting amongst them one Pint of the Spirit of Self-Conceitedness."

But gradually, the public attitude changed. Instead of watching revivalist preachers as they might watch a cockfight, many remained to pray. Among the commonalty, the impression spread that these churches, unlike the church of their betters, had a deep concern for their salvation. The social and political undertones of dissent grew louder. Charges then began to be brought that the dissenters' meetings disturbed the peace.

The first arrest leading to imprisonment took place in Spotsylvania County on June 4, 1768. Taken into custody in the meeting-house yard, John Waller, Lewis Craig, and three others were bonded to appear in Fredericksburg court, where the prosecution declared: "May it please your worships, these men are great disturbers of the peace. They cannot meet a man upon the road, but they must ram a text of scripture down his throat." The justices offered them

15

release if they would promise to preach no more in the county for a year and a day, but ordered them to jail when they refused.

Their transfer from the courthouse was in the nature of a public procession. As they walked, they sang:

> Broad is the road that leads to death,
> And thousands walk together there;
> But wisdom shows a narrow path,
> With here and there a traveller.

Behind bars, the prisoners continued their ministry; people flocked to the jail window and Craig made "very serious impressions on the minds of elevn heads of families and some of their domesticks with many others. The populace did everything they could invent to keep the people off, singing obscene songs, breeding riots, etc. but all in vain; at last they let him out to get rid of him."

Actually, several legal steps preceded Craig's dismissal. After the July court affirmed that these disturbers of the peace had refused to give security for their good behavior, he entered a recognizance that permitted him to go to Williamsburg to petition the General Court.

Commissary Blair sought the advice of Attorney General Randolph. Randolph, while he did not like dissenters, counseled moderation. Blair warned the King's attorney in Fredericksburg that "the Act of Toleration (it being found by experience that persecuting dissenters increases their numbers) has given them a right to apply, in a proper manner, for licensed houses, for the worship of God, according to their consciences; and I persuade myself, the gentlemen will quietly overlook their meetings, till the Court."

Between this first jail sentence, in 1768, and the last case of imprisonment a decade later, fifty-five prison terms were served by Baptist ministers and laymen. Active persecutions, private floggings, and public arrests were visited upon some seventy persons in at least twenty-eight counties. Sometimes the crowds around jail doors entertained themselves by mixing stink bombs of brimstone and black pepper, to be ignited when the wind was right for blowing the mixture into the jail windows; sometimes they listened, rapt and rapturous. Often, when opponents beat drums to drown out the prisoner's message, "sanctified lungs overpowered the rattle of dried sheepskin." But no matter what happened, the imprisonments caused communities to reflect on whether they approved the prevailing treatment of religious dissent.

In mid-July 1771, Lewis Craig was in jail again; arrested in Caroline County, he, two other preachers, and three laymen remained in prison through the summer and early autumn, when he again obtained relief by petitioning the General Court.

Colony-wide discussion of the county incidents took place at the capital. While most Virginia leaders maintained their devotion to the Establishment, a note of conciliation began to appear in the public prints. *The Virginia Gazette* of February 20, 1772, published a long "Address to the Anabaptists imprisoned in Caroline County: You have, I hear, desired to see the Law by which you are condemned. This is what you have a Right to, and in which I propose to give you Satisfaction; though the conduct of one of your champions, in daring, by Letter to the Gentleman who has been discharging the Duty of an active upright Magistrate, in most of your Commitments, to consign him to Perdition, as your Persecutor for that Conduct, might provoke another kind of Treatment. But we have learned another Spirit, from the Charity of that Church we profess ourselves Members of."

However, the month after Craig and his associates were imprisoned in Caroline, the list of Baptists in prison was augmented by a further group of arrests in Middlesex, two counties down the Rappahannock, with John Waller as ranking prisoner.

The Middlesex County Order Book for May 27, 1771, shows grand jury presentations of fourteen citizens for willful absence from church. Their lack of enthusiasm is largely explained by a petition offered at the same sitting by Robert Ware, James Mackan, and ten others to "Establish a place for the publick worship of the Disenters at James Mackan acordind to Law for the peaceable communion of the Christian worship." The back of this petition bears the notation, "The Petition of Robt. Ware & others for to Establish a place of Publick Worship," followed by a three-word account of the court's action: "1771 June Rejected."

They met anyhow. On August 10, Waller, accompanied by William Webber of Goochland who earlier in the year had been jailed for three months in Chesterfield County, came to Middlesex to preach at the home of James Mackan. Thomas Wafford, a layman who often acted as advance man for Baptist preachers, was there too.

Word of the assembly had got round: as Webber preached from James 2:18, "Shew me thy faith without thy works, and I will shew thee my faith by my works," the house was entered by the sheriff, the Church of England rector, several irate citizens, and a magistrate. They were armed with staves and whips and they had a warrant naming Webber, Waller, Ware, Wafford, Faulkner, and Greenwood.

Singly, the named men were taken into another room for questioning. The rector was present. Their "pockets and wallets" were searched "for firearms." When the magistrate established that they had no license, he required them to give bond and security not to preach any more in the county, "which," Waller said, "we modestly refused to do."

Faulkner, not a preacher, was dismissed. Wafford, also not a preacher, was charged "to make his escape out of the county by twelve o'clock the next day on pain of imprisonment"; he was horse-whipped as he departed. The others were taken to prison in Urbanna.

The news traveled, the curious gathered. Next day, "we had a large number of people to hear us preach, and among others, many of the great ones of the land, who behaved well while one of us discoursed on the new birth."

The Virginia Gazette's commentary showed how far opinion had swung:

It will perhaps be alleged that they exhorted or preached in an unlicensed Place; but if the Law of Toleration does not extend here, which is the prevailing Opinion, by what Law were they obliged to have any licensed? If there be no such law, how could they be shut up in close Prison for disobeying it? Another reason for their Commitment might be their being a Pack of ignorant Enthusiasts. This is a common Accusation; and People of little Knowledge, and less Humanity, generally think it is a very good One. . . .

A man may soon be convinced that there are flourishing and happy Governments where the Subjects, though of every Denomination, yet live in Harmony. True Liberty of Conscience is the sacred Property of every Man, which none can take from him without being guilty of Sacrilege and Tyranny.

But next court day, the petition of Ware and his colleagues to license a place of worship was again rejected, and the prisoners remanded back to jail when they refused to agree to cease preaching in the county. This time, they were put on bread and water. After four days of it, friends outside heard of their deprivation, and arrived with so much good food that the prisoners authorized sizeable distributions to the poor of the community. After September 10, they were again permitted exercise in the prison yard.

Then Webber became seriously ill.

Waller, much distressed, wrote the gentleman justice who had signed the order for their imprisonment: "My bro. Webber now in prison, is in a very low state of health & without the divine interposition, must I think, in a few days, launch off the shores of mortality, he is a young man, who when at home, lives with his Mother in Goochland, upwards of 100 miles from this I judge: & the reason of his coming down, into this County to preach, was this, The Ministers that came with me before, are & has been for some time, in Caroline prison, for the very same thing, that I am here: & just before I left home, I was very sick, and pressed on this young man to come with me, to assist me in preaching at my meetings . . . . he is, as well as myself, afraid to sign any Bond, not to preach, for fear of sinning against God; but it is more than probable, if he now had his liberty, that he would never be under obligations, of coming into this County again, for he has not the care of a Church here, as I have, therefore I humbly hope, as you are a Gent. in great power, & much esteem in your County, you will please to procure him, his liberty to return home, to his friends to nurse him."

On behalf of the prisoners, a petition signed by twenty-eight citizens had already been prepared, urging the court to "supercede the aforesaid Order, and Release them . . . to Return home to their Distressed Familyes." On September 26, it was presented. It is marked only, "Petition—Geo. Warwick and others Annabaptists."

No record was entered either of action on the petition or of the court's general handling of the case. The gentleman justices may have decided that the crowds at the biweekly preachings were larger and the public notice given to dissent greater than if the prisoners were to go their several ways and exhort occasional gatherings in private homes. They may have been nervous about a possible martyrdom if Webber died in jail. Coupled with such specific considerations may have been growing doubt that the present laws were the best means of treating religious diversity. Whatever the justification, the prisoners were quietly let go.

By the next year, the public's attitude had changed so much that the Virginia Assembly considered new legislation. Memorials were before it from Baptists in four counties asking for the same indul-

19

gence as Quakers, Presbyterians, and other Protestants. The Amelia County brethren demanded that complete liberty of conscience be assured.

The proposed bill did not go very far. It would have continued registration requirements; confined preaching to registered houses, whose doors must be kept open; prohibited night meetings; and forbidden baptism of slaves without their masters' consent.

It was discussed without action against a background of further arrests. In Chesterfield, when one of Craig's assistants was jailed, a gentleman justice had a high brick wall put up to prevent him from preaching through the window. In King and Queen, two men went to prison singing, "Life is the time to serve the Lord." In Caroline, Ware and Waller were again in custody. A young cousin of James Madison gave a student oration at William and Mary College on "Civil and Religious Liberty."

The following year, leather-lunged John Weatherford bounced his voice over the Chesterfield wall whenever a handkerchief, waved from a tall pole, signaled that his flock was on the other side. Patrick Henry took a hand in his release. Baptists were behind bars in Fairfax, Culpeper, and Orange.

Writing from Orange in January 1774 to William Bradford, Jr., of Philadelphia, James Madison told how the question of toleration agitated his own mind and that of the public: "That diabolical, hell-conceived principle of persecution rages among some and to their eternal infamy, the clergy can furnish their quota of imps for such business. This vexes me the most of anything whatsoever. There are at this [time] in the adjacent county not less than five or six well-meaning men in close jail for publishing their religious sentiments which in the main are very orthodox. I have neither patience to hear, talk, or think of anything relative to this matter; for I have squabbled and scolded, abused and ridiculed so long about it to little purpose, that I am without common patience."

Actually, Madison worked at the matter constantly for the next fourteen years; both in the phrasing of the general declaration of the right to religious liberty in 1776 and in the definitive phases of the debate in the Virginia legislature in the 1780's, where his influence was dominant. In a second letter to Bradford he said: "Our Assembly is to meet the 1st of May, when it is expected something will be done in behalf of the dissenters. Petitions, I hear, are already forming among the persecuted Baptists and I fancy it is in the thought of the Presbyterians also to intercede for greater liberty in matters of religion. For my part, I cannot help being very doubtful of their succeeding in the attempt . . . The sentiments of our people of fortune and fashion on this subject are very different from what you have been used to. That liberal, catholic and equitable way of thinking, as to the rights of conscience, which is one of the characteristics of a free people, and so strongly marks the people of your province, is but little known among the zealous adherents to our hierarchy. We have, it is true, some persons in the Legislature of generous principles, both in religion and politics; but number, not merit, you know, is necessary to carry points there. Besides, the clergy are a numerous and powerful body, have great influence at home by reason of their connection with and dependence on the bishops and the crown, and will naturally employ all their arts and interest to depress their rising adversaries; for such they must consider dissentients who rob them of the good will of the people, and may in time endanger their livings and security."

Madison was right that the Presbyterians intended to force the issue. In 1775, Hanover Presbytery took the initiative with a memorial detailing its objections to the 1772 bill. They wanted "to have and enjoy the full and free exercise of our religion, without molestation or danger of incurring any penalty whatsoever." They wanted the same penalties to be applied to disturbers of their meetings as to those who disturbed the Established Church; freedom of writing and speaking on religious subjects; and the right to hold property for the use of schools and churches. And they underlined their growing economic status in the colonial community by observing that "We are petitioning in favor of a church that is neither contemptible nor obscure." The Bedford Presbyterians proposed that their church be incorporated, in order to hold property and receive public support like the Church of England.

The General Association of Baptists took a different line: in 1775 it petitioned for abolition of the Establishment.

The 1772 bill died on the vine in 1775. The proposals before the legislature were too numerous and too conflicting to permit quick action, and other issues crowded men's minds. An entering wedge for the practice of toleration was inserted when the convention that met in Richmond in August gave dissenting denominations the privilege of conducting services for their members in the army: "for the ease of such scrupulous consciences as may not choose to attend divine services as celebrated by the chaplain."

But the Virginia convention that assembled in Williamsburg in May 1776, after declaring for independence from Great Britain, "Resolved, unanimously, that a committee be appointed to prepare a DECLARATION OF RIGHTS & such a plan of Government as will be most likely to maintain peace and order in this Colony, & secure substantial & equal liberty to the people." And on June 15, the first declaration of rights to be formulated on the American continent contained an assurance of religious liberty.

Its author, Washington's neighbor, George Mason of Gunston Hall, was a gentleman justice of Fairfax County and a vestryman of Truro Parish. He had seen imprisonment for dissent in his own courthouse jail in 1774, when the Baptist Jeremiah Moore had been arrested and sent to Alexandria with a mittimus that read: "I send you herewith the body of Jeremiah Moore, who is a preacher of the gospel of Jesus Christ, and a stroller." As Fairfax County's representative in the Virginia Assembly, Mason had participated in previous discussions of toleration at Williamsburg. The final article of the bill of rights he submitted for the delegates' consideration read: "That religion, or the duty which we owe to our Creator, and the manner of discharging it, can be directed only by reason and conviction, and not by force or violence: and, therefore, that all men should enjoy the fullest toleration in the exercise of religion, according to the dictates of conscience, unpunished and unrestrained by the magistrate, unless, under cover of religion, any man disturb the peace, the happiness, or the safety of society. And that it is the mutual duty of all to practice Christian forebearance, love and charity towards each other."

The convention made very few changes in Mason's draft bill, but a substantial alteration rendered this section still more acceptable to denominations whose members had had specific experience of punishment and restraint by the magistrate. It was proposed by James Madison. The discussion in denominational assemblies and in the legislature had begun to clarify the distinction between freedom as a natural right antecedent to the organization of society and hence not subject to any form of state control, and religious toleration, a liberty granted by the state and hence, at least in theory, subject to revocation. Madison's proposal for change brought this difference into clear view by dropping the word "toleration" and affirming the inalienable nature of religious liberty: the revised text

An Attempt to land a Bishop in America.

that became Article XVI of the adopted declaration read: "That religion, or the duty which we owe to our Creator, and the manner of discharging it, can be directed only by reason and conviction, not by force or violence, and therefore all men are equally entitled to the free exercise of religion according to the dictates of conscience; and that it is the mutual duty of all to practice Christian forebearance, love and charity towards each other."

On passage of the declaration, the Prince William Baptists rejoiced: "The last Article . . . we esteem as the rising Sun of religious Liberty, to relieve us from a long night of ecclesiastical Bondage." But it was some years before that sun reached the zenith. The free exercise of religion had become a tenet of civil society in Virginia, and the affirmation that the manner of expressing religious belief "can be directed only by reason and conviction" implied disestablishment. Yet when the Virginia legislature approached the legal task of giving statutory effect to the principle of religious liberty, a decade of discussion was required to obtain agreement on its form.

Anticlericalism had no part in what was said: all sides, and the dissenters most of all, agreed that organized religion is central to the good society. But though Madison had succeeded in writing his view on the relation between religious bodies and the political structure into the declaration of rights, the other alternative died hard. The assembly was petitioned to maintain, and not to maintain, establishment of the Church of England; to maintain, and not to maintain, an establishment of religion in general under which the state would recognize all churches equally.

Existing property rights required thoughtful consideration. Madison had failed to get the 1776 convention to adopt the principle that "no man or class of men ought, on account of religion to be invested with peculiar emoluments or privileges." A group of Church of England clergy now reminded the house that they had "entered into Holy Orders expecting to receive the several Emoluments which such religious establishment offered; that from the nature of their education they are precluded from gaining a tolerable subsistence in any other way of life."

But the very next day, the Scotch-Irish beyond the Blue Ridge complained: "there is a vast number of Dissenters from the Established Church in this Colony, almost wholly so on the Frontiers whose Duty to God & themselves obliges them to support Gospel Ministers of their own profession at the same time that they & their

Domestick's are charged with the maintenance & all other parochial charges Incident to the Ministry of the Establishment. This unequal Burthen is complain'd of as inconsistent with the spirit of Taxation."

Immediate stopgap legislation exempted dissenters from support of the Established Church and suspended for a year the tax levy for salaries of Church of England rectors—a measure continued annually until 1779, when suspension became permanent.

That was the year of the first substantive effort to treat the issue as a whole. To provide the new state with a body of law rid of British statutes that were no longer applicable, the assembly named a committee of law revisors—Jefferson, Mason, Edmund Pendleton, George Wythe, Thomas Ludwell Lee. Meeting in Fredericksburg, the town where dissenters were first jailed, they proposed a bill drafted by Jefferson and regarded by him at the end of his life, together with his authorship of the Declaration of Independence and foundation of the University of Virginia, as one of his three chief achievements. It provided for complete disestablishment:

Well aware that . . . Almighty God hath created the mind free, and . . . that all attempts to influence it by temporal punishments, or burthens, or by civil incapacitations, tend only to beget habits of hypocrisy and meanness . . . ; that to compel a man to furnish contributions of money for the propagation of opinions which he disbelieves and abhors, is sinful and tyrannical . . . ; that our civil rights have no dependence on our religious opinions; and, finally, that truth is great and will prevail if left to herself, that she is the proper and sufficient antagonist to error, and has nothing to fear from the conflict unless by human interposition disarmed of her natural weapons, free argument and debate . . .

We the General Assembly of Virginia do enact that no man shall be compelled to frequent or support any religious worship, place, or ministry whatsoever, nor shall be enforced, restrained, molested or burthened in his body or goods, nor shall otherwise suffer on account of his religious opinions or belief, but that all men shall be free to profess, and by argument to maintain, their opinions in matters of religion, and that the same shall in no wise diminish, enlarge, or affect their civil capacities.

But a conservative trend was setting in; Jefferson's bill was proposed only to be defeated. Sentiment swerved toward establishment of religion in general, with all denominations to receive pro-rated

25

public support. Patrick Henry, in a reversal of his earlier radicalism, became, along with consistent conservatives like Edmund Pendleton, a highly effective proponent of the general assessment bill.

For several years, opinion see-sawed. Madison joined Jefferson, and when Jefferson became ambassador to France, replaced him as chief advocate of complete disestablishment. But for a time, his side appeared to be the loser.

At the October 1784 session, the general assessment bill passed its second reading in the assembly, and a proposal squeaked through for it to be given a third and final reading before the assembly adjourned.

Madison's only recourse was to play for time while attempting to neutralize Patrick Henry's influence. From France, Jefferson gloomily confided: "What we have to do, I think, is devotedly to pray for his death." But there was an alternative: Henry's influence in the house would be greatly diluted if he were removed from that body by election to the governorship.

The day after the vote for a third reading, Madison implored the house not to enact so crucial a statute as the general assessment bill out of hand. It should, he declared, be held over for decision by the assembly's next session. By a vote of 45-38 he secured postponement until the following November. Ten days before the current session closed, Patrick Henry was made governor of Virginia.

Taking full advantage of the eleven-month recess, friends of disestablishment prevailed on Madison to prepare an extensive *Memorial and Remonstrance* for the assembly. Longhand copies were immediately dispatched to the valley Presbyterians, and, through George Mason, a printed version with spaces for signatures was produced in Alexandria.

The *Memorial* put the case in its strongest form: "We maintain therefore that in matters of religion, no man's right is abridged by the institution of civil society, and that religion is wholly exempt from its cognizance." Church establishments, Madison warned, "have been seen to erect a spiritual tyranny" and to uphold "the thrones of political tyranny" as well. "Either then, we must say that the . . . legislature . . . may sweep away all our fundamental rights; or that they are bound to leave this particular right untouched and sacred."

Actually, the provisions regarding religious liberty that South

Carolina had incorporated in its constitution of 1778 afforded detailed corroboration of Madison's contention. Equal recognition was afforded all religious bodies, just as the Virginia general assessment bill proposed. But then it became necessary to define a religious body, and this function had to be undertaken by the state that was to recognize them.

Article XXXVIII therefore affirmed: "That all Persons and religious Societies, who acknowledge that there is one God, and a future State of Rewards and Punishments, and that God is publickly to be worshipped, shall be freely tolerated. The Christian Protestant Religion, shall be deemed, and is hereby constituted and declared to be, the established Religion of this State. That all Denominations of Christian Protestants in this State, demeaning themselves peaceably and faithfully, shall enjoy equal religious and civil Privileges. . . ."

To constitute a religious society and qualify for such privileges, at least fifteen male persons of at least twenty-one years of age must subscribe to five stated articles:

First, *That there is one eternal God, and a future State of Rewards and Punishments,*

Second, *That God is publickly to be worshipped.*

Third, *That the Christian Religion is the true Religion.*

Fourth, *That the Holy Scriptures of the Old and New Testament, are of Divine Inspiration, and are the Rule of Faith and Practice.*

Fifth, *That it is lawful, and the Duty of every Man, being thereunto called by those that govern, to bear witness to Truth.*

In addition, any person chosen by a religious society as its minister must signify his acceptance, not only of the five articles, but of a long additional declaration stipulating his duties.

By the time Virginians were considering Madison's *Memorial,* experience under this state-stipulated religious framework was leading South Carolinians to favor change. Their new constitution of 1790 abandoned the 1778 specifications in favor of a wording not unlike George Mason's 1776 proposal: "The free exercise and enjoyment of religious profession and worship, without discrimination or preference, shall, forever hereafter, be allowed within this state to all Mankind; provided that the liberty of conscience thereby declared shall not be so construed as to excuse acts of licentiousness, or justify practices inconsistent with the peace or safety of this state."

27

Realization of the difficulties of which South Carolinians had had practical experience spread in Virginia during the summer of 1785 as Madison's exposition passed from hand to hand. Hanover Presbytery changed its earlier position and joined the majority of the denomination in opposition to the general assessment bill. In the autumn, the Methodists, who at the time of the Revolution had declared themselves "not Dissenters, but a Religious Society in Communion with the Church of England," and as such in favor of continued establishment, reversed their stand. The movement snow-balled so rapidly that when the assembly reconvened, its members did not even hold a vote on the general assessment bill.

Years later, at the request of George Mason's grandson, Madison wrote an account of the final victory: "During the session of the General Assembly, 1784-5, a bill was introduced into the House of Delegates providing for the legal support of Teachers of the Christian Religion, and being patronized by the most popular talents in the House, seemed likely to obtain a majority of votes. In order to arrest its progress, it was insisted and with success that the Bill should be postponed till the ensuing session and in the meantime presented for public consideration that the sense of the people might be called forth. Your highly distinguished ancestor, Col. George Mason, Col. Geo. Nicholas also possessing much public weight, and some others thought it advisable that a remonstrance against the bill should be prepared for general circulation and signature [and] imposed on me the task of drawing up such a paper. This draught having received their sanction, a large number of printed copies were distributed, so extensively signed by people of every religious denomination that at the ensuing session the projected measure was entirely frustrated and under the influence of the public sentiment thus manifested the celebrated Bill 'establishing religious freedom' enacted into a permanent barrier against future attempts on the rights of conscience as declared in the great charter prefixed to the Constitution of the State."

So in December 1785, through Madison's efforts, Jefferson's statute of religious freedom gave practical effect to the principle affirmed in Mason's declaration of rights.

On January 19, 1786, Governor Patrick Henry received the engrossed bill from the speaker of the house and affixed his signature. Separation of church and state in Virginia provided the formula that was adopted, nationwide.

CHAPTER II

FREEDOM OF THE PRESS

Congress shall make no law ... abridging the freedom of speech, or of the press ...

BACKGROUND

L earning has brought disobedience, and heresy and sects into the world, and printing has divulged them, and libels against the best government. God keep us from both."
Sir William Berkeley of Virginia, in his 1671 report on the state of the province, expressed a view congenial to many another colonial governor.

A different view was expressed by the First Continental Congress in its open letter to the inhabitants of Quebec in 1774: "The last right we shall mention, regards the freedom of the press. The importance of this consists, besides the advancement of truth, science, morality, and arts in general, in its diffusion of liberal sentiments on the administration of government, its ready communication of thoughts between subjects, and its consequential promotion of union among them, whereby oppressive officers are shamed or intimidated, into more honourable and just modes of conducting affairs."

Seventeenth- and eighteenth-century printers whom those in authority found guilty of publishing seditious libels were very vulnerable. From the time of its invention, the printing press had been subjected to careful control as a dangerous instrument. The regulatory measures adopted under the Tudors were tightened by the Stuarts: in 1637 the court of Star Chamber issued a refinement of its earlier restrictions under which a stringent licensing system effectively prevented the appearance of books of whose contents the authorities disapproved. To aid identification, all publications had to carry the names of author and publisher.

The trial procedures and the punishments meted out under this ordinance in the late 1630's, particularly when John Lilburne was condemned for publishing and importing heretical and seditious books, contributed to the indignation that caused Parliament to abolish the court of Star Chamber in 1641. Its ordinances fell with it. In 1644, John Milton addressed Parliament in favor of unlicensed printing: "As good almost kill a man as kill a good book; who kills a man kills a reasonable creature, God's image; but he who destroys a good book kills reason itself. . . . Though all the winds of doctrine were let loose to play upon the earth, so Truth be in the field, we do ingloriously, by licensing and prohibiting, to misdoubt her strength. Let her and Falsehood grapple: who ever knew Truth put to the worse in a free and open encounter?"

But the Commonwealth proved as chary of criticism as the Crown; it continued previous restrictions.

After the Restoration, a new "act for preventing abuses in printing seditious, treasonable, and unlicensed books and pamphlets, and for regulating of printing and printing presses," the Licensing Act of 1662, was passed. Continued from time to time, it remained in force until 1695.

Thereafter, books and pamphlets no longer had to be examined for seditious content before they went to press, and their texts were consequently seen by numbers of citizens even if action against them were subsequently taken. But once they and their printers were haled into court, several factors made establishment of innocence difficult, especially in the colonies.

In practically all colonial capitals, there was only one press and one printer. Normally, he was brought into the colony to do the public printing; his main source of employment and income was the production of government records, executive and legislative minutes, gubernatorial proclamations, laws. Even if he issued a news sheet, part of his copy was made up of advertisements of sheriff's sales. In these circumstances, the leverage that a governor could apply to keep the views expressed by the printer in line with his own was as definitive as, and more concentrated than, that of today's major advertisers on the contents of the mass media.

Such leverage is clear in the life of William Bradford, publisher of *The New-York Gazette,* who, with only one brief break, maintained his tenure as King's printer in that colony from 1693 until his retirement in 1744 at the age of eighty-two. His attachment to established authority was so faithfully reflected in the paper whose publication he began in 1725 that seven years later some of the then governor's critics determined to start an opposition press. They hired one of Bradford's former apprentices to produce *The New-York Weekly Journal.* Shortly thereafter, in 1735, a charge of seditious libel, brought at the instance of the governor against certain articles in the *Journal,* became the occasion of the trial of its printer, John Peter Zenger.

Throughout this trial, William Bradford stood silent. But Governor William Cosby died on March 10, 1736, and in the March

28 *Gazette,* signing himself "A Friend and Well-Wisher To All Men," Bradford accounted for his recent neutrality with disarming frankness: "Yet as I am and have been above forty years last past a Servant to the Government (and consequently to the several Governours during that Time) so I have according to my duty, some times printed in my Gazette some observations which the late Governour's Friends, thought proper to make upon what the other Party printed against him." He ended by restating his intention to "be obedient to the king, and to all that are put in Authority under him."

But even if a printer enjoyed, like Zenger, private patrons to give him economic independence of the governor, his legal situation was precarious. If an offending item were published in a given colony, little doubt could exist as to who printed it: there was the press and there was the printer. Moreover, jury trial was in such cases a marginal safeguard. When dealing with charges of seditious libel, juries were permitted only to find the fact of publication. They could not consider whether what they found to have been published did or did not constitute a breach of the law.

Nor could a defense be offered on the ground that what had been published was the truth. In cases of libel, injury was held to result whether a statement was true or false—indeed, English lawyers often quoted the aphorism, "The greater the truth, the greater the libel."

The ruling concept of freedom of the press in the mid-eighteenth century, little changed since expiration of the Licensing Act, was accurately stated by William Blackstone in his *Commentaries*: "The liberty of the press is indeed essential to the nature of a free state: but this consists in laying no *previous* restraints upon publications, and not in freedom from censure for criminal matter when published. . . . To punish (as the law does as present) any dangerous or offensive writings, which, when published, shall on a fair and impartial trial be adjudged of a pernicious tendency, is necessary for the preservation of peace and good order, of government and religion, the only solid foundations of civil liberty."

Yet in the New World, at the end of the seventeenth and again at the end of the first third of the eighteenth century, the ruling concept began to be redefined. Even earlier, an English trial had raised the issue of a jury's right to apply law to fact, and the person then tried subsequently became Pennsylvania's proprietor.

In 1670, young William Penn and a companion went to the usual place of Quaker meeting in London's Gracechurch Street. They found its entrance barred by soldiers. Penn addressed the congregation in the street. Arrested on the spot, he was indicted at the Old Bailey for preaching to an unlawful, seditious, and riotous assembly.

At his trial, the jurymen, though instructed to find fact only, asserted a right to consider the charge as it related the law to the facts. They found Penn and his friend guilty of speaking in Gracechurch Street, but not "to an unlawful Assembly."

The court insisted that they produce a clearcut verdict. The recorder assured them: "Gentlemen, you shall not be dismissed till we have a verdict, that the Court will accept; and you shall be lockt up, without Meat, Drink, Fire and Tobacco; you shall not think thus to abuse the Court; we will have a Verdict by the help of God, or you shal starve for it."

Thus badgered, they responded by declaring the defendants not guilty of anything.

The outraged judges fined the jurors forty marks apiece. Quite possibly they could not and in any case they did not pay. They were removed to jail. One of their number, Bushell by name, then brought an action in the court of common pleas, and obtained a judgment that their imprisonment was illegal. This case became the first in a line of precedent establishing a jury's right to determine the legal effect of the facts at bar.

In arguing the Zenger case, Andrew Hamilton, the Philadelphia lawyer who served as defendant's counsel, insisted that against such charges establishment of the truth of what had been published is a valid defense and that a jury's verdict should not be limited to findings of fact. By securing Zenger's acquittal, he started a process of change alike in the law of libel and in the procedure of the common law courts.

Few cases tried in the colonies attracted as wide attention in England as this one did. Copies of the transcript of Hamilton's argument were repeatedly published there, frequently in combination with similar arguments in later English trials. But for more than half a century, its effect burned with a slow fire.

During and after 1776, the several colonies, one after another, affirmed the essentiality of freedom of the press in their bills of rights and successive constitutions, foreshadowing or following the pertinent section in the First Amendment to the federal Constitution that came into force in 1791.

The year after its adoption, Fox's Libel Act became law in England, empowering juries to "give a general verdict of guilty or not guilty upon the whole matter put in issue" and stipulating that they shall not be "directed, by the court or judge . . . to find the defendant or defendants guilty, merely on proof of the publication . . . of the paper charged to be libel."

In 1798, the American Congress, by passing the Alien and Sedition Acts, opened one of the periodic eras of witch-hunting to which the country has been liable. But at the same time, the acts declared the right of an accused person "to offer in evidence in his defense the truth of the matter contained in the publication charged as a libel. And the jury who shall try the cause, shall have a right to determine the law and the fact. . . ."

THE CASE

"You must have heard of two *Scandalous Songs* that are handed about, it is your Duty to enquire the Author, Printer and Publisher of them. Sometimes, heavy, halfwitted Men get a knack of Rhyming, but it is Time to break them of it, when they grow Abusive, Insolent and Mischievous . . ."

Such were the instructions of Chief Justice James DeLancey of New York's Supreme Court to the grand jury in the autumn of 1734. Obediently, the jurymen indicted the ballads, though lacking information as to the authors. The court ordered that at high noon on October 21, the "said *Virulent, Scandalous* and *Seditious Songs* or *Ballads* be burnt before the City Hall, sitting the Court, by the hands of the *common Hangman* or *Whipper*."

A simultaneous request from Governor William Cosby and his council sought the assembly's concurrence in ordering four issues of *The New-York Weekly Journal* to be publicly burnt as "tending to raise Seditions and Tumults among the People." They proposed that a reward be offered for apprehension of the authors of the offending articles, and that the printer, John Peter Zenger, be prosecuted. But this effort was less successful. The assembly tabled the proposal.

At the swearing-in ceremony of New York City's new mayor and aldermen a few days earlier, the governor had remarked that he could not let pass this opportunity to note how the *Journal* had "wickedly insinuated" that the recent elections "were carried against the Governor's interest." He inveighed against "what Industry and Pains are used to raise Uneasiness in the People's minds at my administration by Some Men, who, under the Specious and plausible Pretences of liberty, vent all the licentious bitterness and malice their private Disappointments can suggest."

On November 2, though still lacking the assembly's concurrence, the council ordered the specified issues of Zenger's newspaper to be burnt near the pillory between eleven and twelve o'clock the following Wednesday; proclaimed a reward of £50 for the conviction of the authors of the newspaper articles and £12 for the conviction of the ballad writers; and instructed the mayor and other city magistrates to attend the burning. The aldermen resolved not to go unless they could be shown legal authority for the council's demand. Since the whipper was their employee, they were able to deny the sheriff's request that he be ordered to perform the burning.

Attendance at the ceremony was therefore sparse. The recorder came, and several officers from the garrison. After reading the numbers of the papers, the sheriff "delivered them into the Hands of his own Negroe, and ordered him to put them into the Fire, which he did."

Then on Sunday the seventeenth, in a surprise move under a warrant issued by the council, John Peter Zenger was arrested and jailed "for printing and publishing several Seditious Libels." For three days, he was held incommunicado. Since Monday was his press day, the *Journal* skipped an issue.

On Wednesday, when his attorneys brought him before the court under a writ of habeas corpus and asked for his release on bail, the court set his bail at £400, plus two sureties at £200 each. Zenger demurred, offering an affidavit in which he estimated his net worth at £40. The court declined to lower the figure.

So Zenger was returned to jail and kept there for close to nine months until tried for seditious libel the following August. His wife, to whom he was permitted to speak through a hole in the jail door, took over the printing. The *Journal* appeared regularly.

The forces that confronted each other in this test of freedom of the press had been building up steadily for two years, almost from the moment when H.M.S. *Seaforth* anchored off Sandy Hook at 10:00 P.M. on August 1, 1732, to permit the disembarkation of William Cosby, colonel in the Royal Irish Regiment and former equerry to the Queen, who had duly kissed his sovereign's hands in London as the new governor of New Jersey and New York.

Cosby was a placeman of the Duke of Newcastle, then principal secretary to His Majesty; one of New York's councilmen described him as "a man about 45 and gay . . . has the Earl of Halifax's sister for his wife, 2 daughters almost women and a son." His previous assignment had been to the island of Minorca, where his troubled administration ended in removal for avaricious conduct—as the tenth son of an Irish county family he was without private means.

The new governor's installation was impressive. The *Gazette* reported: "The next Day between the Hours of 11 & 12 his Excellency walked to the City Hall (a company of Halbertiers & a Troop of Horse marching before, and the Gentlemen of His Majesty's Council, the Corporation, and a great number of the Gentlemen and Merchants of this City following, the street being lin'd on each side with the Militia) where his Commission was published, and then his Excellency returned (attended as before) back to the Fort, the Militia then drew up on the Parade, and Saluted him with three Vollies." But the echoes of the volleys had hardly died before trouble began.

Thirteen months previously, Cosby's predecessor, Governor Montgomerie, had died in office. During the ensuing interval, the governor's functions in New York had been performed by the president of the council, Rip Van Dam, a solid and prosperous Dutch merchant with a shipyard just below Trinity Church and thirty years' standing as a councilman. His salary as acting governor was paid by the New York provincial assembly.

But Cosby produced a royal order confirming in him a half-interest in the "salary, emoluments and perquisites" of the governor's office during the interregnum and demanded half of the £1,975 8s. 10d. Van Dam had received. Van Dam refused to turn over the money, countering that the governor had received £6,407 18s. 10d. in emoluments before leaving England. The governor decided to sue.

His difficulty in lodging his case had a Gilbert-and-Sullivan air. New York's three-man Supreme Court, which in spite of its name was, and remains to this day, a court of first instance as well as review, exercised a number of the judicial capacities of the courts in England, but not all of them. It had chancery jurisdiction, but the governor could not bring his suit in chancery since he himself was chancellor. It had jurisdiction in common pleas, but he did not wish to bring such a suit since it would be heard before a jury and Van Dam could cross-file. So, though the court had not previously acted as a court of exchequer, he brought suit before it as guardian of the royal treasury.

The governor's action raised a question of basic principle: acceptance of exchequer jurisdiction would make the supreme court an equity court, and the New York Assembly had consistently held that equity jurisdiction could not be established without its consent. So first of all the court had to decide whether it was empowered to hear the governor's suit in the form in which he had brought it.

Uneasy personal relations on the court made decision difficult.

37

A gap of more than a generation separated the chief justice and the two associate justices. The former, Lewis Morris, Sr., was sixty-one and had been a justice for eighteen years. He was proprietor of the landed estate of Morrisiana in Westchester County, established by an uncle on Bronck's Land in 1670 and made a manor by royal letters patent in 1697. A contentious but able and respected man, he had long moved in the center of government affairs, particularly in the previous decade during the tenure of the popular Scottish governor, William Burnet. Between Governor Montgomerie's death and the coming of Cosby, Morris had exercised in New Jersey the same functions as Rip Van Dam had in New York.

Of the associate justices, James DeLancey, first justice, was the son of a wealthy Hugenot merchant whose home was a show place of New York City. Educated in England at Cambridge and the Inner Temple, he returned to New York to become a councilman at twenty-six and a supreme court justice at twenty-eight. His councilmanic appointment coincided with the dismissal of Lewis Morris, Jr., who was dropped for too outspoken criticism of Governor Montgomerie's drafts upon the revenue.

The second justice, young Frederick Philipse, was the son of an established Dutch family of merchants with a manor in Yonkers; his uncle was speaker of the assembly. The two associate justices enjoyed the confidence of the new governor. The chief justice did not.

When the court sat, the justices had before them both the governor's suit and a lengthy brief denying their jurisdiction in exchequer, filed on Van Dam's behalf by two redoubtable lawyers, James Alexander and his frequent associate, William Smith, Sr.

Alexander had come to America in some haste, after participating on the Stuart side of the unsuccessful rebellion of 1715 on behalf of the Pretender. From his arrival, he was a man of consequence. An engineer by training, he became surveyor general of New York and New Jersey, and in 1720 his fellow-Scot, Governor Burnet, made him a member of the council. He married a prosperous widow. Through his New Jersey activities, he developed a wide acquaintance in Philadelphia; along with Benjamin Franklin, Francis Hopkinson, and Andrew Hamilton, he was a founder of the American Philosophical Society.

William Smith, Sr., had come over on the same boat with Alexander, gone to Yale on arrival, and been admitted to the bar in

1724; his son and namesake became the historian of the colony.

These counsel had made strenuous efforts to file a suit at common law on behalf of Van Dam. First, they requested the governor to enter an appearance; he ignored the request. Then they applied to the judges to follow chancery practice in the case of a peer of the realm and issue a letter summoning the governor; the judges refused. Their third attempt was to seek an ordinary summons from the clerk of court; he declined to affix the seal. So they were reduced to filing a brief denying that the court had exchequer jurisdiction. Not unforeseeably, the court divided two to one on the issue.

Chief Justice Morris "in the presence of a crowded and exasperated audience" delivered a long opinion on the court's lack of jurisdiction; he was overruled by his two juniors. The governor demanded to see Morris' opinion; before handing it over, Morris had it printed. The angered governor removed him as chief justice, commissioned DeLancey in his stead, moved Philipse up to be first justice, left the remaining place unfilled. Cosby took these steps without the advice and consent of the council. In a letter to a friend, Alexander commented: "How the governors of the Plantations . . . King it abroad."

That was in April 1733. At the autumn elections for the assembly, when Lewis Morris, Sr., Westchester County's representative since 1711, announced his candidacy, the two justices canvassed the county for his opposition. In the town of Westchester, Lewis Morris, Jr., was opposed by a Cosby-appointed clerk of the court. By the device of requiring oaths instead of affirmations, the sheriff disfranchised considerable numbers of Quaker freeholders in the area. Nevertheless, the Morrises won. The old judge's next appearance in New York was "announced by the explosion of the cannon of the merchants' ships in the harbour, and by the citizens meeting and conducting him, with loud acclamations, to a public and splendid entertainment."

Meanwhile the tempo of the Van Dam contest quickened. Van Dam wrote a letter to the governor proffering three alternative dispositions of the matter. It was returned as unintelligible with the comment, "Doubt not but I shall hear that those will prove your best Friends on the End, who advised you TO MAKE PEACE ON ANY TERMS." Shortly, the attorney general issued a writ of rebellion against Van Dam with the purpose of making his estate subject to sequestration. A document was circulated for signature in the waterfront bars declaring that "the said Rip Van Dam is not be found." Van Dam replied with a statement, "I am always to be found at my own House," and added that "low means have been taken to bring my Estate thus into the Hands of a Governor that he may cut and carve for himself . . . we are Tenants at Will to Governours, and exposed to be fleeced by them from Time to Time at their Pleasure."

Yet the supreme court, after affirming its jurisdiction in the governor's suit, proved chary of exercising it. The case never came to trial. Dangling in mid-air, it became the symbol of the differences between the popular party and the governor's men, differences that in the late autumn of 1733 were publicly advertised in the new opposition press.

Until then, New York's single source of regular news had been the weekly *Gazette,* published since November 8, 1725, by William Bradford of Hanover Square, a tranquil and well-established gentleman, just past seventy years of age, with four decades of untroubled New York residence behind him. In addition to being official printer to His Majesty for the colonies of New York and New Jersey, he was co-proprietor of a paper factory.

A member—and, over a period, vestryman—of Trinity Church, he had printed the first American edition of the Book of Common Prayer. He produced the first New York paper currency, the first history of the colony, the first copper-plate engraving of the city.

The *Gazette* featured occasional foreign correspondence from "Venice (a beautiful city in Italy)," or "Vienna (a strong city in Germany)." It published official proclamations, custom house notices, news of prices, and announcements regarding runaway slaves or husbands unwilling to meet their wives' debts. Its editorials were gentle homilies, as in the issue of February 8-15, 1731/2: "There is in Human Nature a certain charming Quality, innate and original to it, which is called Simplicity. In later Ages, this has been almost universally exploded, and banished from amongst men, as the Characteristic of Folly; whilst *Cunning* and *Artifice* have prevailed in its Stead. . . But I believe the juster account of the Matter is, that Simplicity is the homespun Dress of Honesty, and Chicanery and Craft are the Tinsel Habits and the false Elegance which are worn to cover the Deformity of Vice and Knavery."

Thus Bradford had managed to get along with royal governor after royal governor. Benjamin Franklin, himself no novice in the

40

arts of subtlety, called him a "crafty old sophister."

The popular party regarded Bradford's paper as a controlled organ of the Fort. Alexander wrote former Governor Hunter that his successor exercises "the privilege of suffering nothing to be in but what he and Mr. Harrison [a council member close to the governor] approve of." The *Gazette's* account of the governor's hospitality on the occasion of His Majesty's birthday was illustrative: "The regular Troops on new mounting, and their Officers in fine regimental Cloathing, being all the time under Arms in the Parade. About Six in the Evening, the whole City was thoroughly illuminated, and all the appartments in the Fort were filled with a numerous Appearance of Gentlemen and Ladies each of whom, as they entered the Room (where they were received by His Excellency's Lady) was presented with a Cockade of Orange coloured Ribbon . . ." Dancing, cards, other diversions were available: "everything was disposed for the Refreshment of the Company with the Greatest Elegance and Plenty . . . the admirable Address which appear'd through the whole render'd this the most agreeable Night that has been known here . . . the Harmony and good understanding between the several branches of the legislature . . . will we hope continue to us all these blessings which we enjoy under a government greatly envy'd and all too often Disturbed by such as instead thereof are Struggling to introduce Discord, and public Confusion."

The above item appeared in Bradford's issue of October 29-November 4, 1733. On November 5, the *Journal* offered an alternative source of commentary to the people of New York.

The backers of the new paper—Van Dam, the Morrises, Alexander, and others—selected as their printer a Palatinate German who in 1710 had come to New York in a shipload of refugees being resettled by the Crown. Mortality on board had run higher than usual: John Peter Zenger's father was among those who died at sea. The governor apprenticed John Peter along with other orphans. For eight years he learned his trade in William Bradford's print shop. Thereafter he went to Maryland, but returned in 1722 and set up his own press. In 1730, he brought out the first arithmetic book in the colonies. His imperfect knowledge of English made his venture a somewhat struggling one and much of what he did print was in Dutch, but his language disability did not disturb his patrons, for while he did the printing, they wrote most of the copy.

In Number 4, their innuendo was directed against Francis Harrison: "a Large Spaneil, of about Five Foot Five Inches High, has lately stray'd from his Kennel with his mouth full of fulsom Panegyricks and in his Ramble dropt them in the NEW-YORK-GAZETTE."

An oblique reference to the Van Dam case enlivened Number 5: "Deservedly, therefore is this Tryal by Juries, ranked amongst the choicest of our fundamental Laws, which whomsoever shall go about openly to suppress, or craftily to undermine, does ipso facto ATTACK THE GOVERNMENT, AND BRING IN AN ARBITRARY POWER, AND IS AN ENEMY AND TRAYTOR TO HIS COUNTRY."

In Number 8, Cosby was the butt of an alleged interview with a magician regarding the initials of governors' names: "the *H* seems to be a fortunate Letter, witness *Hamilton, Hurley* and *Hunter,* Men of Amiable Characters. On the contrary, *C* has always proved unhappy, either to the Government, or to themselves, or both: He instanced *Campbell* and *Carteret* in New Jersey; and *Coot* and *Cornbury* in New-York." It was after this sally that Chief Justice De-Lancey urged the grand jury to take thoughtful note of "Papers printed, with a Design and a Tendency to alienate the Affections of his Majesty's Subjects of this Province from the Persons whom his Majesty had thought it fitting to set over them."

But the focus of public attention shifted abruptly from the printed to the written word when on Friday, February 1, 1734, guests taking their leave of the Alexanders after an evening party found an anonymous blackmail letter on the threshold:

To Mr. Alexander:

I am one who formerly was counted a gentleman, but am now reduced to poverty, and have no victuals to eat; and knowing you to be of a generous temper, desire you would comply with my request, which is, to let me have 10 pistoles to supply my necessaries and carry me to my native country. This is a bold request, but I desire you will comply with it, or you and your family shall feel the effects of my displeasure. Unless you let me have them, I'll destroy you and your family by a strategem which I have contrived. If that don't take the desired effect, I swear, by God, to poison all your tribe so surely that you shan't know the perpetrator of the tragedy. I beg, for God's sake, that you would let me have the money and hinder me from committing such a black deed. I know you can spare it, so desire you to let me have it. Saturday night about seven o'clock, leave it by the cellar door, wrapped up in a rag, and about an hour after, I will come and take it; put it on the ground just where I put the stick. If you don't leave it, I advise you not to drink your beer, nor eat your bread, if you value your life and health, for by my soul I will do what I have mentioned. If I find any watch to guard me in taking of it, I'll desist and not take it, but follow my intended scheme, and hinder you from acting any more on the stage of life. If you comply, I'll never molest you more; but if not, I'll hazard my life in destroying yours, and continue what I am.

The most interesting feature of this document was the hand-writing. A number of responsible people, including the mayor, were impressed with its similarity to that of Councilman Francis Harrison. But members of the popular party were wary of bringing an accusation. An intimate of the governor, in his cups, had been heard to remark that a scheme was afoot to hang Alexander, and Smith as well. (The governor's lady had frequently observed without reticence that "it was her highest wish to see them on a gallows at the Fort gate.")

Longheaded politicians had noted an article, signed "Spectator," in the January 28 *Gazette* saying that the taking away of the good name of another should be punished by death. The idea was repeated in the February 4 issue. The popular party reasoned that the letter might well be a plant. If Alexander accused Harrison of having written it, a scurrilous communication to the governor might be forged in resemblance of Alexander's handwriting, and both alleged authors persecuted. Alexander would be condemned and hanged, Harrison convicted but pardoned by the governor.

Both a grand jury and a subcommittee of the council recommended that the governor issue a proclamation with promise of reward for the detection of the author. The council affirmed that Mr. Harrison was "incapable of being guilty of so foul a deed, and that the letter was a most wicked, scandalous and infamous counterfeit and forgery."

But nothing further happened. The affair of the anonymous letter, like the Van Dam case, remained in the file of unfinished business. Harrison, after being put in an unenviable light in an unrelated lawsuit, shortly left the country permanently for England.

On the surface, the spring of 1734 was a time of détente. The assembly, it is true, held a full dress debate on the assumption of exchequer jurisdiction by the court, but the governor's manner had softened markedly. A correspondent noted that "persons of inferior status were invited to the Fort and dined at his table."

First fruit of the new hospitality on the Battery was a document applauding the current mildness of the Cosby administration, signed by many of those who had recently enjoyed his pleasure; it was published in the *Gazette* as a formal address to His Excellency.

In riposte, the *Journal* carried a letter to the editor: "I Am a poor Man and have been Tenant to several Landlords since I came to this Country . . . and have been well used by all my Landlords except the Last, who has given me several gross Affronts, altho I have paid him by far the greatest Part of his Rents and made him several handsome Presents. But now of late he grows extremely Civil, I am invited, and (when Business allows me to come) entertained after the elegantest Manner. I desire to Publish this for I am at a Loss to know the Reason for this late and extraordinary Civility, is it not to Cajole me to sign a new Lease, or to give him more Rent?"

Members of the New York City Council who were signers of the address complimenting the governor shortly had cause for regret: the popular party entered candidates against them in the autumn elections. Gerald Stuyvesant, who had not signed, was re-elected unanimously, but when the counts were completed—the vote took place on the feast day of St. Michael, the militant archangel—among those incumbents who had had opposition, John Moore alone remained in office.

Overnight, an anonymous broadsheet appeared, setting political words to two popular tunes. By evening, from doors and windows of the town's taverns, beery bursts of cheerful sound brought the words of these catches, sung with gusto by post-election celebrants, to the ears of the governor's men.

The first "Song Made upon the Election of new Magistrates for this City" was a relatively mild ditty, a parody of "To you fair Ladies now on land," beginning

> To you good lads that dare oppose
>   All lawless power and might
> You are the theme that we have chose
>   And to your praise we write:
> You dar'd to shew your faces brave

> In spighte of every abject slave;
> With a fa la la . . .

But every phrase of the second "Song made upon the foregoing Occasion," written to the tune, "Now, now, you Tories all shall Stoop," was packed with political innuendo. Item by item, it reviewed the accumulated grievances of the past two years:

> Come on brave boys, let us be brave for liberty and law
> Boldly despise the haughty Knave that would keep us in aw.
> Let's scorn the tools bought by a sop and every cringing fool.
> The man who basely bend's a sop a vile insipid tool.

> Our Country's Rights we will defend, like brave and honest men:
> We voted right and there's an end, and so we'll do again.
> We vote all signers out of place as men who did amiss,
> Who sold us by a false adress, I'm sure we're right in this.

> Exchequer courts, as void by law, great grievances we call;
> Tho' great men do assert no flaw is in them; they shall fall,
> And be contemn'd by every man that's fond of liberty
> Let them withstand it all they can, our Laws we will stand by.

> Tho' pettyfogging knaves deny us Rights of Englishmen;
> We'll make the scoundrel raskals fly, and ne'er return again.
> Our Judges they would chop and change for those that
>   serve their turn,
> And will not surely think it strange if they for this
>   should mourn.

> Come fill a bumber, fill it up, unto our Aldermen;
> For common-council fill the cup, and take it o'er again.
> While they with us resolve to stand for liberty and law,
> We'll drink their healths with hat in hand, Whoraa!
>   Whoraa! Whoraa!

After the burning of these ballads and the arrest of the *Journal's* printer, the issue between the popular party and the governor was squarely joined.

Zenger's defense attorneys were Alexander and Smith. Alexander prepared a careful brief for his defense. At the April court, they began by challenging the legality of the commissions of the two supreme court justices on the double ground that the governor had made their appointments without the advice and consent of the council and that their commissions read "during pleasure" instead

45

of "during good behavior."

Chief Justice DeLancey was outraged. Addressing Smith, he said: "You thought to have gained a great Deal of Applause and Popularity by opposing this Court, as you did the Court of Exchequer; but you have brought it to that Point, That eithtr, We must go from the Bench, or you from the Barr; Therefore We exclude you and Mr. Alexander from the Bar."

The two lawyers were dumbfounded. Disbarment, as they pointed out in formal complaint to the next session of the assembly, deprived them of their means of livelihood: "Had we err'd; must a Man loose his Livelihood for an innocent Mistake? Must we be put out to starve, or seek our Bread in a new Country or in a Manner of Life, for one Contempt? . . . Instead of consulting our Law Books, and doing what we think consistent therewith, for the Benefit of our Clients, we must study in GREAT MEN'S CAUSES, only what will PLEASE the Judges, and what will most flatter Men in Power."

The court assigned John Chambers, one of the signers, to replace the disbarred men as Zenger's counsel. (He later became second justice of the supreme court.) The date for trial was set as August 4.

Alexander prepared two statements to be made by Zenger in his own defense, but he and Smith determined to find other counsel for their client, seeking a man who not only was not one of the governor's coterie, but also was not a New Yorker and thus not subject like themselves to peremptory disbarment.

Two Philadelphia lawyers, John Kearsley and Andrew Hamilton, were widely known outside their colony. The former was unavailable because currently engaged in negotiations with Cosby. A concerted letter-writing campaign was planned to induce the latter, with whom Alexander had been associated in many past cases, to accept the brief.

Hamilton was thoroughly accustomed to dealing with men in high places. Emigrating to Virginia's Eastern Shore near the turn of the century, he began practice as an attorney, acquired considerable property, married a well-to-do Quaker widow. In 1709 he moved to Kent County, Maryland; his new plantation was very close to the disputed line between Maryland and the three lower counties on the Delaware, of which William Penn had secured possession. Practice at Dover, the capital of the middle of these counties, and frequent transactions in Philadelphia shortly led to Hamilton's being retained as attorney for the Penns.

In 1712-13, he crossed the Atlantic to read law at Gray's Inn, but his standing was promptly recognized: he had been there less than two weeks when he was called "per favor" to the bar.

Back in America, he made a further move, to Philadelphia. He was then named attorney general of Pennsylvania and speaker of the three lower counties, representing the area in its boundary negotiations with Lord Baltimore.

A few years later he went to England again, to probate the will of Pennsylvania's proprietor, William Penn; on his return he served as recorder of the city of Philadelphia, prothonotary of the supreme court, and Bucks County representative in the assembly, where, with the exception of one session, he was annually chosen speaker for over a decade following 1729.

Yet Hamilton suffered from two handicaps. A heavyset, florid man he endured acute pain from gout, and while only fifty-nine he gave the appearance of being well along in years. The journey to New York, in the heat of August, was bound to be tiresome, and the assignment vexatious. When word came that he would take the case, the popular party, keeping his acceptance quiet for the shock effect of his entry into the courtroom, looked forward to Zenger's trial with confidence.

Alexander briefed Hamilton on their difficulties. This was a political trial, and the supreme court justices were governor's men. Zenger had indeed printed the offending newspapers. If the court would not permit the jury to do more than ascertain the fact of publication, the judges would apply the law as the governor wanted, and a conviction was unavoidable.

Hamilton determined to go into the courtroom and argue that truth could not be libelous and that a jury should be authorized not only to find the facts but to consider them in relation to the law as well.

Actually, his intention was not wholly without support. In addition to Bushell's case in England, there had been a more recent trial in Pennsylvania; if it had ended in a clear-cut verdict, Hamilton would have had a telling citation at hand.

The Philadelphia case was exceptionally pertinent to his argument, for it concerned a printer who, forty years before, had been sent to jail charged with printing a seditious libel, exactly as Zenger was now charged. Arguing his own case, this defendant had rested on the very grounds that Hamilton planned to use; on truth as a defense and on the jury's right to apply law to the facts. The case ended with a hung jury, but the arguments had all been made.

Its pertinence to the New York trial, moreover, had a further dimension: the Zenger drama contained a play within a play. The printer who went to jail in Philadelphia and the man who now basked in Governor Cosby's confidence as the publisher of *The New-York Gazette* were one and the same.

William Bradford, the elderly Episcopalian who throughout the Zenger trial printed the governor's proclamations and made no reference to his Philadelphia story, had been the Quaker lad of whom, in 1685, George Fox wrote to Friends in Philadelphia: "This is to let you know that a sober young man whose name is William Bradford, comes to Philadelphia to set up the trade of printing Friends' books."

The young Bradford had recently completed his apprenticeship under Andrew Sowle, London's chief printer of Quaker tracts, had adopted his patron's religion (Bradford had been raised an Anglican), and had married his daughter. He was already familiar with Pennsylvania affairs: at William Penn's request, under his own name though doubtless on his employer's press, Bradford had printed the first "Frame of Government" for the tract of land that Charles II granted to Penn in 1681. The grant was in recognition of a £16,000 loan made to the Stuart cause by the admiring admiral, Penn's father; the name, Pennsylvania, was in his honor.

By the end of 1685, Bradford was set up in Philadelphia, and had printed an almanac with the preface: "Hereby understand that after great Charge and Trouble, I have brought that great Art and Mystery of Printing into this part of America believing it may be of great service to you in several respects. . . . Some Irregularities, there be in this Diary, which I desire you to pass by this year; for being lately come hither, my matereals were Misplaced, and out of order, whereupon I was forced to use Figures and Letters of various sizes. . . ."

But after his "letters" were sorted, his printing continued to run into difficulties. His 1686 almanac, though the data in it had been compiled by another man, brought a rebuke from the Quakers, initiated by Penn's cousin, William Markham, the secretary of the council. The reference to "the beginning of government by ye Lord Penn," he was informed, should have read, "by Mr. Penn";

Quakers disapprove of titles. The offending words were ordered to be inked out, and Bradford was warned not to print anything "but what shall have lycence from ye Council."

His 1688 issue was also unsatisfactory: the Friends' Philadelphia Quarterly Meeting paid him £1 for copies confiscated and destroyed as containing "light, foolish and unsavoury paragraphs."

The Friends' Yearly Meeting, moreover, disappointed Bradford in his desire to print an edition of the Bible; he offered to do so at forty shillings the copy, half to be paid in specie and half in goods at the price of specie. (The Friends' enthusiasm may have been tempered not only by the price but also by Bradford's plan to include the Anglican Book of Common Prayer as an appendix.)

Next the civil authorities rebuked him. William Penn arrived

49

in 1682 to see to the governance of his province, but returned to England in less than two years. Even before he left, his revisions of the colony's charter had caused restlessness in the assembly; it increased while Penn continued in London enjoying high court favor under James II.

In the course of one of the local disputes that flourished under his deputies, Bradford printed the revised charter, along with Magna Carta and an abstract of Penn's patent, at the initiative of a Friend who wanted copies available for a contest with the vice-governor. Haled before council, for again printing without license by the government, this time he was bound under a £500 penalty.

Meanwhile, he had allied himself spiritually with George Keith, a prominent and controversial Friend, founder of the Penn Charter School. Keith was the author of numerous polemical pamphlets directed at other sects—he and Cotton Mather exchanged anathema —and other factions within the Friends. His religious views, including his proposal to include celebration of baptism and the Lord's Supper in the Friends' order of service, were of lasting influence on Bradford. But the controversy in which his writings involved the printer concerned Quaker policy in a secular situation.

Pirates were preying lucratively on Philadelphia's growing volume of shipping. When the provincial government ordered armed vessels fitted out to suppress them, Keith castigated their decision as a use of force that denied Quaker principles. Replying, twenty-eight Quaker preachers collectively castigated his castigation. Keith, saying that he had been condemned without a trial, wrote a document for advance circulation before the Friends' Yearly Meeting in mid-summer 1692: "An Appeal from the Twenty-eight Judges to the Spirit of Truth." Bradford printed it.

At the end of the meeting, the town crier circulated a "Publick-writing" about the incident, and the justices of the county of Philadelphia issued a warrant for Bradford's arrest. On August 24, he and John McComb, keeper of an ordinary, each of whom was found to have sold a copy of Keith's pamphlet, were sent to jail under a mittimus that declared: "Whereas William Bradford printer, and John McComb Taylor, being brought before us, upon an Information of Publishing, Uttering and Spreading a Malicious and Seditious Paper," refuse to give bail, they are to be taken into custody by the sheriff and safely kept "till they shall be discharged by due Course of Law." Two of the justices, who were not Quakers, insisted that the dispute was a sectarian disagreement and not a proper subject for court action, but were overruled.

The accused remained in jail, and the sheriff, according to a Bradford sympathizer, "took away a good quantity of Bradford's Letters" from his printery, and from his bookshop, "half as much more as the said Warrant was for."

Bradford and McComb appeared before the court next quarter sessions, "desired they might come to a Trial, it being greatly to their Prejudice, to be kept Prisoners . . . it is provided by Magna Charta, that Justice shall not be delayed on any and we being free born English subjects claim this as our priviledge, and hope this Court will not deny us it, because not only our Persons are restrained, but William Bradford's working Tools are detained from him, with which he should work to maintain his Family."

The following interchange then took place between the justices and the prisoners:

JUSTICE COOK: What Bold, Impudent and Confident Fellows are these, to stand thus confidently before the Court?

McCOMB: You may cause our hats to be taken off, if you please.

BRADFORD: We are here only to desire that which is the right of every free-born English subject, which is speedy Justice, and its strange that that should be accounted Impudence, and we Impudent Fellows therefore, when we have spoken nothing but words of Truth and Soberness, in requesting that which is our Right, and which we want, it being greatly to our Prejudice to be detained Prisoners.

JUSTICE COOK: If thou hadst been in England, thou wouldst have had thy back slasht before now.

BRADFORD: I do not know wherein I have broke any Law, so as to incur any such Punishment.

JUSTICE JENNINGS: Thou art very ignorant in the Law surely; does not thou know that there's a Law, that every Printer shall put his Name to the Book he prints, which thou hast not done.

They still pressed for a trial.

JUSTICE COOK: A trial you shall have, and that to your Cost, too, it may be.

JUSTICE JENNINGS: A Tryal you shall have, but for some Reason known to us, the Court defers it to next Session; and that is the Answer we give, and no other shall you have.

51

So back they went to jail. When the council suspended Mc-Comb's license to keep an ordinary, symapthizers raged, "his Wife was but two days delivered of a Child, and in danger of Death, by a Flux, . . . and yet he could not prevail so much as to go home to take leave of his Wife, or set his House in order. . . ."

Actually, in Bradford's case at least, the confinement did not amount to more than house arrest during the next months. His press brought out a number of items, including the new almanac and further treatises by James Keith, in one of which he developed the doctrinal basis for a new sect known as the Christian-Quakers.

The case came to trial at the December quarter sessions. Of the eight justices present that day, including Justices Jennings and Cook, six were Quakers. David Lloyd, an assemblyman from Chester, served as special attorney for the prosecution; Bradford presented his own case.

Called before the bar, he was charged with printing a seditious paper, of which the ninth to twelfth articles were said to be "of a tendence to weaken the hands of the Magistrates."

BRADFORD: Justice Cook told us last Court that one reason why ye deferred our Trial then, was, that we might have time to prepare ourselves to answer it; but ye never let me have a copy of my Presentment, nor will ye now let me know what Law ye prosecute me upon.

ATTORNEY LLOYD: It's not usual to insert in Indictments against what statute the offence is, when its against several Statutes and Laws made, and if thou wilt not plead guilty or not guilty, thou wilt lose thy Opportunity of being Tried by thy Country.

The clerk was ordered to note that Bradford refused to plead. As he was making the notation, Bradford asked that they not take advantage of him, and several of the justices agreed. He then pled not guilty.

The jury was summoned. The proper functions of a jury became an issue when Bradford was asked if he had objections to any of the jurors.

BRADFORD: Yes, I have and particularly against two of them, . . . Joseph Kirle and James Fox; for at the time when I was committed to Prison Arthur Cook told me, that Joseph Kirle had said, that if the proceedings of the Magistrates was thus found fault with, that they must not defend themselves against Thieves and Robbers, Merchants would be discouraged of coming here with their vessels.

Bradford himself had heard the other juror, on the day after one of the principal pirates was captured, find fault with a fellow citizen who disapproved of Quakers commanding men and pressing them to pursue privateers.

ATTORNEY LLOYD (*holding such objections irrelevant*): Hast thou at any time heard them say that thou printed the paper? For that is only what they are to find.
BRADFORD: That is not only what they are to find. They are to find also whether this be a seditious paper or not, and whether it does tend to weaken the hands of the magistrates.
ATTORNEY LLOYD: Nay, that is matter of law, which the jury is not to meddle with, but find whether William Bradford printed it or no, and the Bench is to judge whether it be a seditious paper or not; for the law has determined what is a Breach of the Peace, and the penalty, which the Bench only is to give judgment on.
JUSTICE JENNINGS (*to the jury*): You are only to try whether William Bradford printed it or not.
BRADFORD: This is wrong, for the Jury are Judges in Law, as well as in matter of fact.

Everyone began to talk at once. Members of the jury desired to know what they were attested to try, declaring they "did believe in their consciences, they were obliged to try to find whether that Paper was Seditous, as well as whether William Bradford printed." Some of them asked to be discharged. Some of the justices wanted to accept Bradford's objections to the two jurors.

JUSTICE COOK (*attempting to secure order*): I will not allow of it; is there four of us of a mind?

Lloyd then presented the government's case, not only against Keith's pamphlet but for the decision to arm vessels· against the privateers. He denied that men had actually been hired to fight—they were only to fetch back a captured sloop from the pirates. He emphasized that they had not been given a commission, but only a hue-and-cry warrant. And furthermore, "what was done was in a case of great necessity, when a Company of Rogues had Pyratically stolen away a Sloop to the great terror of the People of this place; and if the Magistrates must be blamed for their proceedings herein, what do you think will be the consequences thereof, but to encourage all manner of Wickedness? And Will Bradford is presented for printing and publishing this Seditious Paper, whereof you of the Jury are to find him guilty if it appears to you that he has printed it."

BRADFORD: I desire you of the Jury and all here present, to take notice that what is here contained in the Paper is not Seditious, but wholly related to a Religious Difference, and asserting the Quakers Ancient Principles, and is not laid down positive, that they ought not to have proceeded against the Privateers, but laid down by way of query, for the People called Quakers to consider and resolve at their Yearly Meeting, Whether it was not a Transgression of the Quakers Principles to hire and commission men to fight.

JUSTICE COOK: If it was intended for the yearly meeting at Burlington, why was it published and spread abroad before the meeting?

BRADFORD: Because it might be pursued and considered of any Friends before the Meeting, even as the Bills that are prepared to be passed into laws, they are promulgated a certain number of days, before the Assembly meets, that all may have opportunity to consider them.

Before summing up, Lloyd read the Act of 14 Charles II against books being printed without the printer's name and noted that for this, too, Bradford was prosecuted. Then, reaffirming the sedition, he reminded the jurors "it was evident William Bradford printed it, he being the printer in this place; and the frame on which it was printed was found in his House."

BRADFORD: I desire the Jury, and all here present to take notice, that there ought to be two evidences [witnesses] to prove the matter of Fact, but not one evidence has been brought in this case.

JUSTICE JENNINGS: The frame on which it is printed is evidence enough.

BRADFORD: But where is the Frame, there has been no Frame produced here, and if there had, it is no Evidence, unless you saw me print on it.

JUSTICE JENNINGS: The jury shall have the Frame with them, it cannot well be brought here: and besides, the season is cold, and we are not to sit here to endanger our health; you are minded to put tricks upon us.

BRADFORD: I say the Jury ought not to hear or have any Evidence whatsoever, but in the presence of the judge and prisoner.

Justice Jennings ignored the point, but his charge to the jury, which followed, was unexpectedly in Bradford's favor: contrary to his and Justice Cook's previous reasoning, he accepted the broad interpretation of the juryman's function and instructed it to find:

First, whether or not that Paper, call'd the Appeal, had not a tendency to the weakening of the hands of the magistrates, and encouragement of wickedness.

2dly, whether it did not tend to the Disturbance of the Peace, and

3dly, whether William Bradford did not print without putting his name to it, as the law requires.

Had the jury brought in a verdict on these counts, the case would have been a legal milestone: the judges had charged them to apply law to the facts. But the jury could not agree. It split as between the nine Quakers and the three non-Quakers. After being out forty-eight hours they returned to the courtroom to ask: "Whether the Law did not require two evidences to find a man guilty?"

The prosecutor read them a passage out of a law book: they must determine guilt by evidence, or on their own knowledge, or otherwise. "Now this otherwise," said he, "is the Frame which you have, which is Evidence sufficient."

BRADFORD: The Frame which they have is no Evidence, for I have not seen it, and how do I know that that which was carried in to them is mine?

But the frame no longer existed. When it was taken to the jury room, a near-sighted juror had tilted it up, the better to read the inky lettering. One noisy and horrifying instant later, he was holding an empty rectangle; in an unintelligible printer's pie, the loosened type littered the floor.

The jury was ordered to retire again, and an officer instructed to keep them without meat, drink, fire, or tobacco until they should agree. That afternoon, they reaffirmed their inability to do so and were discharged.

In the absence of a conviction, Bradford expected to be discharged also, but Justice Jennings surprised him with the statement: "No, thou shalt not have thy things now, thou standest in the same capacity to answer next Court as before." So Bradford remained under house arrest, and his press remained confiscated.

Meanwhile, the political status of Pennsylvania had altered. In Britain, when the Glorious Revolution of 1689 replaced James II with William and Mary, Penn's activities on behalf of the outgoing monarch led him close to the borderline of what the new succession regarded as treason. In 1692, an order in council deprived him of his province. Colonel Benjamin Fletcher, the new governor of New York, was commissioned to take over the Pennsylvania government —though Penn warned him to "tread softly" and recovered his proprietorship in 1694.

Fletcher arrived with suitable pomp in Philadelphia in April 1693. Bradford promptly lodged an appeal to the new governor. He received a most cordial hearing; New York was without a printer. In fact, just before Fletcher left for Philadelphia, his council had resolved "that if a printer will come and settle in the City of New Yorke for the printing of our Acts of Assembly & Publick papers he shall be allowed the Summe of forty pounds Current money of New Yorke per annum for his salary & have the benefits of his printing besides what serves the publick."

With this in view, on April 23, the governor of New York, in his capacity as governor of Pennsylvania, ordered restoration of the tools of William Bradford. Before the month was out, the prisoner, his family and his Blau press had a new address at 81 Pearl Street and a commission retroactive to the time of the governor's arrival in Philadelphia. One of his first New York publications, over and above his official printing, was a full account of his trial and a rhymed attack on Justice Jennings in twenty-four stanzas.

Bradford's return to the religion of his childhood on reaching New York is less subject to a charge of opportunism than his silence during the Zenger case. True, Governor Fletcher was an ardent

Anglican, to whose newly erected church inside the Fort Queen Mary sent suitable prayerbooks, plate, and furniture. But Bradford's friend George Keith had moved in the same direction. Disowned by the Friends' Yearly Meeting of London, he affiliated with the Church of England in 1702 and returned to America as an agent of the Society for the Propagation of the Gospel in Foreign Parts. Bradford published the sermons he preached in Trinity Church in that capacity.

Such was Bradford's Philadelphia story. But on the morning of August 4, 1735, few New Yorkers were thinking about the past of William Bradford. This was the day for the trial of John Peter Zenger. All sorts and conditions of men milled around the corner of Nassau and Wall streets, trying to wedge their way into the city hall for the spectacle. Inside, Chief Justice DeLancey and First Justice Philipse sat robed and wigged on the bench; the jury waited attentively, with one Thomas Hunt, mariner, as foreman. The choosing of these twelve good men and true had been the occasion of a wrangle in which Zenger's representatives had successfully forced the sheriff to draw his names from a complete roll of freeholders rather than a select panel. The Dutch ancestry of a majority of the men chosen was significant against the background of the Van Dam case.

Richard Bradley, attorney general and member of the council, was holding his brief for the prosecution; young John Chambers, his for the defense. Then way was made for Andrew Hamilton to enter. At sight of him, the crowd sucked in its breath and packed itself more tightly.

Opening the proceedings, the attorney general announced that the charge concerned "printing and publishing a false, scandalous and seditious libel, in which his Excellency the Governor of this Province, who is the King's immediate Representative here, is greatly and unjustly scandalized as a Person that has no Regard to Law nor Justice." He informed the court that the prisoner pleaded not guilty.

Mr. Chambers initiated the defense. He set forth the nature of libel, emphasizing the importance of great allowances being made for what men spoke or wrote. In the case of an alleged libel, there should be no doubt about who is being attacked by the offending statement. He hoped the attorney general would fail in his proof.

Hamilton forestalled the prosecution's next move by announc-

57

ing that he freely admitted his client to have published the documents in question; it was unnecessary to summon witnesses.

The attorney general saw an opportunity: since the publication of the statements is admitted, "I think the Jury must find a Verdict for the King, for supposing they were true, the Law says that they are not less libellous for that; nay indeed the Law says, their being true is an Aggravation of the Libel."

Hamilton denied that the fact of printing necessarily made the paper libelous: "The Words themselves must be libelous . . . or else we are not guilty."

Bradley countered with citations. In the eyes of the law both of God and of man "it was a very great Offence to speak evil of, or to revile those in Authority over us." The governor and council had finally decided that Zenger "ought not to be suffered to go on . . . and therefore they had directed this Prosecution."

Hamilton picked up a new theme. He himself, he said, had not even been sure that much of the material was directed against the governor. Now he finds that it is the governor and council who are directing the prosecution. "From the extraordinary Appearance of People of all Conditions, which I observe in Court upon this Occasion, I have Reason to think, that those in the Administration have by this Prosecution something more in View, and that the People believe they have a good deal more at Stake, than I apprehended."

He found it also worthy of note that the cases just cited by the attorney general concern the libeling not of an appointed official, but of the King himself. "Is it not surprising to see a Subject upon his receiving a Commission from the King to be a Governor of a Colony in America, immediately imaging himself to be vested with all the Prerogatives belonging to the sacred Person of his Prince?"

Bradley returned to his previous line of attack: "Nothing is plainer than that the Words in the Information are scandalous, and tend to sedition, and to disquiet the Minds of the People of this Province."

Hamilton observed that the attorney had not said the words were false: "If he can prove the Facts charged upon us, to be *false* I'll own them to be *scandalous, seditious* and a *Libel*." The chief justice intervened: "You cannot be admitted, Mr. Hamilton, to give the Truth of a Libel in Evidence. A Libel is not to be justi-

fied; for it is nevertheless a Libel that it is true."

Hamilton offered cases where the falsehood of a libel had been the ground for judgment. The court considered these for some time. The chief justice asked the attorney general what he thought of Hamilton's offer to prove the papers "to be true, at our peril."

THE ATTORNEY GENERAL: The Law in my opinion is very clear; they cannot be admitted to justify a Libel.

THE CHIEF JUSTICE: Mr. Hamilton, the Court is of the Opinion, you ought not to be permitted to prove the Facts in the Papers.

HAMILTON: These are Star Chamber Cases, and I was in hopes that Practice had been dead with the Court.

THE CHIEF JUSTICE: Mr. Hamilton, the Court have delivered their Opinion, and we expect you will use us with Good Manners; you are not to be permitted to argue against the Opinion of the Court.

HAMILTON: With Submission, I have seen the Practice in very great Courts, and never heard it deemed unmannerly to . . .

THE CHIEF JUSTICE (*cutting in*): After the Court have declared their Opinion, it is not good manners to insist upon a Point, in which you are overruled.

HAMILTON (*turning from the court to the jury*): It is to you we must now appeal . . . The Reason of your being taken out of the Neighbourhood is, because you are supposed to have the best Knowledge of the fact that is to be tried. And were you to find a Verdict against my client, you must take upon you to say, the Papers referred to in the Information, and which we acknowledge we printed and published, are false, scandalous and seditious: but . . . you are really what the Law supposes you to be, honest and lawful Men, and, according to my Brief, the Facts which we offer to prove were not committed in a Corner; they are notoriously known to be true; and therefore in your Justice lies our Safety.

Re-examining the definition of libel, Hamilton then worked the chief justice around to agree that words must be interpreted as they are understood.

THE CHIEF JUSTICE: All Words are libelous, or not, as they are understood. Those who are to judge of the Words, must judge whether they are scandalous or ironical, tend to the Breach

of the Peace, or are Seditious: there can be no Doubt of it.
HAMILTON: I thank your Honour; I am glad to find the Court of
this Opinion. Then it follows that these twelve men must
understand the Words in the Information to be scandalous,
that is to say, false . . . and when they understand the Words
to be so, they will say we are guilty of publishing a false libel,
and not otherwise.

THE CHIEF JUSTICE (*reaffirming the point that Justice Jennings had
made in the Bradford case*): No, Mr. Hamilton, the Jury may
find that Zenger printed and published those Papers, and
leave it to the Court to judge whether they are libellous . . .

HAMILTON: I know, may it please Your Honour, the Jury may do
so, but I do likewise know, they may do otherwise. I know
they have the Right beyond all Dispute, to determine both
the Law and the Fact . . . This leaving it to the Judgment
of the Court, whether the words are libellous or not, in
Effect makes Juries useless (to say no worse) in many Cases
. . . in the reign of an arbitrary Prince, where Judges held
their Seats at Pleasure, their Determinations have not always
been such as to make Precedents of, but the Contrary.

He reviewed the great changes that have occurred in law over
time: "There is Heresy in Law, as well as in Religion, and both
have changed very much; and we well know that it is not two
Centuries ago that a Man would have been burnt as a Heretick for
owning such Opinions in Matters of Religion as are publickly wrote
and printed at this Day . . . From which I think it is pretty clear,
That in New York a Man may make very free with his God, but
he must take special Care what he says of his Governour."

As a final instance to support a jury's right to find law as well as
fact, Hamilton cited the Bushell case. Summarizing its outcome,
he pressed home his point: "It is established for Law, That the
Judges, how great soever they be, have no Right to Fine, imprison
or punish a Jury, for not finding a Verdict according to the Direction of the Court. And this I hope is sufficient to prove, That Jurymen are to see with their own Eyes, to hear with their own ears,
and to make use of their own Consciences and understandings, in
judging of the Lives, Liberties or Estates of their fellow Subjects."

Returning to the interpretations that may be put upon words,
Hamilton warned the jury—and the crowd—of the danger that might

61

be run by a man who merely reads parts of the Bible in public: "What of Isiah LVI, verses 10 and 11? The words are, 'His watchmen are all blind, they are ignorant, &c. Yea, they are greedy Dogs that can never have enough.' " The attorney general, Hamilton suggested, might interpret a reading of this passage as libelous: "As for Instance; His Watchmen (innuendo, the Governour's Council and Assembly) are blind, they are ignorant (innuendo, will not see the dangerous Designs of His Excellency) Yea, they (the Governour and Council meaning) are greedy Dogs, which can never have enough (innuendo, enough of Riches and Power.)"

Resuming his seriousness, Hamilton closed: "Power may Justly be compared to a great River, while kept within its due Bounds, is both Beautiful and Useful; but when it over flows it's Banks, it is then too impetuous to be stemm'd, it bears down all before it, and brings Destruction and Desolation wherever it comes . . . I hope to be pardon'd Sir for my Zeal upon this Occasion; it is an old and wise Caution that when our Neighbour's House is on Fire, we ought to take Care of our own. For tho' Blessed be God I live in a Government where Liberty is well understood, and freely enjoy'd; yet Experience has shewn us all (I'm sure it has to me) that a bad Precedent in one Government, is soon set up for an Authority in another. . . You see, I labour under the Weight of many Years, and am born down with great Infirmaties of Body; yet Old and Weak as I am, I should think it my Duty, if required, to go to the utmost Part of the Land, where my Service would be of any Use in assisting to quench the Flame of Prosecutions upon Informations, set on foot by the Government, to deprive a People of the Right to Remonstrating (and complaining too) of the arbitrary Attempts of Men in Power."

When Hamilton had done, the attorney general reiterated that all the jury had to do was to consider the fact of printing and publishing; since Hamilton had admitted his client had done this, Zenger was without doubt guilty.

The nettled court asked the jury to observe "the great pains Mr. Hamilton had taken, to show how little Regard Juries are to Pay to the Opinion of the Judges." Once again, the court stressed that the facts were confessed, and the determination of the libel must be left to the judges.

The jury was out only briefly. When Thomas Hunt led it back, it was to announce a verdict of not guilty. Former Chief Justice

Morris' son-in-law led the huzzas that burst the courtroom.

Zenger was free. The *Journal* was in business at the old stand as the opposition paper of New York. A new principle had been sustained in the law of libel, and a new procedure for juries.

Hamilton was borne away to a festive dinner tendered him by forty citizens at the Black Horse Tavern in Smith Street. Next day, when he went down to the waterfront to embark on his return voyage to Philadelphia, the guns of New York's merchantmen barked salute.

Forthwith, James Alexander edited and Zenger published a detailed account of the trial. Neither Attorney General Bradley nor John Chambers supplied the full transcript of their arguments that was requested, but Hamilton's complete brief was reproduced. Many copies of this 1736 edition were sent to London; a reprint there sold out four editions in three months in 1738. Other prints were run off in Boston and in Lancaster, Pennsylvania.

In July 1737, a careful rebuttal of Hamilton's brief, based on accepted principles of English law, was published in Keimer's *Barbadoes Gazette* by "Anglo-Americanus" and reprinted by Bradford in New York and by Franklin's *Pennsylvania Gazette* in Philadelphia. Immediately afterwards, Franklin published James Alexander's response.

In 1765, in London, Zenger's account was combined with a description of a similar case, concerning William Owen, bookseller in Temple Bar, "who was also charged with the Publications of a libel against the government, of which he was honourably acquitted by a jury of freeborn Englishmen." In 1770, a further edition appeared in New York at the time of the indictment of Alexander MacDougall.

It was eighty-six years after the trial, however, before the principle enunciated in the Zenger case was given official form in a New York declaration of rights.

In 1776, the revolutionary convention of New York had instructed a committee to draw up and report a bill of rights and a frame of government, but its report was read from atop a barrel to a harried convention assembled for safety in Kingston-on-Hudson's town square—the British held New York. This hasty document supplied only the new state's most immediate needs: a legislative and an executive arm. The judiciary was given no more than a passing note, and the bill of rights was left out altogether.

Yet the absence of a bill of rights from the proposed federal Constitution as presented for ratification in 1788 was the main reason why, as the New York convention began deliberations, sentiment was estimated as perhaps two to one against adoption. Eventually the combined persuasiveness and parliamentary skill of Alexander Hamilton and John Jay produced a final vote of thirty to twenty-seven in favor of accession. The slender affirmative margin was largely due to a commitment to prefix the ratifying statement with a draft declaration of rights for immediate consideration by the first Congress as amendments to the document.

The draft ran to twenty-eight articles, of which one affirmed "That the People have a right peaceably to assemble together to consult for their common good, or to instruct their Representatives, and that every person has a right to petition or apply to the Legislature for redress of grievances—that the Freedom of the Press ought not to be violated or restrained."

Then, and only then, "Under these impressions and declaring that the rights aforesaid cannot be abridged or violated, and that the Explanations aforesaid are consistent with the said Constitution, and in confidence that the Amendments which shall have been proposed to the said Constitution will receive early and mature Consideration: we the said Delegates, in the Name and on behalf of the People of the State of New York Do by these presents Assent to and Ratify the said Constitution." But New York still lacked a declaration of its own.

Meanwhile the legal impact of the Zenger case continued. In England, Fox's Libel Act, passed by Parliament in 1792, established beyond further challenge the right of juries considering sedition to judge both law and fact.

A few years later, the willingness of the young American republic to countenance criticism of its government comparable to the criticism of royal rule by colonial patriots was tested in turn, and a key case was brought in New York. Section 2 of the Federal Sedition Act of 1798 sounded rather like a governor in council: "scandalous and malicious writing or writings against the government of the United States, or either House of Congress of the United States, or the President of the United States with intent to defame . . . convicted before any court of the United States having jurisdiction thereof, shall be punished by a fine not exceeding $2,000 or by imprisonment not exceeding two years,"

The Habeas Corpus, or The Wild Geese flying away with Fox to America.

Pub. by J. Sparrow, August. 27. 1782. No. 84. Dorset Street, Salisbury Court, Fleet Street.

Nº 9.

though the statute also specified that "the jury who shall try the case shall have the right to determine the law and the fact, under the direction of the court, as in other cases."

Under this statute, in 1804, the editor of *The Hudson Wasp,* a Federalist paper in New York, was brought into court for seditious libel after an attack on President Jefferson. He was represented by another lawyer named Hamilton—Alexander, this time—who repeated his predecessor's contention. Liberty of the press, he insisted, includes "the right to publish, with impunity, truth, with good motives, for justifiable ends, though reflecting on government, magistracy, or individuals."

This brief supplied draft wording when, in 1821, New York finally adopted a complete constitution. In its Article 7, devoted to "Rights and Prohibitions," Section 8 recognized both the principle and the procedure which Andrew Hamilton's brief had relied on and Alexander Hamilton's had re-affirmed: "Every citizen may freely speak, write and publish his sentiments, on all subjects, being responsible for the abuse of that right; and no law shall be passed to restrain or abridge the liberty of speech, or of the press. In all prosecutions or indictments for libels the truth may be given in evidence, to the jury; and if it shall appear to the jury, that the matter charged as libellous, is true, and was published with good motives, and for justifiable ends, the party shall be acquitted; and the jury shall have the right to determine the law and the fact."

CHAPTER III

THE RIGHT TO BEAR ARMS

The Bill of Rights: A well regulated militia, being necessary to the security of a free state, the right of the people to keep and bear arms, shall not be infringed.

BACKGROUND

The preference for a citizen army expressed in the American bills of rights had deep roots in historic subsoil. Down the centuries, a conviction that for the defense of liberty a militia was far sounder than a professional force had been ingrained in the English yeoman. He was sturdily opposed to standing armies in peacetime; he had observed that the military all too easily became makers of kings, initiators of policy, independent repositories of power. He was proud that the eyes and arms of the longbowmen of Agincourt were trained in the butts of England's villages, proving that a citizen army was not only a constitutionally sound defense but a militarily effective one as well. Conviction that the common man had a right to keep and bear arms came to the New World with its English settlers.

The unusual circumstances of frontier life gave new sweep to their conviction. In their island past, where a firm frame of custom and law surrounded the individual's every action, a gun was either an instrument of sport or the equipment of the infantry. To the frontiersman, a rifle was an essential of individual survival. He needed it to live off the country—to bring down deer and partridge, coon and possum. And he needed it to stay alive in the country—it was his means of exercising the immemorial right of self-defense, his response to the Indian arrow, his weapon in encounters with bear and moose, water moccasin, alligator, rattlesnake. In using it, he relied and had to rely on his own vigilance. He lived so far out on the fringes of organized society that authorization of his actions could only be retroactive and help could come only too late; the seventeenth- and eighteenth-century frontiersman too could say with his Bourbon contemporary, "L'état, c'est moi." The right to keep and bear arms was in his eyes a natural right, antecedent to and underived from the permissions of government. And when he and other individuals associated spontaneously—in vigilante bands or as minute men—they held their actions to be justifiable self-defense on self-assumed authority.

These were largely inchoate assumptions, but at the time of the Revolution, Jefferson phrased them into a philosophy. According

o its frontier interpretation, the right to bear arms extended all
he way to a right to revolution: when man's natural rights are in-
ringed by his sovereign, the social compact is dissolved and he
nust undertake the defense of his own safety. As draftsman of the
declaration justifying the Revolution of 1776, Jefferson elaborated
a long bill of particulars reciting the wrongs done by George III in
violation of the safety and happiness of the American colonies, then
added: "whenever any form of government becomes destructive of
these ends, it is the right of the people to alter or to abolish it, and
to institute a new government, laying its foundation on such principles, and organizing its powers in such form, as to them shall seem
most likely to effect their safety and happiness."

Jefferson's view was not solely an *ad hoc* argument. Eleven years
later, he reaffirmed the right of revolution as a basic general principle: "What country before, ever existed a century and a half without a rebellion. What country can preserve its liberties if its rulers
are not warned from time to time that its people preserve the spirit
of resistance. Let them take arms. The remedy is to set them right
as to facts, pardon and pacify them. What signify a few lives lost
in a century or two? . . . The tree of liberty must be refreshened
from time to time with the blood of patriots and tyrants. It is its
natural manure." With time, however, the American revolutionaries' concept of the right to bear arms has been nullified, alike by
technical development and by thickening settlement.

Except for heavy artillery, eighteenth-century arms were man-
ageable by individuals. In the narrow defile of the Avenue de
Versailles, some of the staves and pitchforks carried by the Paris
revolutionaries of 1789 were shattered by the firepower of the professional palace guard, but the advancing forest of indignation was
not halted. In assaults on established authority, a rough parity
between attack and defense still existed.

The Hungarian Revolution of 1956, by contrast, showed how
futile, against the caterpillar-treaded firepower of a modern state,
is the attempted exercise of the right of redress through use of
small arms by the general citizenry. Today, if a government gets
out of the control of its citizens, domestic correction of the abuse is
impossible without the assistance of at least part of the military
establishment.

The desirability of individual possession of firearms is being
increasingly reassessed, now that the United States has become a

closed society. The rifle in the jeep of a western cattleman is a vestigial remainder. Preservation of personal and public safety is today held to be a function of public authority, exercised internally by the police forces of state and local governments and externally by a military establishment that relies largely on the specialized expertise of professional components.

Though real guns or toys enliven the sport or play of autumnal hunters or junior suburban cops and robbers, it is accepted that the privately owned revolver and the sawed-off shotgun have become the weapons of the criminal. Sales and shipments of firearms are still unregulated, but most modern metropolitan areas license ownership and make the carrying of a concealed weapon illegal.

While recent realities are constantly coming into sharper focus legally, modern facts are still not reconciled with ancient guarantees. Ordinances limiting the right to keep and bear arms are subject to constitutional challenge. The shots in Dallas at the time of President Kennedy's assassination were facilitated by the judicial disallowance, fourteen months earlier, of an ordinance forbidding possession of firearms in the city. The words in which the court struck down this regulation repeated colonial ideology verbatim, declaring it "an unconstitutional and unauthorized invasion of a natural right the citizens of this state have never relinquished to their rulers."

Collective exercise of the natural right to bear arms had occurred in all the colonies except Pennsylvania long before 1776: in Virginia and the northern section of Carolina in 1676-77; in the "Dominion of New England" formed in 1686 and extended in 1688 to include the territory from present-day Maine through New York to the Jerseys; in New York when the "Dominion" disintegrated; and in Maryland and the southern section of Carolina thereafter, the powers of government were at least temporarily exercised by citizens who had taken matters into their own hands. In each case the insurgents issued reasoned justifications of their action.

The basis for most of these insurrections was desire for greater local self-government, in resistance either to mismanagement by colonial governors or lords proprietors or to centralizing efforts by the Crown.

Three revolts occurred in sequence at the transfer of power from the Stuarts to William and Mary. In 1688, Sir Edmund Andros, governor of Massachusetts, was deposed and the "Dominion" dissolved. In New York, news of Andros' fate touched off a successful uprising against the incumbent government; here the rebels ruled for over a year. Finally, in 1689, amid rumors of a popish plot to kill Protestants in Maryland, an insurgent force captured the capital at St. Marys and conducted the government for two years, until the arrival of a new royal appointee.

Carolina's first uprising, the Culpeper Rebellion of 1677, marked the settlers' reaction to high taxes, inadequate local government, revocation of direct tobacco trade with New England. The rebels imprisoned council members, seized public funds and records, and instituted governmental reforms. Forty-two years later, the assumption of power by the Charleston assembly was in both cause and effect similar to the 1689 revolt in Maryland, although without its religious element. Both brought about the end of proprietary rule.

In Bacon's Rebellion of 1676 in Virginia, civil grievances were a component, but the revolt began as a frontier muster to mount against the Indians an initiative that was not forthcoming from the capital. The right to bear arms had been assumed in all of the insurrections, but in this case more than any other it was exercised to conduct prolonged military activity. The rebels first assembled to force from the governor a commission to recruit military strength and go into action against the Indians, though they shortly obtained legitimate political control of the assembly through the ballot box and instituted numerous measures of enduring governmental reform.

At their moment of maximum power, in the summer of 1676, the insurrectionists dominated all of Virginia except the two counties on the peninsula across Chesapeake Bay. But the governor neither left the colony nor came into the rebels' power; in less than eight months, sudden death had left them leaderless and the governor had resumed executive authority. The courts-martial and civil processes then instituted and the legislation passed specifically extinguished the right to bear arms in concert, which Bacon's successive manifestoes had justified.

In its extreme form, the right claimed in these various uprisings was a right to revolution beyond what any government can willingly tolerate. But the initial episode in Virginia, and its successors up and down the coast, were visible warnings of what happens when the distance grows too great between a government and its people. A hundred years later, the fact that many of these earlier affirma-

71

tions of popular sovereignty had been successful bulwarked the con
viction that the security of a free state should be in the keeping of
a citizen militia.

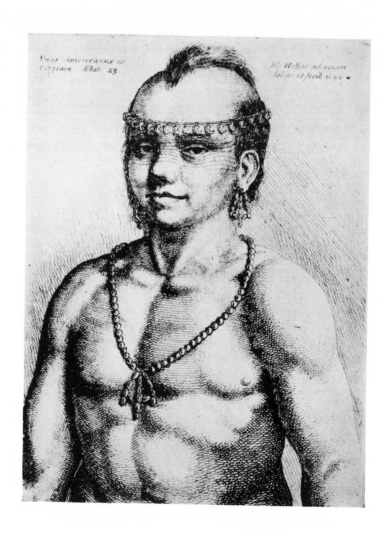

THE CASE

In the summer of 1675, on the edge of the Potomac River in the upper reaches of Virginia settlement, a little quarrel broke out between a white man and some Indians over title to a few hogs. Their dispute was like the friction of two twigs on the floor of a parched forest: wisps of grey smoke curl from the stiff leaf-scatter —and soon miles of tree-tops hiss in torching flame.

The first red flick showed when a group of churchgoers, sauntering home from Sunday service, found Robert Hen, recently hired herdsman on the plantation of Thomas Mathew, sprawled across his doorstep, blood-soaked from tomahawk wounds.

Stumbling into a run across the stumpy clearing, they stooped low, their faces close to Hen's: "Who?"

"Doegs, Doegs," Hen whispered, and died. Indoors, stiff with terror, his little boy crawled out from underneath the bed.

On horse and foot, the Stafford County captains of militia, Colonel George Brent and Colonel George Mason, gave hot pursuit across the Potomac into Maryland. They located two Indian forts. The fort approached by Colonel Brent's troops belonged to Doegs; they shot the chief, took his young son prisoner. But the too-quick fire poured by Colonel Mason's troops into the other fort murdered hitherto friendly Susquehannocks. The injury was compounded when a joint Maryland-Virginia force—the Virginia contingent led by Colonel John Washington—beseiged a further Susquehannock stronghold and murdered four of the tribe's Great Men who came out to parley.

After that, vengeance was assured. During the early weeks of winter, the Susquehannocks brooded their wrongs, assembled allies. On January 25, 1676, retaliatory massacres butchered thirty-six members of settlers' families in the first raid. By February 10, as colonists were killed or withdrew from the frontier to less exposed positions, the number of inhabited plantations in a single parish of the northern neck of Virginia dropped from seventy-one to eleven. Over the year, casualties had reached the three hundred mark. In settlements and in men, the colony was shrinking.

At Jamestown, Sir William Berkeley, the royal governor, vacillated. He commissioned a member of his council to lead a force in defense of the frontier, then rescinded the commission. The matter, he said, could wait until the March meeting of the General Assembly. But the assembly merely ordered additions to an existing series of frontier forts at the fall lines of the rivers, with mounted patrols between them; their garrisons were immobilized by a requirement that commanders consult the governor before making sorties.

New raids then rimmed the frontier as far south as Henrico County (modern Richmond) where Colonel William Byrd I commanded the fort at the falls of the James. Three of his men were killed. So was the overseer on a nearby plantation belonging to Nathaniel Bacon, Jr.

By April, down the James in Charles City County, a self-assembled defense force was gathering. After consultation with other western landowners, Bacon offered himself as leader of this militia.

The young commander was only twenty-nine years old and had been in the colony less than two years. But as the King's commissioners subsequently noted, he was "of no obscure family"—Sir Nicholas Bacon, Queen Elizabeth's lord keeper of the great seal, and his still more famous son, Francis, were collateral ancestors, and baronets were frequent in his direct line. Lady Frances Culpeper Berkeley, wife of the governor, was a relative and so was Nathaniel Bacon, Sr., who had come to Virginia in the 1650's. He was president of the governor's council, to which young Bacon was appointed upon arrival.

Before emigrating, at home at Friston Hall in Suffolk, Nathaniel, Jr., had run true to eighteenth-century form as the feckless only son of a well-to-do county family. A member of St. Catherine's College, Cambridge, he had interrupted his desultory studies to make the grand tour, tutored by the naturalist, John Ray, who commented that his charge was of "very good parts and a quick wit," but "impatient of labour." Later, he read law at Gray's Inn.

He also went through a regrettable amount of money. A neighboring baronet, Sir Edward Duke, disinherited his daughter, Elizabeth, when she married Bacon over his fully expressed opposition in 1670.

Marriage did not increase Bacon's financial responsibility; more money troubles followed. A fresh start elsewhere seemed advisable. Endowed by his family with £1,800, the young couple sailed for Virginia in 1674. A land purchase, on a loan from a council mem-

)er, enabled them to establish a plantation at Curle's Neck, some
orty miles above Jamestown. "Bacon's Quarter," where the over-
,eer was massacred, was a subsidiary holding further upriver.

The history of the seven-month period between Bacon's taking
:ommand of the Charles City County troops in April and his
death of the bloody flux in October, like the history of any civil
war, bristles with irreconcilable evidence. Both sides committed
excesses; among them, partisan accounts selected their preferred
items.

The Burwell Manuscript, a contemporary chronicle of the rebellion written for a friend by an unknown author (generally
thought to be John Cotton of Queen's Creek), presents the conflict
in its literary form: "There was many coppes of Verces made after
his departure, calculated to the Lattitude of there affection who
composed them; as a relish taken from both appetites, I have here
sent you a cuple."

The "cuple" consists of twin odes on the occasion of Bacon's
death, whether composed by Cotton himself or by two other authors
is uncertain. The first, identified as "Bacon's Epitaph, made by
His Man," shows Bacon as he appeared to hundreds on hundreds
of now-nameless frontiersmen who proclaimed him "General of the
People":

> Death why soe crewill ! what, no other way
> To manifest they splleene, but thus to slay
> Our hopes of safety; liberty, our all
> Which, through thy tyranny, with him must fall
> To its late Caoss. . . . .
> Here let him rest; while wee this truth report,
> Hee's gone from hence unto a higher Court
> To pleade his Cause: where he by this doth know
> Whether to Ceaser hee was friend, or foe.

The second ode, in answer, displays the side of the coin that had
currency with the governor:

> Whether to Caesar he was Friend or Foe ?
> Pox take such Ignorance, do you not know ?
> Can he be Friend to Caesar, that shall bring
> The Arms of Hell, to fight against the King? . . . . . .

Among more factual documents, Bacon's proclamations exist;
so do those of the governor. His addresses to his men are available

in full; so are their counterinstructions from Jamestown. Copious personal correspondence, particularly letters sent to London on behalf of Bacon and Berkeley, shows what was heard at court. A number of contemporary histories provide a rough chronology. The reaction of British officialdom is of record, all the way up to the throne. It includes the findings of the commission of inquiry sent out from London at the end of 1676. Before the commissioners arrived, the rebellion was over and its leader dead. Much of what they report was necessarily hearsay. Yet their account is probably as reliable as any single document.

They described Bacon as "indifferent tall but slender, black-hair'd and of an ominous, pensive, melancholey Aspect, of a pestilent & prevalent Logical discourse tending to atheisme in most companyes, not given to much talke, or to make suddain replyes, of a most imperious and dangerous hidden Pride of heart, despising the wisest of his neighbours for their Ignorance, and very ambitious and arrogant."

With parts of this description, his up-country followers gladly agreed. If he swore a good deal, so did they. When he addressed them, even though they might be hungry and very tired, his logic prevailed. And when his oath was, "If the redskins meddle with me, God damn my blood, but I will harry them, commission or no commission," they, with the Charles City County volunteers, were ready to yell, "A Bacon! A Bacon! A Bacon!" and gulp approval of his leadership in fiery rum.

Clear and present danger of Indian attack produced Bacon's first following. But the frustration that emboldened his men to military action was not solely due to the governor's failure to organize their protection. In their minds, inadequate defense of Virginia's borders was tightly interlocked with abuse of privilege in the colony's domestic society. For this reason, once social unrest began to receive expression, Bacon's campaign turned quickly into a two-front operation; one front fighting Indians on the western borders and the other fighting a civil war in tidewater. In mid-1676 Berkeley wrote Councilman Thomas Ludwell: "How miserable that man is who governs a people when six parts of seaven at least are Poore Endebted Discontented and Armed."

The domestic grievances of the community bore familiar names: favoritism and corruption, monopoly and exploitation, burdensome and inequitable taxation. They merged with the defense issue because the same Indians who killed remote settlers also killed pelt-bearing animals—and there was money in the fur trade. The men on the periphery of settlement were by no means sure whose protection the governor had most at heart, theirs or the Indians'. "No bullets would pierce Bever skins," frontiersmen said knowingly to one another.

Recently, the fur trade had been reorganized. Where the Dan and Staunton rivers unite to form the Roanoke, the Occaneechees occupied a fortified island to which Indians brought furs from five hundred miles around. The Dutch, until ousted from New York twelve years previously, had run lines of exchange all the way down the western mountains to this terminal. Thereafter, the trade became open to British exploitation.

Governor Berkeley made exceptions to the general prohibition forbidding Virginians to engage in any form of exchange with the Indians, licensing various persons of substance to deal with them for furs. A portion of the gains under these licenses accrued to the governor. H.B.M.'s commissioners concluded that "This made the People jealous that the Governor for the lucre of the Beaver and otter trade &c. with ye Indians, rather sought to protect the Indians than them."

What the Indians wanted most—and got—from these transactions was firearms and ammunition. Back-country settlers resented deals that left their adversaries in possession of firepower comparable to their own. As the 1676 raids extended, they blindly ceased to distinguish between one Indian tribe and another: to them the only good Indian was a dead Indian. Ruthlessly, they abandoned all distinction, turning on Indian friends who had formerly fought side by side with them against other Indians.

When the governor upbraided them for having murdered the Great Men of the Susquehannocks in cold blood—"If they had killed my Grandfather and Grandmother, my father and Mother and all of my friends, yet if they had come to treat of Peace they ought to have gone in Peace"—they were unmoved. Listening, they stolidly wondered if justice were being wrapped in a beaver skin against the frontier weather.

And their doubts about the governor's desire to protect them were paralleled by certainties about the futility of such protection as he and the assembly saw fit to sponsor. Backwoodsmen fully understood the Indians' tactics of ambush and evasion. Against

77

such tactics, a chain of forts was no defense—indeed by immobilizing manpower that might otherwise be available in infiltrated settlements, it actually weakened their condition. They called the forts "mousetraps," and held them to be "a great grievance, juggle and cheat."

The special assessment levied to build more forts was resented as a double injury. The incidence of taxation in the colony was sharply regressive: since revenue was raised by flat-rate poll taxes, the poor man was liable for the same amount as the landed proprietor.

The funds for the new forts permitted the governor to award additional public works contracts to well-to-do settlers, many of whom already enjoyed substantial income from the public purse for the erection of courthouses and tobacco warehouses and the care of highways. Taxpayers of the common sort, whose levies had recently risen from forty or fifty pounds of tobacco to two hundred pounds a year, looked on the forts, H.B.M.'s commissioners observed, as "merely a Designe of the Grandees to engrosse all their Tobacco into their owne hands."

In the 1640's, the Virginia colony had been warmly sympathetic to the Royalist cause; when England passed under Cromwellian rule, the Old Dominion became a major haven for refugee Cavaliers. But after the Restoration, the local counterparts of the favoritism and corruption in Whitehall under Charles II caused rising resentment. The colony raised a special fund to send an agent to England to protest the royal grant of the Virginia colony to Lords Arlington and Culpeper in 1663. When Governor Berkeley threatened to confiscate the estates of settlers who took up arms in 1676, the up-countrymen again said knowingly, "Rebels forfeitures would be Loyall Inheritances."

The increased domestic tension in the colony was largely due to the governor's recent manner of exercising his very considerable power. Few disagreed when Councilman Philip Ludwell said, "The sole author of the most substantial part of the government, whether for laws or for other inferior institutes, is the governor."

Sir William Berkeley had been in the colony for a generation and a half. His first gubernatorial administration lasted a decade. He was appointed two years before the beheading of Charles I and it was 1652 before the Cromwellian Parliament made its authority effective in Virginia. Speaking to the assembly in March 1651, he

may himself have been in a rebellious mood: "Gentlemen by the Grace of God we will not so tamely part with our King, and all these blessings we enjoy under him; and if they oppose us, do but follow me, I will either lead you to victory, or loose a life which I cannot more gloriously sacrifice than for my loyalty, and your security." And although through the 1650's successive Cromwellian commissioners officiated by Parliamentary authority in Jamestown, Berkeley maintained his residence a few miles away at Green Spring, a commodious manor built from public funds for the use of the governor, where he welcomed Royalists, held a miniature court of exiles, planted extensive orchards, grew oranges under glass.

This courtier's devotion to the throne—he had been gentleman of the bedchamber to Charles I before coming to Virginia—redoubled in intensity with the Restoration. The divine right of kings, cynically espoused by Charles II as a useful doctrine, was to Berkeley a central verity. In 1661, while affairs were still uncertain in England, the assembly asked him to resume the governorship on the death of the Parliamentary incumbent in Jamestown. He did so, casting himself on the royal mercy for taking office in advance of receipt of the commission that arrived in due course.

Always, Berkeley had held that the best government is government by the rich and well-born. He admired conformity—in his first administration he moved to eradicate heresy by passage and strict enforcement of laws authorizing deportation of dissenters. But in those earlier years he also showed courage, decision, and resourcefulness. At the time of the Indian massacres of 1644-46 he personally took the field and captured the formidable Chief Opechancanough in a daring charge. To halt the decline in tobacco prices he made a vigorous effort to secure a crop-control program jointly adhered to by Maryland, Virginia, and North Carolina. He encouraged diversification of the economy through development of local industries such as glassmaking and tanning. He ended his first term a popular man.

The Berkeley of the Restoration was different. In his old age, he grew blind to the needs and aspirations of the generality of citizens. During the sixteen years of his second term, he governed largely on behalf of what became known as the "Green Spring faction," the grandees who had gathered round him during the Cromwellian years. In his 1671 report to the commissioners of the plantations, he was able to thank God that in Virginia "there are no free schools nor printing and I hope we shall not have, these hundred years."

Many observers charged part of the change in the governor to his marriage in 1664 with Frances Culpeper, kinswoman of the King's friend who had just become the colony's co-proprietor. The governor was fifty-six; she, though already a widow, was only thirty. The Lady Frances was a woman of ingenuity and daring who understood power and had a taste for it. The Green Spring faction's ready inference that it stood somewhat above the law was augmented by her coming.

Both branches of the legislature had long been Berkeley's creatures. In 1661, he had called for the election of a new House of Burgesses, and in the colony's first flush of enthusiasm for the Restoration all but eight of the members elected during the Cromwellian period were thrown out. The returns were so highly acceptable that the governor allowed fifteen years to elapse without further reference to the voters: "Men were more valuable in any calling in proportion to their experience."

The burgesses became less and less representative of the freeholders whose taxes supported them in Jamestown: they increased their salaries and per diems (including allowances for one servant and two horses) until they averaged ten to twelve thousand pounds of tobacco and absorbed about a third of a county's annual budget.

To the smaller, appointive governor's council, it was said that Berkeley named only those who did not in the least "thrust or cross his humor," with the result that he "thus layde aside his maties. councell here, and in the stead thereof formed a councell of his owne, the better to support his single power."

Berkeley's patronage extended far down into the localities. Appointments to sheriff's offices were valuable: over and above salary, their holders got a tenth of every hogshead of collected tax tobacco. Government contracts permitted small initial amounts of capital to be parlayed into sizeable fortunes. The bill of particulars that Charles City County citizens submitted to H.B.M.'s commissioners lists as successive awards to the Edward Hills, father and son, of Shirley Plantation:

11,000 pounds of tobacco awarded to Colonel Hill, Sr., to build
   a tannery of which Colonel Hill, Jr., had the use;
25,000 pounds awarded to the Hills and others to clear highways;

81

21,373 pounds of a county levy totaling 33,322 pounds awarded to the Hills to build a courthouse.

With the tobacco earned under this last award, the son established an ordinary where he sold liquor. He also housed, at suitable fees, drunkards condemned to prison for their debts. If a prisoner escaped owing him money, the taxpayers became liable for the defaulted sum.

As a prestige measure, young Edward prevailed on Governor Berkeley to name him not only colonel and commander of the county's forces, but also president of the court, "a style unknown in this country before." Yet at Jamestown, and later at Williamsburg, he was a respected figure who moved from preferment to preferment: attorney general, councilman, treasurer, speaker of the House of Burgesses.

Popular resentment against Berkeley's second administration was thus compounded of envy and resentment arising from the aggrandizement of the local gentry, suspicion of complicity in the profits of the fur trade, and wrath at the unavenged frontier massacres. The indignation of the Charles City County volunteers who raised huzzahs at Bacon's arrival included all these explosive elements.

Bacon's flamboyance—his flair for stirring words and conspicuous actions—made him exactly the man for their purposes. Even at that first rally, he gave a cloak-and-dagger touch to the enrollment ceremony: instead of making an ordinary list he inscribed the names of his volunteers in a large circle, without beginning or end, "that their Ring Leaders might not be found out."

The chronology of his military enterprises through the summer of 1676 is the chronology of a pendulum. His militia were inadequate to man two fronts, one on the frontier and one in tidewater, so his force swung back and forth, east to west, west to east. By late autumn, it had stopped on dead center.

In April, before starting west to make contact with the Indians, the vigilantes issued *A Humble Appeal of the Volunteers to all Well-minded and Charitable People*. They cited the absurdity of the frontier forts and their intention themselves to put an end to Indian harassment: "Judge therefore all unprejudiced men, for to you only do we appeal, whether anything of greater consequence for the country's good could be offered than with our persons and fortunes freely to redeem our country, & become both actors and paymasters of this necessary defensive war, and whether this our proffer be not wholly clear from any dregs of rebellion and mutiny . . ."

But on May 10, the governor declared that the volunteers were indeed "rebels and mutineers"; he ordered them to disband and go home. He likewise removed Bacon's name from the governor's council, assured Mrs. Bacon that her husband would hang, and started west in pursuit.

The governor's proclamation frightened certain of the men with Bacon into going home, but some three score stayed by the undertaking, and with them Bacon struck southwest through the forest to the Occaneechees' trading center. On arrival, he parleyed with the Occaneechee warriors, engaging them to undertake a foray against a nearby Susquehannock fort. The Occaneechees returned from this expedition with both Susquehannock prisoners and other Indians who had been enslaved by the Susquehannocks. According to one of Bacon's men, the Susquehannocks were then "putt to death, after their way for that Wee refused to take that office, which they offered to us."

But disagreement about disposition of the slaves prolonged negotiations, and Bacon's men were running out of provisions. As the Indians delayed furnishing them, suspicion spread among the whites that they had been reached by an emissary of the governor—a later proposal to the King by two council members, Thomas Ludwell and Robert Smith, is known to have urged letting the Indians "know yt. he [Bacon] was at that time and still is a rebell and that if they shal bee assistant in the taking or killing of him they shall have peace on good tearmes . . . and that if they bring him in they shall see him executed."

According to Bacon's man, in the midst of this triggered waiting a shot from across the river "killed one of our Men, which we quickly repaid them, firing in at all their men, ports holes, and other places soe thick that the groans of Men, Women & Children were so loud, that with all their howling, & singing, could not hinder them from being heard." Shortly, they added fire to the fort's horrors. Next day, the trading post where a thousand beaver skins had been assembled was a smouldering bed of deserted ashes.

In this engagement, only three of Bacon's volunteers were killed, against a hundred and fifty Indians. Plunder-laden and proud, the expedition turned back to the settlements. News of their exploit preceded them. They "returned with a greater victory from sharper conflict than ever yet had been known in these parts of the world," expecting and finding a heroes' welcome.

Governor Berkeley, in Jamestown, deflected blame to the House of Burgesses on the grounds that in March it was they who voted for more forts. He dissolved the assembly and called for a new election and a session in June.

Virginia voters relished the long-absent opportunity to return representatives consonant with their current mood. Upsets were general; survivors of the long assembly could be counted on the fingers of two hands. In the eyes of the Green Spring faction, the result was a disaster. Berkeley wrote that only "eight of the Burgesses . . . were not of his [Bacon's] faction," and the commissioners reported that "At this new election (such was the Prevalency of Bacon's Party) that they chose instead of Freeholders, Free men that had but lately crept out of the condition of Servants . . . for their Burgesses and such as were eminent abettors to Bacon, and for faction and ignorance fitt Representatives of those that chose them."

Bacon and Captain James Crewes were elected to represent Henrico County. When they sailed down the James to attend the June assembly, Bacon prudently anchored his sloop upriver from Jamestown, sending his fellow-burgess to convey assurances of his loyalty to the governor and to see if it were safe for him to land. When His Excellency's response was to order guns fired on the sloop, Bacon withdrew upstream, waited until dark, then slipped into town to make his own estimate of the situation.

Jamestown had two reasons for its existence: as a port of entry for ocean commerce and as the colony's place of public business. Besides the state house and the church, it numbered perhaps a dozen brick houses and many more wooden ones; during sessions of the assembly, most of their owners engaged, as one burgess remarked, in "keeping ordinaries at extra-ordinary rates."

Here Bacon had two consequential friends, Richard Lawrence and William Drummond. With the exception of William Kempe's, their houses were regarded as the finest in the capital. An Oxford man, Lawrence had "Married a Wealthy Widow who kept a large house of public Entertainment unto which resorted those of the best quality and such others as Businesse Called to that Town."

Drummond was "a sober Scottish gentleman of great repute," established for several decades as an importer.

Both had long been at outs with the governor. According to Berkeley's supporter, Councilman Richard Lee, Lawrence "had been partially treated at Law, for a Considerable Estate on behalfe of a Corrupt favorite" and had borne Berkeley an active grudge thereafter, referring to him as an "old treacherous villian."

Drummond and Berkeley had been close in the early sixties: Berkeley, as one of the lords proprietors of Carolina after Charles II's grant in 1663, designated Drummond to serve the northern section as governor. But in 1666, the two fell out over a lease of land near Jamestown that Drummond had rented from Berkeley.

Throughout the Rebellion, these two Jamestown citizens gave Bacon substantial support and counsel.

Bacon's consultations likewise included a talk with his elderly cousin. According to one of H.B.M.'s commissioners, Nathaniel, Sr., was "soe desirous and Industrious to divert the evil consequences of his Rebel kinsman's proceedings, that at the beginning hee freely proposed and promised to invest in him a considerable part of his Estate in present, and to leave him the Remainder . . . upon condition hee would lay downe his Armes, and become a good subject to his Majestie, that the colony might not be disturbed or destroyed, nor his owne ffamily stained with soe foule a Blott."

Following this reconnaissance, Bacon decided to return to his plantation, but the governor ordered one Captain Thomas Gardner to intercept and bring him forcibly back to Jamestown. When Bacon was led into Berkeley's presence, his excellency remarked: "Now I behold the greatest rebel that ever was in Virginia."

Bacon, urged "by ye importunity of my cousin, & to shew my cleanesse from any ill intencons as also to reconcile ye people and the Governr., who found my party too universall," concluded to "submitt & doe soe generous an Act (as my cozen formed it) as to acknowledge yt. my actions were unjust & unwarrantable, to beat up drums with out ye Governrs. leave, which if I should doe, all should be well."

So next day, kneeling before the governor in council, Bacon threw himself on the executive mercy: "I am and have been guilty of diverse late unlawful, mutinous and rebellious practices, contrary to my duty to his most sacred majesties governour and this country . . . not only without order and commission, but contrary

85

to the express orders and commands of the Rt. Hon. Sir William Berkeley, Knt. his Majesties most worthy governour and captain general of Virginia." He offered bond of £2,000, the equivalent of his whole estate, for his good behavior for a year.

So abject a confession brought prompt results: Berkeley forgave Bacon and all who were with him, put him back on the council, promised him a commission, fined Captain Gardner £70 for seizing Bacon's sloop.

After this opening flurry, the assembly got down to business. Desiring the aid of friendly Indians in the frontier war, the governor summoned the queen of the Pamunkeys, whose tribe formed an enclave within the settled area of the York River. Her husband had been killed fighting with the English beside Edward Hill, Sr., a decade earlier. She "entered the Chamber with a Comportment Gracefull to Admiration, bringing on her right hand an Englishman Interpreter, and on her left her Son, a Stripling Twenty Years of Age. She having round her head a Plat of Black and White Wampumpeague Three Inches broad, in imitation of a Crown, and was Cloathed in a Mantle of dress't Deerskins with the hair outwards and the Edge cut round 6 Inches deep, which made Strings resembling Twisted frenge from the Shoulders to the feet; Thus with grave Court-like Gestures and a Majestisk Air in her face, she Walked up our Long Room to the Lower end of the Table, Where after a few Intreaties, She Sat down; th' Interpreter and her Son Standing by her on either side, as they had walked up." But she would promise no more than twelve warriors.

In the House of Burgesses, the new majority was in full control. As draft bills began to be considered, it became clear how much the temper of the body had altered. It had been customary, for instance, for two members of the council to sit with the house committee on Indian affairs, to keep the assembly's thinking in line with that of the governor. But according to Thomas Mathew, who with Colonel George Mason represented Stafford County, "Mr. Presley my Neighbour an old Assembly Man, sitting next to me, rose up, and (in a blundering manner replied) 'tis true, it has been Customary, but if we have any bad Customes amongst us, We are come here to mend 'em! which Set the house in Laughter."

Rumor spread that Berkeley was about to order Bacon's rearrest. Just in time to avoid a search in which swords were thrust through the featherbeds at Richard Lawrence's in an effort to discover him, Bacon left town.

His absence was brief. When he came back, he had with him 400 foot and 120 horse. He ranged his men in position before the state house, while his fellow-burgesses, in session on the second floor, gaped from the windows.

Berkeley came out, met Bacon on the green. The two harangued each other. Berkeley, after baring his breast and crying, "Here! Shoot me, foregod, fair Mark, Shoot!" desired to duel.

Bacon declined: "God damne my blood, I came for a commission, and a commission I will have before I goe!" As the governor hesitated, he threatened: "I'll Kill Governr, Council, Assembly and all, and then Ill Sheath my Sword in my owne heart's bloud." Turning to his troops he ordered: "Make Ready! Present!"

From an upstairs window, a burgess waved a white handkerchief: "You shall have it! You shall have it!"

The moment was so tense that Thomas Mathew reports: "So near was the Massacre of us all that very Minute, had Bacon in that Paroxism of Phrenetick fury but Drawn his Sword, before the Pacefick Handkercher was Shaken out at Window."

Next day, the governor provided a commission to Bacon's liking, together with blank forms commissioning subordinate officers for Bacon to fill out himself. Berkeley likewise wrote a letter to the King explaining and excusing Bacon's action, and assured indemnity to all.

During the next weeks, the assembly passed twenty laws. In addition to stricter controls over the Indians and repeal of the law passed in March permitting five persons in each county to trade with them, the new statutes set up a much more democratic governmental structure and procedures in respect to taxation, representation, and defense.

The civil measures were probably not primarily due to Bacon's inspiration. Thomas Mathew suggests that their contents were strongly influenced by conversations taking place at Richard Lawrence's hostelry. The weight of the host's view would have been augmented by the fact that he represented Jamestown in the assembly: "his Parts with his even Temper made his Converse Coveted by Persons of all Ranks; So that being Subtile, and having these advantages he might with lesse Difficulty discover mens Inclinations and Instill his Notions where he found these woud be imbib'd with greatest Satisfaction."

Bacon, Mathew felt, "was too young, too much a Stranger there, and of a Disposition too precipitate, to Manage things to that length those were Carried, had not thoughtful Mr. Lawrence been at the Bottom."

The author of the Burwell Manuscript, though disapproving Lawrence's morals, corroborates this impression, saying that he and Drummond were those "by whose Councell all transactions were, for the greater part, managed all along on that Side. Drummond was . . . all ways esteemed a Parson [person] of such induments, where Wisdom and honisty are contending for supriority; which rendred him to be one of that sort of people, whose dementions are not to be taken by the line of an ardnary Capassety. Larance was late one of the Assembly, and Burgis for Towne, in which he was a liver. He was a Parson not meanely aquainted with such learning (besides his natureall parts, that inables a Man for the management of more then ardnary imployments, Which he subjected to eclips, as well in the transactings of the present affaires as in the darke imbraces of a Blackamoore, his slave. . ." In addition to these two, William Sherwood names Thomas Blanton of Spotsylvania County as "Bacon's great engine" in the assembly and James Mingo, the clerk of the assembly, as "Bacon's great friend in forming the laws."

In county government, the substantial reforms initiated at the June 1676 session included greater local control and an enlarged basis for the franchise. Freemen as well as freeholders and housekeepers were authorized to participate in elections. Prior to 1670 they had done so but an act of the assembly that year had restricted the franchise to conform to English practice. Sheriffs were to hold office for one year only. The gentlemen justices appointed to county courts by the governor were to have resided for three years in the county, to serve in rotation, and to hold only one office at a time.

A new representative element was added in the tax power. County levies were to be voted jointly by the appointed justices and an equal number of elected freemen; these freemen were likewise to vote in the making of other local regulations. The county courts were to appoint their own collectors. The act exempting members of the governor's council from payment of taxes was repealed.

The right to bear arms was recognized by detailed provision for

88

a citizen army. A thousand men were to be raised on a county quota basis. They were to choose their own officers and enjoy specified emoluments including plunder, Indian slaves, and pensions for the wounded. Bacon was to be commander-in-chief, with the personal right to raise volunteers. As one of the governor's men wrote: "the intent of which soe neere as all sober men Judge, is ye subvercon of the Laws and to Levell all, this Mr. Bacon being Styled by the rabble theire Generall."

On June 25, when these changes were accomplished facts, word arrived that hostile Indians were at the York River. Next day, Bacon, as General of All the Forces of Virginia Against the Indians, started west on a second military venture.

To the west and to the east, the pendulum of the Rebellion had now completed its highest arc. On June 29, Mrs. Bacon wrote her sister in England: "After Mr. Bacon was come in hee was forced to keep a guard of soldiers about his house, for the Governr. wd certainly have had his life taken away privately if hee Could have had opportunity; but all the country does so really love him, that they would not leave him alone anywhere; there was not any body against him but the Governr.; & a few of his great men, which have gott their Estates by the Governr.; surely if your brother's crime had been so great, all the country would not have been for him, you never know any better beloved than hee is. . . ."

But at home in Suffolk, Bacon's father sensed disaster. On behalf of his son, he prepared a petition to the King: "in persuance of the Governours order to keep the people Quiet hee was enforced to accompany them not being able to restragne or perswade them from comeing downe to press Governour & Assembly with much Earnesness to grant his Commission. . . . Yor. Petr. therefor being under an Apprehention & feare of the Exteremities of Yor. Maties. displeasure & Justice against yor. Petrs. said son, humbly Implores Yor. Maties. Mercy, beseeching you not to cast him into dispaire by exempting him from yor. fforgiveness. . . ."

With the dog days of midsummer, the pendulum began to bobble.

At the falls of the James, Bacon, reaffirming his men's loyalty, took himself, and gave to them, an oath of allegiance. He then required of them a second oath of fidelity to himself including a promise not to divulge his plans and to have no truck with Indians.

But the governor as well as Bacon was afield. When Gloucester

County citizens protested the high-handed methods used by Bacon's men to obtain requisitions, Berkeley departed to fan their grievance, declaring that Bacon's commission had been "extracted from the Assembly, which in effect is noe more than if a Thiefe should take my purse and make me owne, him I gave itt freely."

But on arrival, Berkeley sustained a rude shock. The assembly of citizens to whom he proposed pursuit of Bacon replied with shouts of "A Bacon! A Bacon!"; the governor, according to the commissioners, "Ffainted away on horseback in the Ffield, and hearing of Bacons being on his march to Gloster, hee was feigne to fly thence to Accomack [one of the two Virginia counties on the detached peninsula that forms the eastern shore of Chesapeake Bay] leaving now the Seat of the Government lyable to . . . Usurpation."

When told that the governor had fled across the bay, Bacon entered Jamestown and took over full exercise of the executive power. He garrisoned the capital and dispatched an appeal to the people of Accomac to relinquish the governor and unite with the rest of the colony.

Commandeering the best available ship, he mounted extra guns, placed Giles Bland and Captain John Carver in command, ordered them to cross the bay and arrest the governor, who was lodged at the home of Colonel John Custis, so that he might be returned to England.

Giles Bland and the governor had long been at loggerheads. Bland was H.B.M.'s collector of customs for Virginia, his father was a well-known London merchant, and his father-in-law, master of requests to the King. From the first, he had been favorable to Bacon. His direct line of communication to London, independent of the governor, made possible prompt presentation of Bacon's side of the struggle to Whitehall officials and upon occasion to the King.

At the same time, Bacon called for a constitutional convention to meet at Middle Plantation (later Williamsburg) in August. He then issued a *Declaration of the People* drafted in the form of a bill of particulars against Berkeley. He signed it, "Nathaniel Bacon, Gen'l By the Consent of ye People."

The governor was accused:

Of raising taxes upon specious pretense of public works to the advancement of private favorites and without improvement of the colony's fortifications, towns, or trade;

Of having rendered the magistrates contemptible by advancing scandalous and ignorant favorites to positions of judicature;

Of monopolizing the beaver trade, bartering lives and country for this gain, protecting the emboldened Indians;

Of calling back troops on the track of the Indians, altering the commission, recalling the forces a second time.

The governor and nineteen others were ordered to surrender in four days: "Thus wee the Commons of Virginia doe declare, desiring a prime union among ourselves, that wee may Joyntly and with one Accord defend ourselves against the Common Enemye."

This was heady stuff. Next week, reduced attendance at the constitutional convention revealed that people were drawing back from a resort to arms that had become first a rebellion and then a provisional government.

Bacon proposed a further oath, to be taken by all Virginia citizens, under which they would agree to:

Oppose forces sent from England until Bacon had acquainted the King with their cause and received a reply;

Swear that what the Governor and Council have enacted is illegal, and that what Bacon has done is in accord with the laws of England;

Declare Bacon's commission to be lawfully and legally obtained;

Promise to divulge anything they might hear against Bacon, and keep his secrets.

Only by threatening to resign could he obtain acceptance of this oath, though it was given thereafter by the regular magistrates to citizens of most counties. He had just summoned the assembly to meet on September 4 when news of an Indian raid broke up the meeting. Abandoning his executive for his military role, Bacon left for the west again.

This time, he and his men proved unable to make contact with the marauders. When the search for Susquehannocks and Occaneechees gave out, dreading to return empty-handed, Bacon invoked the volunteers' past declarations of enmity even to friendly Indians. He moved into the York freshes to attack the Pamunkeys.

Once more, food was running short. Before starting Bacon gave to all "full leave to returne, the heate of whose courage and resolu-

91

tions for the Suppressing of the heathen, and revenge for the Bloods of their Ffriends and Acquaintance they had shed, were not above and more than the particular regard and care they had for theire Belly." Only three men left, and the force was shortly augmented by the arrival of Colonel Giles Brent with men from northern Virginia.

Hot August rains then bogged them down. Food became even scarcer. Bacon divided his army. Brent went home.

Finally, some scouts discovered an old Indian woman, nurse of the queen of the Pamunkeys. Like a killdeer protecting her nest, she led them for two days in a false direction. Bacon, detecting the ruse, "gave command to his Soldiers to knock her in the head, which they did, and they left her dead on the way."

Bacon told his men, "All you gentlemen that intend to abide with mee must resolve to undergoe all the hardships this wilde can afforde, dangers and successes and if need be to eate chinkapins and horse flesh before hee returns. Which resolve I have taken therefore desire none but those which will so freely adventure, the other to Returne in."

But the remaining troops made a capture of forty-five Indians, including the queen of the Pamunkeys. With these prisoners and some plunder for a show, Bacon started back to the settlements.

Meanwhile in Accomac, the governor had turned the tables on him. Philip Ludwell, with the aid of Captain Thomas Larrimore, had captured Giles Bland, Captain Carver, and their ship; three mornings later, Berkeley hanged the captain at the water's edge. Relieved of seige, he returned to the mainland with troops raised on the eastern shore. On September 7, offering amnesty to all inhabitants except Lawrence and Drummond, he reoccupied Jamestown, fortified it, again proclaimed Bacon a rebel and traitor.

Bacon had "136 tyr'd men" with him when he heard the news. For a third time he harangued them: "Gentlemen and Fellow Soldiers. How I am transported with gladnesse to find you thus unanimous, Bold and daring, brave and Gallant; you have the victory before you fight, the conquest before battle. . . . The Indians we beare along with us shal be as soe many motives to cause Reliefe from every hand to be brought to you. . . . I know you have the Prars and wellwishes of all the People in Virginia, while the others are loaded with their curses."

Thus inspired, and gathering fresh recruits as they came through

New Kent, his troops reached Green Spring on September 13 after covering between thirty and forty miles since daybreak. As they approached Jamestown, he shouted, "Come on, my hearts of gold, hee that dyes in the field lyes in the Bedd of honour."

With night, they moved to within firing range, and with two axes and two spades dug a ditch beyond the palisade erected before the town by the governor's forces. They then lined the ditch with stakes.

Next day, to complete their preparations undisturbed, they kidnapped the wives of several council members and stationed them as hostages—"dear white guards of the devil"—in the line of possible fire while they worked.

On the fifteenth, Berkeley ordered a sortie. It failed. His Accomac army "went out with heve hearts" and very shortly "returned hom with light heels," scattering to the winds. Deserted, Berkeley decided to "weigh anchor in the night and silently fall downe the River, thus flying from the fface of an enemy that during this siege (which lasted one whole weeke) lay exposed to much more hardships, want and inaccommodation than themselves, besides the fatigue of a long march at their first coming to Towne."

On the night of September 19, Bacon entered Jamestown and burned it to the ground. Drummond set fire to his own house; so did Lawrence, "with all its wealth and a faire cupboard of plate." By morning the colony was without a capital.

Moving to Green Spring and there formulating a further oath of fidelity to his cause, Bacon denounced the governor as "having betray'd his Trust to the King by flying from his seate of Judicature." He then set up headquarters at Tindalls Point in Gloucester at the home of the assembly speaker and began belated work on the establishment of committees to take charge of the colony's civil affairs.

But the popular movement was disintegrating. News came from northern Virginia that Colonel Brent had changed sides and was making his militia available to the governor. His rumored descent on Bacon's stronghold did not materialize, but the switch witnessed a change of mood on the frontier. Citizens summoned to take the current oath at Gloucester Courthouse proved recalcitrant.

Dissolution of the Rebellion accelerated as word spread that Bacon "lay sick at one Mr. Pate's in Gloster County of the Bloody Flux and (as Mr. Pate himself affirms) accompanyed with a Lousey

Disease; so that the swarmes of Vermyn that bred in his Body he could not destroy but by throwing his shirts into the Fire as often as he shifted himself." When he died, his partisans spirited his body away to prevent its exposure on a gibbet. Some said they weighted it with stones and sank it in the York River.

In the end, it was Berkeley who won the siege of Jamestown. H.B.M.'s commissioners were informed "this very service was supposed to be the Death of Bacon, who by lying in a wett season in his Trenches before Towne contracted the Disease whereof hee not long after dyed."

Berkeley commented that "his usual oath which he swore at least a Thousand times a day was God damne my Blood and god so infected his blood that it bred lice in an incredible number so that for twenty dayes he never washt his shirts but burned them. To this God added the Bloody flux and an honest minister wrote this Epitaph on him

> Bacon is Dead I am sorry at my hart
> That lice and flux should take the hangman's part."

Promptly, the governor reassumed control. Bacon's followers—Captain Ingram, who succeeded him as titular leader, and the various groups of men holed up for last stands in plantation houses such as the Allen home in Surry County, thereafter known as Bacon's Castle—were killed or taken prisoner.

In the Chickahominy swamp, Drummond was discovered and apprehended. Lawrence either escaped or died in the snow-silenced woods. Resistance ended.

In London, by the beginning of October, the news from Virginia had led from anxiety to action. For weeks, letters and dispatches had brought various versions of what was going on, together with proposals for an investigation. Bacon himself, in June, had urged that the colonists' complaints be "audited, either by agents from hence to England, or there by commers. from thence: & his Mty. & ye world will quickly pceive how ye case stands between the Governour, and the country."

On October 3, Whitehall announced the appointment of a royal commission of inquiry to go to Virginia on behalf of the Crown. A contingent of troops was to accompany them. The members were Francis Moryson, a Royalist who had gone to Virginia during the civil war, served as speaker of the house and as acting governor when Berkeley made a trip to England in 1661-62, then returned to London as Virginia's agent to negotiate repeal of the royal grant of the colony to the Lords Arlington and Culpeper; Colonel Herbert Jeffreys, a friend of Secretary of State Williamson, designated commander of the troops; and Captain Sir John Berry of the Royal Navy, charged with transport of the troops and naval support of their operations. This announcement was followed by a royal proclamation dated October 27, granting amnesty for all who had taken up arms except Bacon. Early in November, Jeffreys was given a commission to succeed Berkeley as governor of Virginia. On November 24, a little in advance of Jeffreys, Berry and Moryson sailed for Jamestown.

These two commissioners landed on January 29, 1677, to learn that Bacon was dead and to discover that while they were at sea Berkeley, with those of his council who were available, had sat five times as a court-martial and hung a considerable number of the prisoners.

On January 11, on board Captain John Martin's ship in York River, they had condemned Thomas Hall to death and set up a gallows on shore to hang him immediately.

On January 12, they had dispatched Thomas Young, Henry Page, and James Wilson.

On January 19, under guard, Drummond was brought before the governor, then lodged at Nathaniel Bacon, Sr.'s, plantation at King's Creek. Drummond had been Bacon's man all the way. Some time previously, Thomas Mathew had warned him "to be very Wary, for he saw the Governour had put a brand on him. He (gravely expressing my Name) answered, 'I am in over Shoes, I will be in over Boots.' "

When he was brought into the governor's presence, Berkeley made him a mocking low bow: "Mr. Drummond, you are very welcome. I am more glad to see you than any man in Virginia. Mr. Drummond, you shall be hanged in half an hour."

His prisoner replied: "What your Honour pleases."

Actually, the governor reserved Drummond's formal condemnation until the next day, when a court-martial sat at the house of councilman James Bray at Middle Plantation. The Burwell Manuscript gives an account of what followed: "If the Governour was soe [glad] to see Drummon, Drummon was no less sad to see [his h]on-

95

our, the sight of whom (with out the help of an As[trol]egr, might inform him of what death he should [die], and that he had not many days to live. That night [he] was sent aborde a Ship in Irons, while the Governour [re]moved the next day in his Coach to Mr. Bray's, a [jour]nye of some 5 Miles. The next day after, being Sater[day] Drummon was, by a party of Horss (who recev[ed him] at Coll: Bacons) conveyed to his tryall. In his way [thi]ther he complained very much that his Irons hurt [him], and that his fine Cloake, as he called it, a green- . . . for the H[a]ngman had taken his fur'd Coate from [him,] (a bad presage) did much hinder him in his way. [When] proffer'd [a h]orss, to ride, he refused, and sade he [would] come to . . . e to his port before he was preparde [wi]th his Anc[hor]: ading that he did very much feare [Sir Wil]iam w[ould] not al[low h]im time to put of his dir[ty cl]othes b[efore] he went to lye downe upon his ev[en]ing b[e]d. [He s]aide, welcom be the Grace of God, for [it would clea]nse him from all his filth and pollution. He ex[pressed] abundance of thanke for being permitted to res[t hi]mselfe upon the Roade, while he tooke a pipe of Tobacco. He discoursed very much with that parson who comm[anded] his gard concerning the late troubles, affirming that he was wholly innoscent. . . ."

Condemned at one o'clock, he was hanged at four, as soon as work could be completed on the scaffold.

At this session, a death sentence was, also passed on John Baptista.

January 22 saw the governor home again at Green Spring, with the assembly members who were not dead, fled, or under arrest called to meet him there in February. Two days later he held a court-martial whose six death sentences led off with that of James Crewes, Bacon's fellow burgess from Henrico. Henry West was declared banished with his estate forfeit except £5 for passage money.

During February, the governor was occupied with the arrival of His Majesty's commissioners and a busy session of the reconvened assembly, but in March, new trials—this time, civil processes—started at Green Spring.

On March 1 and 3, three men were heavily fined.

On March 8, with the commissioners present, and for the first time before a jury, death sentences resumed, Giles Bland's leading a list of executions that mounted to nine before the hangman's trap had opened under its last victim.

When Edmund Chisman, a major under Bacon, was brought

forward, his wife, Lydia, threw herself at the governor's feet and asked to be hanged in his stead, declaring it was at her instigation that he joined the Rebellion. He died in prison.

Thomas Hansford, who had been commander of four counties and president of Bacon's court of sequestration, fruitlessly asked that he "might be shot like a soldier and not hanged like a dog"; on the scaffold he urged those present to note that he "died a loyal subject and a lover of his country." Fourteen others were banished, or fined heavily in pork to be used by the royal troops.

Altogether, these records of reprisal enrolled the names of forty men, of whom more than a score had been turned into wry-necked corpses tiptoeing thin air.

The restored Green Spring faction did not take the royal commissioners very seriously. It did not occur to the governor that the actions of so great a loyalist as he could fail to find approval in the eyes of his King. The Berkeleys declined to recognize Jeffrey's gubernatorial commission: since Berkeley had been ordered to return to London, they treated it as an interim appointment and styled him the lieutenant governor. Philip Ludwell called him "a pitiful little fellow with a periwig."

The assembly that met at Green Spring between the military and the civil hangings endorsed everything Berkeley asked in respect to the Rebellion.

First, he promulgated with its assent an act of very limited amnesty, differing materially from the royal proclamation of October 27 that had been transmitted to him for publication when the commissioners arrived. The King had granted amnesty to all except Bacon. Berkeley's document excepted fifty-eight men and women. Berkeley justified the discrepancy by the King's instructions to him dated October 10, which contained a discretionary power to pardon.

His second initiative applied a posthumous bill of attainder to the rebels' dead leader, with the comment that "in the height of their monstr'ous rebellion, it pleased Almighty God of his infinite mercy and goodness to this poore country, by a just and most exemplary death, to take the said Nathaniell Bacon out of this world."

A third act inflicted "paines and penalties upon greate offenders." Numbers of Virginians who had taken sides with Bacon were condemned to appear either before the general court at Williamsburg or the courts of their own counties, with ropes around their

97

VIRGINIA

AND

MARYLAND

As it is Planted and
Inhabited this present
Year 1670 Surveyed and
Exactly Drawne by the
Only Labour & Endeavour
of *Augustin Herrman*
Bohemiensis

Significations of some remarkable Letters in this Mapp
C Denotes Countys in several Colonies
M Mannours but are not all inserted
R Rivers Cr Creeks Pt Points of Land
⊕ Plantations notifying only the manner of situation
▥ Indian Houses and Plantations
▨ The smaell littel Pricks resemble the Sands and
Shoals whereof some perhaps may alter but
the long ones marcked thus ▨ denotes certain Marches
The Cyphers denotes the Channels and certain Soundings

necks, to acknowledge on their knees their wrong-doing in bearing arms. In some counties, the requirement was parodied: the general court record notes that at Rappahannock the prisoners "did, in contempt of the said law and the King's majesties authority in this his colony, appear in the said court with small tape (instead of halters) about their necks, which was allowed and accepted by the magistrates then sitting."

The assembly's fourth statute, conforming to the King's instructions, repealed all the laws passed the previous June by Bacon's assembly. (But later in the session, they re-enacted a considerable number of the provisions, including those enlarging the franchise, providing for rotation in office, decentralizing and democratizing local government, and reducing the salaries and emoluments of the burgesses.)

Then, after compensating loyalists for losses suffered during the rebellion, Berkeley developed the sanctions under which he proposed to prevent further disorder.

For the "prevention of seditious and scandalous libels, the usuall fore runners of tumult and rebellion," new legislation specified that any persons who "shall presume to speake, write, disperse or publish by words, writeing or otherwise, any matter of thing tending to rebellion, or in favour of the late rebells or rebellion . . . . shall be fined one thousand pounds of tobacco & caske, & stand upon the pillory two howers with capitall letters of their crimes affixed on their foreheads or brest." A second offense doubled the fine; a third invited prosecution as a "rebell & traitor to his most sacred majesty."

In case of libel that included abuse of the governor, his council, justices of the peace, or commissioned officers, special penalties attached to a third conviction: "to be whipped on the bare back with thirty-nine lashes, and stand in the pillory two howers, or pay double the before recited ffines, all which said ffines as aforesaid shalbe and belong the one halfe to the informer. . . ."

The final section of this act abrogated the collective right to bear arms in Virginia: "And whereas by a branch of an act of assembly made in March last, liberty is granted to all persons to carry their arms wheresoever they goe, which liberty hath beene found to be very prejudicial to the peace & welfaire of this colony. Bee it therefore further enacted . . . that if any person or persons shall, from and after publication of this act, presume to assemble together in arms to the number of five or upwards without being legally called

99

together . . . . they be held . . . riotous and mutinous and . . . proceeded against and punished accordingly."

Initially, Berkeley's personal triumph could hardly have been greater. But it was short-lived. The commissioners began a county-by-county series of open hearings, at which people's grievances were presented in cumulative review. Friction between the commissioners and the governor mounted, and they condemned many of the governmental abuses protested by the makers of the Rebellion in their resort to arms.

By the end of April or early May, Berkeley at last obeyed the summons to London, leaving behind a letter to Jeffreys in which he signed himself "Governor of Virginia til his most sacred Majesty shall please to determine otherwise of me," and looking forward to putting his own case before his King.

In mid-summer his wife forwarded the intelligence: "As soon as your back was turned, the Lieut. Governor said he would lay 100 £ that you would not be permitted to see the King, but would be sent to the Tower."

Sir William never read this letter: by the time it reached England he was dead. Thomas Mathew ends his history of these times with a poignant vignette of the failure of this overloyal old man's mission: "The Governour went in the Ffleet to London, (whether by Command from his Majesty or Spontaneous I did not hear), Leaving Col'. Jefferyes in his Place, and by next Shipping Came back a Person who waited on his Honour in his Voyage, and untill his Death, from whom a report was Whisper'd about, that the King did Say, 'that old fool has hang'd more men in that naked Country, than he had done for the Murther of his Ffather', whereof the Governor hearing dyed soon after without having seen his Majesty; Which shuts up this Tragedy."

May 4, 1677, was designated by the Virginia Assembly as a statutory fast day "for the pardon and remission of our manifold sinns." During the nights of that week, looking up into the dark spring sky, Virginians watched in awe the stream-tailed course of an enormous comet. They talked of it long afterwards, likening it to Bacon's transit of the previous summer: breathtaking, brilliant, brief.

A hundred years later, the collective right to bear arms that had been affirmed in Bacon's manifestos was again asserted in Virginia. This time, the rebellion turned into a revolution whose limited de facto success endured to receive lasting de jure recognition.

CHAPTER IV

QUARTERING OF TROOPS

The Bill of Rights: No soldier shall, in time of peace, be quartered in any house, without the consent of the owner; nor in time of war, but in a manner to be prescribed by law.

BACKGROUND

In the drawing room of the Carlyle House in Alexandria, Virginia, in April 1754, the governors of five major colonies conferred on grave military matters. Major General Edward Braddock had arrived as commander-in-chief of His Majesty's forces in North America.

For the active prosecution of the war against the French and their Indian allies, His Majesty's troop strength in North America was to be rapidly increased to around ten thousand men. The forces were to be augmented not only by local recruitment, but also by the dispatch of professional regiments from the British Isles. Their coming raised two related questions: where could they be quartered, and how could the expense of their maintenance be met? Governor Shirley of Massachusetts expressed the view that the colonists should be required to bear the cost of their own protection.

In London, pressure for such an arrangement was mounting—the drain of colonial administration on the British budget had increased alarmingly in recent years. Yet to devolve on the colonists the expenses of the anticipated military activity in America was a touchy matter. Most of them did not regard the global struggle for empire between Britain and France as their affair. As to protection, American frontiersmen held the British regulars' capacity for Indian border warfare in a contempt quite equal to General Braddock's professional disdain for the ununiformed and uncouth sharpshooters of whom American contingents were composed. They considered their opinion substantiated when the general died at Great Meadows within six months of his arrival surrounded by casualties numbering more than half his officers and almost half his men and murmuring of the Indians, "We shall better know how to deal with them another time."

But the origins of the conferees' difficulties lay much further back than colonial indifference to the objects of this war and colonial mistrust of professional tactics. The quartering of troops combined personal inconvenience and inequitable taxation. Resistance to it was recorded in detail in the great English documents of the preceding century and a quarter.

102

Charles I's effort to maintain his armies for the unpopular Spanish War by prerogative taxation and forced quartering after Parliament had refused to vote him funds was the occasion of the Petition of Right of 1628. Its bill of particulars included as its sixth item: ". . . of late great companies of soldiers and mariners have been dispersed into divers counties of the realm, and the inhabitants against their wills have been compelled to receive them into their houses, and there to suffer them to sojourn, against the laws and customs of the realm and to the great grievance and vexation of the people." Its specification of remedies, to re-establish "rights and liberties, according to the laws and statutes of this realm," proposed, "That no man hereafter be compelled to make or yield any gift, loan, benevolence, tax, or such-like charge, without common consent by act of parliament; . . . and that your Majesty would be pleased to remove the said soldiers and marines, and that your people may not be so burthened in time to come. . . ."

When the new sovereigns, William and Mary, came to the throne with the Glorious Revolution, the Bill of Rights of 1689 listed among the wrongdoings of James II "raising and keeping a standing army within this kingdom in time of peace, without consent of parliament, and quartering soldiers contrary to law." It required that in future such raising or keeping be only with Parliament's consent.

Lord Loudoun, who arrived in January 1756 to resume the military campaign in America, was well aware that the legal basis of his demands for military appropriations was ill-defined. The proper handling of troop supplies had been specified in detail in the Mutiny Act of 1689 with respect to troops in England: soldiers on the move or stationed in areas where regular barracks did not exist were to be accommodated at inns and public houses, with the innkeepers recompensed by their quartermasters from funds voted by Parliament. Only in Scotland, where public accommodations were few, did the law stipulate that officers and men be given coals, candles, and lodging in private houses, and its application there had been infrequent.

But for America, no clear regulations existed. Acts of Parliament passed after settlement of the colonies were normally held not to apply to them unless specifically extended. And though Loudoun made repeated requests for clarification, Parliament did not act on the matter until after the end of the war. At the time of Braddock's

103

expedition, the secretary of state had merely informed the colonial governors that "quarters must be taken in the plantations as they are in England in time of war," without instructing them how to sequester lodgings or how to get the owners reimbursed.

In America, neither barracks nor inns existed in adequate numbers. When one of the English battalions reached Charleston the only shelter obtainable was a damp, half-finished church, where the troops slept without straw or blankets. On arrival, they numbered one thousand with only thirteen sick; by the end of a month, five hundred were sick and sixty dead. So with little authority beyond his firm belief in the royal prerogative, and in the face of recalcitrant legislatures from Massachusetts to South Carolina, Loudoun had to act.

New York, with its port and its strategic location, was scheduled to receive the heaviest concentration of troops. In New York City, after encouraging cooperation by paying handsomely for lodgings for his own use and assuring Governor Hardy that in wartime "not even the people of first fashion in England are exempted" from quartering, Loudoun called on the mayor and council to provide funds. The mayor raised objections, but when Loudoun threatened to march in three or four battalions and quarter by force, the city corporation voted to pay their costs for bedding and firing, but not beer. His lordship privately observed that "the People in this country, tho' they are very obstinate, will generally submit when they see you are determined."

In Albany, Loudoun used the power to quarter with full force. The city was his staging point for operations against Canada. Its inhabitants were largely Dutch and heavily engaged in Canadian trade. The mayor was obdurate, formally announcing that he and they would die rather than submit. Loudoun ignored him. He ordered a house-to-house, room-to-room canvas of the dwellings of the town's 329 families. The result indicated a capacity to accommodate 146 officers and 1,443 men or, with close packing, 190 officers and 2,082 men. Loudoun demanded beds, firing, and candles for 1,300, use of the Dutch church (with pews removed) for a powder magazine, and space in the local jail. He proceeded with forced billeting, reporting to London that he refrained from billeting officers until a "Canadian trader threw an officer's baggage into the street, and barricaded the door, and I sent a file of men, and put the officer into Possession; my resolution is, if I find any more of this work, whenever I find a leading man, shut out any of the people, to take the whole house for a hospital, or a storehouse, and let him shift for himself." But he also began construction of barracks to be paid for by the Crown.

By December 1756, the New York Assembly had been induced to pass an act that legalized quartering in public houses, or in private houses if available public houses were insufficient, and instructed local magistrates to set rates to be paid proprietors from funds appropriated by the colony. Two months later, Governor Hardy wrote the board of trade: "it is with pleasure I can acquaint your Lordships that little or no difficultys have arisen in quartering the Forces." In the course of the year, new barracks, in addition to those at Fort George, were built on the New York City common, with the assembly footing the £3,500 bill.

The erection of barracks at central locations and the cessation of military operations in the American theater with the signing of the peace treaty of 1763 removed most of the individual friction-points of billeting in colonists' homes. The quartering of troops became solely a fiscal issue. But Parliament's specific extension of the Mutiny Act to the colonies in 1765, at the request of General Thomas Gage, created new disquiet. Its terms were clear. Soldiers were to be lodged in barracks; if space in barracks was insufficient, they were to be billeted in inns, livery stables, ale houses, and other public buildings. If these accommodations too did not suffice, the governor and council could authorize taking, hiring, and making fit enough privately owned buildings to quarter the residue.

The reason of its enactment was also clear: to strengthen the general's hand not as commander in a foreign war but as enforcement officer of recent unpopular legislation, particularly the Stamp Act. Required military expenditures then became a double grievance: self-taxation to support troops engaged in sustaining legislation passed without consent of those concerned.

THE CASE

In New York in the mid-1760's, times were hard. An acute shortage of ready money hampered all transactions. Most exports were exchanged not for money but for other goods in the mother country; what cash was available came chiefly from side deals in the West Indies. Stricter enforcement of the Navigation Acts was drying up this money supply at the very time when the Stamp Act imposed new taxes, payable in cash, for the stamps required on land titles and commercial documents. Projects for relief from the currency crisis, inconclusively canvassed from docksides to assembly corridors, even included unabashed resort to inflation by setting up a public loan office to emit bills of credit, with the interest earned on them used to defray the expenses of government.

Against this background, when General Gage, at the end of 1765, requested supplies under the Quartering Act, the assembly refused to vote the full measure. During the next summer, repeated scuffles took place between citizens and soldiery. In one such fracas, Isaac Sears, a popular leader was wounded. The assembly of December 1766 refused to make any military appropriations whatever.

At the news, Parliament suspended the validity of all acts of the New York Assembly until it should comply, the suspension to become effective October 1, 1767. The governor did not enforce it since £3,000 had been voted while the act was on the way over. But in 1768, the assembly balked again.

Compliance or noncompliance became the central issue in the hotly fought political campaign of 1768-69. Elections were due both for the assembly, where the terms were seven years, and for the city council.

Over two generations, political control in New York had seesawed, the ups and downs divided between a conservative faction, normally close to the royal governors, in which the DeLancey and Philipse families were conspicuous, and a progressive faction, led chiefly by Morrises and Livingstons. The two differed in religion and in old school ties as well as in politics. The conservatives were upholders of the Church of England and sponsors of the King's College (later Columbia) under the Establishment. Among the

106

progressives, Yale-trained Presbyterian lawyers were prominent—various Livingstons, William Smith, Jr., and John Morin Scott. The Livingston faction had controlled the assembly from 1761-68; the DeLancey faction was now determined to make a comeback.

In the progressive group, the nucleus of well-to-do and long-established landowners, merchants, and lawyers had recently been augmented by a more popular element, many of whom, vigorous recent arrivals eagerly working their way up, were ready proponents of direct action.

Alexander MacDougall was typical of the newer membership. He started as a delivery boy making rounds with his father's milk cart. He then went to sea and became master of a sloop. Next he married a wealthy widow and established himself as a New York merchant. He ended life as the first president of the Bank of New York.

He and others—Isaac Low and Isaac Sears among them—were leaders in the Sons of Liberty, an association taking its name from a speech in the House of Commons in praise of America's resistance to the Stamp Act. Its ebullient members demonstrated at mass meetings in the Fields (the New York Common, later City Hall Park), carried remonstrances to the governor at the gates of Fort George, and exchanged fisticuffs with British soldiers quartered on the common, where a liberty pole in conspicuous view of the barracks celebrated repeal of the Stamp Act.

But if the progressives had gained in numbers, the conservatives had had time to reorganize the close-knit political structure built and led by James DeLancey, Sr., during the years after the Zenger trial. His power had been successively augmented by the chief justiceship with permanent tenure (1744), the lieutenant governorship (1753), and two periods as acting governor; but his death in 1760 left his faction unprepared for the next year's polls. Now, the gap in leadership had been filled by his son.

Thus fortified, the factions fought it out. When the votes were counted, the conservatives were found to have made a decisive sweep, with safe margins in both council and assembly.

In New York City and its adjacent counties, not a progressive remained in the assembly. In a battle of ranking lawyers, exchanging charges of libel and corruption, James Jauncey had defeated John Morin Scott. Philip Livingston, the speaker, had been defeated by John Cruger, the former mayor of New York City who had co-operated with Loudoun in quartering troops; he became speaker of the new house. Captain James DeLancey, Jr., declined appointment on the council in order to remain as floor manager of the new majority in the twenty-seven-man assembly.

Only upcountry, in the manors along the Hudson and in Albany and Schenectady, did the Livingston-Schuyler group retain representation, and the new majority quickly cut this down.

A recount in the borough of Westchester, where Lewis Morris, Jr., had won 59-55, put John DeLancey in his place. Philip Livingston's representation of the manor of Livingston was challenged on the ground of nonresidence in his district, as was that of Abraham Ten Broeck, uncle and guardian of Livingston's young son-in-law, the lord of the manor of Rensselaerswyck. Ten Broeck's fiduciary relationship enabled him to hold on. But though in all but three of the past fifty-three years the incumbent of Livingston's seat had maintained residence in New York City rather than in the family's holding on the river, he was "excused from further attendance in this House," and the assembly confirmed the residence requirement by statute.

After these changes, the new majority prepared to fulfill its election promises.

The conservative group had an active ally in Cadwallader Colden, allied by marriage with the DeLanceys, and acting governor in November 1769 because of the recent death of Governor Hardy. Born in Scotland in 1688, he emigrated to Philadelphia in 1710, but moved to New York in 1718, where Governor Robert Hunter made him surveyor general in 1720. Named to the council in 1721, he began a membership that lasted fifty-five years. On the death of James DeLancey, Sr., in 1760, his long ambition to be lieutenant governor was at last fulfilled. He was seventy-three at the time, but pronounced himself sound as a nut. One correspondent wrote to a long absent friend: "He fairly lives himself into office, being, they tell me, as hearty as when you knew him." Now, as acting governor, he asked the assembly to make up the arrearage in military supplies.

Though the Sons of Liberty might rail outside, urging New York to follow the lead of Massachusetts and South Carolina in a refusal, the conservatives affirmed the assembly's willingness to undertake this form of taxation in a classic demonstration of the smooth management of political power.

For the better part of the morning of December 5, the house stayed in executive session; the speaker did not take his chair, and the public was never admitted until he had done so. A deal was in the making: in return for support of military appropriations, De-Lancey's men were promising support for easement of the financial stringency by establishment of a loan office. The previous spring, when the loan office was first discussed, most members had agreed that so inflationary a measure was certain to be disallowed by White-hall. But the prospect had grown more tempting to representatives as their constituents became increasingly hard pressed.

As soon as the deal was worked out, a delegation was dispatched to seek formal approval by the acting governor. On its return, the speaker took his chair, admitted the public, and entertained a care-fully planned series of motions.

First, with the house sitting as a committee of the whole, Captain DeLancey obtained a unanimous vote in favor of hearing a motion to grant "money to his Majesty, for furnishing troops with neces-saries." A member of his faction then moved that a sum not exceed-ing £2,000 be granted for this purpose, to be taken from the loan office money when the bill establishing the office should have been passed. The vote on this motion resulted in a 11-11 tie.

The speaker broke the tie to defeat the motion.

Another member of the faction then offered a substitute mo-tion, that would also grant £2,000, but would take the first £1,000 from money currently in the treasury, replacing it with money from the loan office when available; the second £1,000 would come direct-ly from the loan office. Such an arrangement assured £1,000 for the troops even if establishment of the loan office was disallowed.

The DeLancey faction summoned its strength; the motion passed 12-11.

Sitting now as the house, the assembly confirmed this act, 12-11, the speaker not voting.

Public reaction was rapid. On the night of the seventeenth an anonymous broadside in the form of an open letter addressed *To the betrayed inhabitants of the City of New York* and signed "A Son of Liberty," was pasted on city walls; it condemned the assembly's action and urged citizens to hold a public meeting and convey their indignation to their representatives:

Our granting money to the troops, is implicitly acknowledging the authority that enacted the revenue acts, and their being obligatory on

109

us, as these acts were enacted for the express purpose of taking money out of our pockets without our consent. . . .

To what other influence than the deserting of the American cause, can the ministry attribute so pusillanimous a conduct, as this is of the Assembly; so repugnant and subversive of all the means we have used, and opposition that has been made by this and other colonies, to the tyrannical conduct of the British Parliament. . . .

Hence it follows that the assembly have not been attentive to the liberties of the continent, nor to the property of the good people of this colony in particular, we must therefore attribute this sacrifice of the public interest, to some corrupt source . . . Mr. Colden knows from the nature of things, that he cannot have the least prospect to be in administration again; and therefore, that he may make hay while the sun shines, and get a full salary from the Assembly, flatters the ignorant members of it, with the consideration of the success of a bill to emit paper currency; when he and his artful coadjutors must know, that it is only a snare to impose on the simple; for it will not obtain the royal assent . . . The De Lancy family knowing the ascendency they have in the present house of Assembly, and how useful that influence will be to their ambitious designs, to manage a new Governour, have left no stone unturned to prevent a dissolution. The Assembly, conscious to themselves, of having trampled on the liberties of the people, and fearing their just resentments on such an event, are equally careful to preserve their seats. . . .

Is this a state to be rested in, when our all is at stake? No, my countrymen, rouse! . . . Imitate the noble example of the friends of liberty in England; who, rather than be enslaved, contend for their right with k--g, lords, and commons . . . What I would advise to be done is, to assemble in the fields, on Monday next, where your sense ought to be take on this important point . . . After this is done, go in a body to your members, and insist on their joining with the minority to oppose the bill . . . let the notification to call the people be so expressed, that whoever absents himself, will be considered as agreeing to what may be done by such as shall meet;—and that you may succeed in the unfeigned desire of

A SON OF LIBERTY

Next day, the mayor formally brought this broadside to the attention of the assembly. The following morning, a briefer communication along similar lines, signed "LEGION," was also submitted.

On the nineteenth, the house resolved that the broadside was "calculated to inflame the minds of the good people of this colony, against the Representatives . . . and contains scandalous reflections on the three branches of the legislature"; that its proposal of a visitation to the assembly was "introductive of anarchy and confusion, and subversive of the fundamental principles of our happy constitution." The acting governor promptly complied with its request that he issue a proclamation stating that the assembly had declared "that the said paper is a false seditious and infamous libel" and offering £100 reward for identification of "A Son of Liberty" and £50 for identification of "Legion."

Over fourteen hundred people attended the meeting to which the broadside summoned them; they appointed a committee of eight, including prominent members of the Sons of Liberty, to take their grievances to the New York City assembly delegation.

On the twentieth, the house issued a warrant for John Lamb, the man who had moved the resolutions adopted by the meeting, to appear before its bar so they might determine whether his actions had been in response to the two libels. He succeeded in claiming that they were not and was discharged.

The £100 reward proved tempting. The colony's paper of the time, *The New-York Gazette; or, The Weekly Post-boy,* was published by James Parker, who also worked as clerk in the post office. Among his apprentices was one Michael Cummins, recently arrived from Cork. Turning informer, Cummins gave evidence that the broadside was printed in Parker's shop and that its author was Alexander MacDougall. A warrant was issued for Parker to appear before the lieutenant governor and council. When threatened with loss of his post-office job, he corroborated what Cummins had said.

Next day, Alexander MacDougall was arrested and brought before Chief Justice Horsmanden. His account of their interchange runs:

Tho' no Questions were put to me upon my being presented to the Chief Justice, yet immediately on my Entrance into the Chamber, his Honor said to me, "So you have bro't yourself into a pretty Scrape."

To which I replied, "May it please your Honor, that must be judged by my Peers." He then told me that there was full Proof, that I was the Author or Publisher of the abovementioned Paper, which he called a "false, vile, scandalous Libel." I replied again, "This must also be tried by my Peers."

His Honor thereupon informed me, that I must either give Bail or go to Gaol. I answered, "Sir, I will give no Bail." He was then pleased

111

to order the Sheriff to take me to Gaol, and made out a Mittimus, charging me as the Author and Publisher of a certain false, scandalous, seditious and infamous Paper, addressed, directed to the betrayed Inhabitants of the City and Colony of New-York, and subscribed a Son of Liberty; and commanding the Sheriff therewith to receive me, and safely keep me in Gaol, until I shall thence be delivered by due course of Law . . .

This description is part of the open letter "To the Freeholders Freemen and Inhabitants of the Colony of New York; and to all the friends of liberty in North America," written in New Gaol, February 9, 1770, in which MacDougall gave a full account of the events leading up to his imprisonment. It was published in *The New-York Gazette* of February 15 and republished in *The Massachusetts Gazette; and the Boston Weekly News-Letter* of February 22 and elsewhere along the coast. Its final passages read: "And now, my Fellow Citizens, and Fellow Americans, when the infamous Star Chamber Doctrine of Libels, has so long been exploded in the Mother Country, I rejoice to think that I may in the least contribute to prevent its Appearance in these happy Regions! Once indeed! it attempted in this Land of Light and Liberty to rear its baneful Standard, and round it flocked the Adherents of the very Party who now endeavour to re-introduce it. But Liberty herself, in the form of ZENGER, instantly prostrated the infernal engine, and gained an illustrious Triumph. . . . I shall estime my Confinement a singular Felicity. . . ."

His estimation was correct. The jail was a new and imposing building on the common close to the military barracks and to the new liberty pole. (Destruction of the old pole by soldiers from the barracks a few weeks earlier had set off a brawl that left one man dead on Golden Hill. The Sons of Liberty, denied permission to replace the pole on the common, made a private purchase of a narrow strip of land directly across the way.)

MacDougall's quarters became a social center. In order to have time for writing without interruption, he was obliged to enforce visiting hours; but from three to six in the afternoon callers bearing delicacies crowded his cell. Acting Governor Colden wrote Lord Hillsborough: "He is a person of some fortune, and could easily have found the Bail required of him, but he chose to go to Jail, and lyes there imitating Mr. Wilkes in Everything he can."

A "second Wilkes" was a description much applied to Mac-

John Wilkes Esqr.

Drawn from the Life and Etch'd in Aquafortis by Willm Hogarth.

ice 1 Shilling.

Publish'd according to Act of Parliament May ye 16 1763.

Dougall in the public prints. John Wilkes, agitator and reformer, member of Parliament and publisher of the *North Briton,* enjoyed an immense popularity among the commonalty on both sides of the Atlantic. Arrested in 1763 at the instigation of the Court party on the grounds that his paper's commentary on that year's address from the throne constituted seditious libel, he was subsequently expelled from the House of Commons. He had become particularly conspicuous in 1769, when he was re-elected and re-expelled on three occasions by a house that finally seated a candidate whom he had just defeated by nearly three to one. During his periods in jail, popular demonstrations occurred repeatedly in his favor. Subscriptions for his defense were raised on both sides of the Atlantic.

The publication for which Wilkes had been arrested was Number 45 of the *North Briton;* by coincidence, this was also the number of the page of the *Journal of the New York Assembly* on which MacDougall's offending broadside was recorded. So the number *45* became a symbol. In his *History of New York,* the conservative Thomas Jones wrote: "The public papers announced that on such a day 45 gentlemen dined with him, that on such a morning 45 ladies breakfasted with him, that on such a night 45 tradesmen supped with him . . . Sometimes we were told of 45 bottles of wine being drank at a sitting, of 45 pounds of beef being eaten, and 45 patriotic toasts given . . ." On March 19, the anniversary of the repeal of the Stamp Act, the Sons of Liberty, after toasting Wilkes and MacDougall 45 times at their favorite tavern, went in a procession to the jail and saluted MacDougall as a martyr to liberty with 45 cheers.

While this merriment proceeded, the time came for the spring meeting of the supreme court. Attorney General John Kempe prepared a careful brief itemizing what MacDougall would have to prove in order to demonstrate his innocence. Much hinged on the composition of the grand jury which would be asked to indict MacDougall: Acting Governor Colden wrote Loudoun that "when he comes to his Tryal it will appear what dependence we may have in a Jury of this place." Isaac Sears is said to have approached the sheriff in the interest of selecting a panel friendly to the popular side, but Thomas Jones affirms with satisfaction that the jury was a body "consisting of the most impartial, reputable, opulent, and substantial gentlemen in the city."

MacDougall's friends and attorneys had attempted to smother

114

indictment of the broadside by bringing into court at the same time a miscellany of other publications which they insisted were libelous, hoping that all would be thrown out together. But in MacDougall's case, the jurymen found a true bill.

John Morin Scott, MacDougall's attorney, then proposed that the defendent should enter his plea in person. Enthusiastic partisans formed an escort for his half-mile walk from the jail to the city hall. Pleading not guilty, he was released on £1,000 bail.

Shortly thereafter, the acting governor in council named the mayor and the recorder as attorneys to assist the attorney general in the prosecution of this case. William Smith, Jr., who had succeeded his father on the council in 1769, was named but refused to serve, remarking that the broadsides, far from being libelous, represented the views of the majority of the people.

Meanwhile, popular resentment shifted to the young apprentice who had turned informer. By the time he collected his reward on May 2, MacDougall's friends were offering other rewards for information as to his whereabouts. Fearful of their wrath, the lad slipped away to Boston, made contact with General Gage, and was spirited out of the country.

With his departure, the government's key witness became unavailable. On July 2, the printer, James Parker, its other source of information, died suddenly in New Jersey.

But the charge against MacDougall was not withdrawn. He was out, but out on bail.

After six months of inaction, on December 13, an assembly member suddenly moved to summon MacDougall before the bar of the house. The motion passed with only one contrary voice. The sergeant-at-arms was sent to bring him in.

When he appeared, the assembly's journal shows,

Mr. Speaker acquainted him, that he was charged, by a member of the house, with being the author or publisher of a certain paper, entered on the printed journals of this house, on the 18th day of December, 1769, page (45) . . . and the same being read, Mr. Speaker asked him, whether or not he was the author or publisher of the same? To which said M'Dougall replied. "That as the grand jury and house of the Assembly had declared the paper in question to be a libel, he could not answer the question. Secondly, that as he was under prosecution in the Supreme court, he conceived it would be an infraction of the laws of Justice to punish a British subject twice for one offence. . . ."

And upon Mr. Speaker's asking whether the foregoing words of said M'Dougall were not a contempt of the authority of this house, a debate arose, and the question being put thereon, it passed in the affirmative . . . And the said M'Dougall refusing to ask pardon of the house for the said contempt . . . Ordered that the Speaker issue his warrant to the gaol keeper of the city and county of New York, commanding him to receive the said M'Dougall into safe and secure custody, and him to keep the prisoner in the common gaol of the said city and county, until he shall be thence discharged by due course of law; and that the sergeant at arms convey the said M'Dougall, and deliver him to the keeper of the said gaol.

So at year's end, MacDougall was back in the familiar building on the common, confined this time by order of the assembly. Promptly, he wrote a vindication. Equally promptly, moves were undertaken for his release.

On January 19, 1771, the sheriff appeared at the door of the assembly and informed the house that he had been served with a writ of habeas corpus, to take MacDougall from the jail and bring him before the supreme court. The assembly declined to permit the sheriff to produce the prisoner, responding with an order, "that the judges of the supreme court be acquainted that the said Alexander M'Dougall is committed by warrant of the Speaker for a contempt of the authority of this house."

Perhaps house members were uncertain of the propriety of imprisonment under such an order. Perhaps some of the supreme court judges indicated discontent that their habeas corpus had been ignored. In any case, at the next sitting of the house, Captain DeLancey introduced a motion for the appointment of a committee "to search the journals of the House of Commons, for precedents in cases where writs of habeas corpus have been issued, to bring persons committed by the commons, before other courts."

Speaker Cruger designated four members from his faction, including Captain DeLancey and two Livingston men. They were to report "with all convenient speed." On February 16 this committee, with Captain DeLancey as spokesman, brought in a fat docket of precedents. The last, quoted from the records of Parliament for March 8, 1704, ran:

The serjeant at arms attending this house, having acquainted the house, that he had received two writs of Habeas Corpus, under the great seal of England, to bring before the lord keeper, the bodies of James Montague, Esq. and Alexander Denton, Esq. who are committed to his custody, by warrants from the speaker of this house, for a breach of privilege.

Resolved, That no commoner of England, committed by the house of commons, for breach of privilege, or contempt of that house, ought to be by writ of habeas corpus, made to appear in any other place, or before any other judicature, during that session of parliament, wherein such person was so committed. . . .

Resolved, That the serjeant at arms attending this house . . . do make no return of, or yield any obedience to the writs of habeas corpus, and for such his refusal . . . that he have the protection of the house of commons. . . .

Resolved, That the lord keeper be acquainted with the said resolutions, to the end, that the said writs of habeas corpus may be superseded, as contrary to the law and privileges of this house.

On the strength of these precedents, MacDougall was left in jail for the rest of the session; his second imprisonment lasted eighty-one days. On March 4, Governor Dunmore prorogued the house, and the prisoner was released.

John Morin Scott then successfully applied to the supreme court for a discharge of the case. By the end of April, MacDougall was free to partake of the relative tranquility of the years 1771-72.

At the time that MacDougall's imprisonments were dramatizing appropriations for the quartering of troops as a specific instance of taxation without representation, the duties assessed under the Townshend Acts of 1767 were being resented on the same grounds up and down the coast. Resistance was expressed in nonimportation resolutions, and though compliance was far from complete, these were sufficiently effective for Lord North's ministry in 1770 to rescind all but one of the offending duties. That on tea was retained to assert Parliament's right to place such imposts.

In 1773, the Tea Act was reaffirmed and landings of cargo arranged for four key ports: Boston, New York, Philadelphia, and Charleston.

The New York Sons of Liberty, with MacDougall as one of their leaders, resolved in November "That whoever shall aid, or abet, or in any manner assist in the introduction of tea, from any place whatsoever, into this colony, while it is subject, by a British Act to parliament, to the payment of duty, for the purpose of raising a revenue in America, he shall be deemed an enemy to the liberties of America." The tea shipped to New York was not landed. The Boston Tea Party took place on December 16.

The following March, Parliament passed the measures that the colonists termed the "Intolerable Acts." Among them, the Quartering Act of 1774 gave the British commander and the governor of a province authority to quarter troops wherever their presence might be needed; the Boston barracks were too far from the center of town for troops lodged there to be readily available for riot duty.

News of these acts had not reached New York when, on May 16, a public meeting, called for Fraunce's Tavern but moved to the Broad Street Exchange to accommodate the crowd, heard Isaac Low put two questions:

Whether it is necessary, for the present, to appoint a committee to correspond with the neighbouring Colonies on the present important Crisis?

Whether a Committee be nominated this Evening for the Approbation of the Public?

And, after both had been rousingly carried in the affirmative, "Whether the Committee of 50 be appointed, or 25?" The crowd approved fifty; a second meeting, to confirm or supplement the nominations, was set for the nineteenth.

But on the seventeenth, an express rider clattered in from Boston with a letter from the committee of correspondence there, transmitting the new acts. At once, the fifty nominees, plus one addition, were endorsed by acclamation.

The committee of fifty-one included both representatives of the conservative merchants—John Alsop, James Duane, James Jauncey —and members of the Sons of Liberty—Isaac Sears, Alexander Mac-Dougall, and Isaac Low, who was chairman. A subcommittee, consisting of John Jay, Duane, MacDougall, and Low, drafted a reply that was dispatched to Boston on the twenty-third, proposing the calling of a continental congress.

At the election of five deputies to represent New York at this congress, however, the old factional division revived. The differences between the two groups concerned personalities, not the substantive issue; the ranking merchants were merely worried lest the situation get out of hand. After the meeting at the exchange on the sixteenth, Gouverneur Morris wrote Governor John Penn of Pennsylvania:

> I see, and I see it with fear and trembling, that if the disputes with Britain continue, we shall be under the worst of all possible dominions, We shall be under the dominion of a riotous mob.
>
> It is the interest of all men, therefore, to seek for reunion with our parent state. A safe compact seems in my poor opinion to be now tendered. Internal taxation to be left with ourselves. The right of regulating trade to be vested in Britain, where alone is found the power of protecting it.

The election results were reported to the Earl of Dartmouth by Cadwallader Colden, once more acting governor: "The Persons named are James Duane and John Jay, two eminent Lawyers, Isaac Low, Phillip Livingston and John Alsop, Merchants—I am told a Violent Effort was made in the Committee to have John Scott, an eminent lawyer, and Alexr. M'Dougal, the Wilkes of New York, named, in the place of Jay and Alsop . . . These Transactions are dangerous, my Lord, and illegal; but by what means shall government prevent them."

The congress met in Philadelphia on September 5, 1774; on October 14, it issued a "Declaration and Resolves" whose recital of grievances opens: "Whereas, since the close of the last war, the British parliament, claiming a power, of right, to bind the people of America by statutes in all cases whatsoever, hath, in some acts, expressly imposed taxes on them . . ." Its fourth resolve runs: "That the foundation of English liberty, and of all free government, is a right in the people to participate in their legislative council: and as the English colonists are not represented, and from their local and other circumstances, cannot properly be represented in the British parliament, they are entitled to a free and exclusive power of legislation in their several provincial legislatures, where their right of representation can alone be preserved, in all cases of taxation and internal polity. . . ." Its final section lists the acts regarded as infringement of these rights. The last statute cited is the Quartering Act of 1774.

In the interval between the close of the French and Indian War and the British capture of New York in 1776 the quartering issue concerned military appropriations as a form of taxation. But its cruder aspect of forced placement of troops in people's houses again became an actual, vivid grievance as soon as General Howe and his redcoats occupied city and province. When the Poughkeepsie Convention of 1788 concluded its deliberations on ratification of the proposed federal Constitution, the preamble of its accession contained a series of affirmations, among them, "That in time of Peace no Soldier ought to be quartered in any House without the consent of the Owner, and in time of War only by the Civil Magistrate in such manner as the Laws may direct."

CHAPTER V

SEARCH AND SEIZURE

The Bill of Rights: The right of the people to be secure in their persons, houses, papers, and effects, against unreasonable searches and seizures, shall not be violated; and no warrants shall issue, but upon probable cause, supported by oath or affirmation, and particularly describing the place to be searched, and the persons or things to be seized.

BACKGROUND

Pine-blackened coves, where a quick dark sloop could slip in and out like a minnow; lonely projecting sandspits where the rhythm of wind and surf obliterated imprint—at the end of a homeward voyage with highly dutiable cargo the eighteenth-century New England sea captain had wide choice of natural harbor. The Navigation Acts controlling colonial commerce gave him ample incentive to exercise it.

In stony New England, where town and sea were main sources of livelihood, the impact of the acts regulating trade was far greater than in the southern colonies. There, the plantation was the economic base: one-crop agriculture on virgin soil yielded generous exportable surpluses of tobacco, wheat, rice, and indigo and smaller amounts of naval stores and cotton. Southern colonists felt no particular hardship in the requirement that their produce be shipped to British ports: they needed the manufactured goods obtainable by this exchange. But New Englanders, whose thin soil grudged them little more than self-sufficiency, were constantly frustrated. An early historian, William Tudor, noted "they were not allowed to manufacture, because the manufactures of the parent country would be injured; they were confined in their navigation, because the shipping interest in England would suffer; they were not allowed to sell their fish for French and Spanish molasses, because the sugar colonies would not have the monopoly of supplying them; they could not import teas from Holland because it interfered with the East India Company; they could not trade with Spain and Portugal nor any other nation, because it infringed the navigation laws."

That was why, from Newburyport to Marblehead, the mariners and merchants of Massachusetts gave careful consideration to all means of lessening the impact of the law on the natural course of commerce, and why port towns understandingly commended their activities as evidence of business prudence.

Delivery of outbound cargo to forbidden ports was relatively easy. A master needed only to change course at sea after clearing for a legal destination. But the landing of cargo required discretion. Goods could be smuggled ashore informally, without clearance. Or

122

they could be put through customs under the eye of an inspector who had been paid to wink. Since customs officers were legally possessed of considerable discretion in assessing duties, an overlay of bribery on discretion was not unduly difficult. The naming of such officials was part of the patronage enjoyed by the King's friends and the lords of trade; more often than not, their placemen did not themselves come to the colonies, but subcontracted their privileges to subordinates who welcomed supplementary sources of income. In Virginia, Purdie's *Gazette* called them "needy Wretches who found it easier, and more profitable, not only to wink but to sleep in their Beds; the Merchants' Pay being more generous than the King's."

By mid-century, on a volume of trade which if assessed at statutory rates might have yielded up to £25,000, the collection of customs cost £2,000-£8,000 and yielded £1,000-£2,000. For every five hundred hogsheads of molasses—basic raw material of the rum trade and subject to special regulation since 1733—imported from the British West Indies, some fourteen thousand hogsheads were landed from forbidden, lower-priced sources in the French West Indies. During the French and Indian War, William Pitt noted that while such purchases constituted trading with the enemy, they nevertheless continued in "open contempt of the Authority of the Mother Country as well as to the most manifest Prejudice of the Manufactures and Trade of Great Britain."

To halt illicit trade and to exercise surveillance over legal commerce was the task of Thomas Lechmere, surveyor general of H.B.M.'s customs of the northern district of America, and his subordinates such as Charles Paxton, who in 1752 had been appointed surveyor of all rates, duties and impositions in Boston.

To facilitate inspection, in June 1755, Paxton applied to the Massachusetts Superior Court for issuance of a writ of assistance. This writ was a general warrant authorizing entry and search of premises for contraband, without specifying either the informer or the places where "uncustomed" goods were expected to be found. The court granted Paxton's request.

In the King's name, this legal instrument ran: "We therefore command you and each of you that you permit ye said Charles Paxton and his Deputies and Servants from Time to time at his or their Will as well in the day as in the Night to enter and go on board any Ship, Boat or other Vessel riding lying or being within or coming to the said Port or any Places or Creeks appertaining to the said Port, such Ship, Boat or Vessell then and there found to View and Search and strictly to examine in the same, touching the Customs and Subsidies to us due, And also in the day Time together with a Constable or any other public officer inhabiting near unto ye Place to enter and go into any Vaults, Cellars, Warehouses, Shops or other Places . . . and to open any Trunks, Chests, Boxes, fardells or Packs made up or in Bulk, whatever in which any Goods, Wares, or Merchandises are suspected to be packed or concealed . . . Fail not at your Peril."

Authority for this writ, which contravened the ancient common law rule that a man's privacy could not be invaded unless the official entering his premises possessed a warrant specifying exactly the place and purpose of his search, derived from a 1662 statute regarding uncustomed goods. It authorized enforcement officers to board vessels, and ordinary citizens obtaining a writ of assistance from the court of exchequer and accompanied by a public officer to enter premises to look for contraband, and to break in by force in case the occupant resisted. In 1696, such powers were specifically extended to apply in America.

Over the years 1756-59, several writs similar to Charles Paxton's were given to collectors at other ports. In November 1760, an application for such a writ was made by James Cockle, collector at Salem.

This application ran into difficulty. The four associate justices of the superior court indicated a disposition to grant the writ, but Stephen Sewall, chief justice for the past eight years, though he had presided when Paxton's first writ was issued, now expressed doubts as to the legality of these instruments. He ordered a hearing on the matter at the next term of court, in February, in Boston.

The Cockle case took on new importance when, on December 27, news reached Boston that George II had died in October. When a British monarch dies, all writs in his name expire if not renewed within six months. The court's decision in the Cockle case would therefore affect the renewal of all outstanding writs; besides Lechmere and Paxton, the collectors in Newburyport, Marblehead, and Falmouth currently possessed them.

Meanwhile, death had also altered the composition of the court; before the Cockle case was argued, a new judge had replaced Chief Justice Sewall.

The appointment was made by a new governor. In August,

Francis Bernard, then governor of New Jersey, was promoted to govern Massachusetts Bay; among special charges in his instructions was an admonition to "be aiding and assisting to the collectors and other officers of our admiralty and customs, in putting into execution" the acts of trade.

Governor Bernard's choice for the new judge, whom he designated as chief justice, was the lieutenant governor, Thomas Hutchinson. This gentleman's loyalist proclivities had long been amply demonstrated and amply rewarded: in addition to the lieutenant governorship, which had twice enabled him to serve as acting governor, he was a member of the governor's council and a judge of probate. Various members of his family held other posts.

The popular elements in the colony resented Hutchinson's newest appointment; feeling was particularly violent in the family of the James Otises, father and son.

Colonel James Otis was considered a good attorney, but he was self-made, not a Harvard man. His son James Otis, Jr., Harvard '43, was recognized as a leading lawyer—he was advocate general of the admiralty court, with the prestige of having tried cases at Halifax. But the family was nevertheless outside the ruling group.

It was common talk that in 1752 Governor Shirley had given Colonel Otis an assurance that the next appointment to the court should be his; but, as Hutchinson records in his *History of Massachusetts Bay,* in 1756 "a vacancy happened, and Mr. Shirley, from a prior engagement, or for some other reason, disappointed him."

So this time, Hutchinson continues, "he made application to Governor Bernard, that the first surviving judge might be appointed chief justice, and that he might take the place of a judge. His son also, with great warmth, engaged in behalf of his father, and, not meeting with that encouragement which he expected, vowed revenge, if he should finally fail of success."

The associate judges of the superior court, in order of seniority, were Benjamin Lynde, Jr., John Cushing, Chambers Russell, and Peter Oliver. All belonged to the small group of distinguished, long-settled, Harvard-trained families who had supplied the court with judges for several generations. A manuscript in the Cushing family papers conveys their general temper; it notes that the appointments of Russell and Oliver "were the appointments, particularly of the former, which excited the vengence of James Otis, &, arousing his patriotism . . . changed a courtier into a troubled and fiery mili-

125

tant . . . Sewall, who in 1752 succeeded Dudley as Chief Justice died and Thos. Hutchinson was appointed Chief Justice—he was an exceedingly unpopular man—friendly to ye Royal party . . . Judge Cushing and his friend Judge Lynde were no friends to the popular spirit now raging. They had long been a part of the Govt. & were warmly interested in it, & Bernard, Hutchinson & Oliver were their intimate friends; they were as Zealously & firmly devoted to their Country's welfare as any alive: and they believed B.H. & O & the others were so likewise—they believed that no evil was intended ye Country & that whatever evils seemed to threaten it, might be peaceably averted, without bloodshed or commotion. They believed too that ye country, then just emerging from a Wilderness into settled Status, would be crushed in a contest with ye mother country & reduced to ruin & Servile dependency. & they did not give credit to the patriotism of the leading men on ye popular side, some of them urged on by disappointed ambition, others courting popular favour in every way & aiming to be demagogues; seeing them act from such selfish motives they could not believe their purposes to be good: & such was the opinion of nearly all the professional, well educated and more respectable classes of the day."

The respectable merchants of Boston, however, regarded James Otis, Jr., as a very suitable attorney for their purposes, when, in the year of all these changes, sixty-three of them formed the "Society for Promoting Trade and Commerce within the Province" and engaged him as their counsel.

The society had several pieces of unfinished business in the courts. One was a smuggling case concerning the brigantine *Sarah*, owned by John Erving of the governor's council. In April, she had been found guilty in the admiralty court and a forfeiture declared to the value of half her cargo.

Owners could contest such a judgment by bringing a suit for damages at common law, on grounds of false arrest, against the customs officer lodging the complaint. The process was expensive, for costs were assessed against the owner even when he was successful, but it permitted a public hearing in a court where, unlike the admiralty court, there was a jury. For this reason the merchants' group decided to support a protest of *Sarah's* forfeiture.

The society likewise determined to challenge Commissioner Paxton's method of paying informers. Under the law, receipts from forfeitures were split three ways: one-third to the King, for use by

126

the provincial treasury; one-third to the governor; and one-third to the successful customs officer. Paxton was making a practice of paying informers for tip-offs out of the third that went to the provincial treasury rather than out of his own portion. The merchants decided to contest this arrangement. When, at its December meeting, the Massachusetts legislative assembly—the general court—held hearings on Paxton's practices, Otis presented the society's view.

The day after the close of these hearings the ship with news of the King's death arrived. The society immediately decided to lodge a collective protest against the issuance of any new writs of assistance and to be represented before the superior court when the Cockle application came up.

Equally promptly, Thomas Lechmere officially requested to "be heard on his Majesty's behalf upon the same Subject . . . that Writs of Assistance may be granted to him and his officers as usual."

THE CASE

The council chamber in Boston's Town House is spacious, but on the morning of February 24, 1761, it was crowded far beyond capacity: all seats sat on, standing room bulging, deeply recessed window sills jammed. Hearing of argument on the legality of general search warrants was the day's agenda.

A twenty-four-year-old law student named John Adams, admitted to practice at this term of court, and another fledgling attorney, his friend Samuel Quincy, had squirmed their way in: the crabbedly abbreviated notes taken by Adams and his expansion, in his years of recollection, both of them and of his general impressions of the scene, provide an eyewitness record.

Even some very small fry had slipped in among the legs and greatcoats of the standees: Israel Keith, then nine and still at the Boston Latin School, was present with a notebook. He too wrote about the occasion later.

Both sides had moved quickly to secure legal talent. Each attempted to retain Benjamin Pratt, but this ranking Boston lawyer declined both requests on the grounds of having just been named chief justice of the supreme court of New York.

Four attorneys were finally selected: Jeremiah Gridley, attorney general of the province, assisted in the second phase of the hearing by Robert Auchmuty, was counsel on behalf of Lechmere; James Otis and Oxenbridge Thacher, counsel on behalf of the merchants.

Otis had a conflict of interest. His government post as advocate general for the admiralty court made him a natural representative of the customs collectors; his obligations as counsel for the merchants put him on the other side. He severed his government tie.

In combining Otis and Thacher, the merchants chose astutely. Otis could present their case with fire fed alike by the conviction that had led him to resign his lucrative admiralty post and by his indignation at the governor's slight to his father. The impact of what he said on citizens attending the trial and on the general populace would create a political atmosphere to which the judges could hardly be indifferent.

But the court itself would not give his views the weight that

128

would accrue to the same arguments if made by one of their own social circle. Oxenbridge Thacher provided the necessary counterpoise; the Thachers belonged to the gentility. Most of them, including this one, had been trained for the ministry. He had turned to law when his voice proved unequal to the strain of preaching. William Tudor wrote: "The opposition of Thacher gave the government great uneasiness. . . . There was no pretext for assigning any unworthy motive for the part he took; and he was therefore the more to be dreaded."

In Jeremiah Gridley, this team had a formidable opponent. He was the grand old man of the legal profession. Few indeed were the lawyers of the colony who had not received at least part of their training in his chambers, as had Auchmuty, Otis, and Thacher. By a gesture, he could indicate that his opponents were promising young men, whereas he was seasoned counsel.

When the day came, Benjamin Pratt had no intention of missing the argument. He was a cripple: a serious injury had ended his early life as a mechanic and turned him to the law. Now, Adams says, "In a corner of the room must be placed as a Spectator and an auditor, wit, sense, imagination, genius, pathos, reason, prudence, eloquence, learning, and immense reading, hanging by the shoulders on two crutches, covered with a great cloth coat, in the person of Mr. Pratt, who had been solicited on both sides, but would engage on neither."

Mr. Pratt's retention of his greatcoat witnesses the bite of New England winter, for after commenting pridefully that the "Council Chamber was as respectable an apartment as the House of Commons or the House of Lords in Great Britain, in proportion, or that in the State House in Philadelphia," Adams notes that "round a great fire, were seated five Judges, with Lieutenant-Governor Hutchinson at their head, as Chief Justice, all arrayed in their new, fresh, rich robes of scarlet English broadcloth, in their large cambric bands, and immense juducial wigs. In this chamber were seated at a long table all the barristers at law of Boston, and of the neighboring county of Middlesex, in gowns, bands, and tie wigs . . . Two portraits, at more than full length, of King Charles the Second and of King James the Second, in splendid golden frames, were hung up on the most conspicuous side of the apartment . . . The pictures were stowed away in a garret, among rubbish, till Governor Bernard came, who had them cleaned, superbly framed, and placed in council for the admiration and imitation of all men—no doubt with the advice and concurrence of Hutchinson and all his nebulla of stars and satellites."

Gridley led off the argument: "I appear on behalf of Mr. Cockle and others, who pray 'that they cannot fully exercise their Offices in such a manner as his Majesty's Service and the Laws in such cases require, unless your Honors who are vested with the powers of a Court of Exchequer for this Province will please to grant them Writs of Assistance . . .' "

In upholding the superior court's power to issue general writs of assistance, Gridley based his case on the assumption that the Parliament of Great Britain was the sovereign legislature for the entire British Empire: "If it is law in England, it is law here." When the Massachusetts legislature set up the colony's judicial system, he declared, it had recognized in the superior court all the powers "that the court of King's Bench, Common Pleas and Exchequer have within his Majesty's Kingdom of England, or ought to have." Parliament had authorized the issuance of general warrants in its statutes of the thirteenth and fourteenth years of the reign of Charles II. In the seventh and eighth years of the reign of William III, it extended to revenue officers in the colonies the powers enjoyed by their counterparts in England: "Pity it would be," Gridley commented, if the Massachusetts officers "should have like Right, and not like Remedy," with their colleagues in Britain; "The Law abhors Right without Remedy."

Oxenbridge Thacher followed Gridley. He contested the extent of the powers that Gridley had declared to be vested in the superior court, arguing that it "did not possess all the powers of Exchequer even in matters of revenue." He submitted that there is "only one proper writ of Assistance, that issued from the King's own Court of Exchequer . . . No other officers but such as constitute that Court can grant it . . . that this Court is not such a one . . . this Court has in most solemn manner disclaimed the Authority of Exchequer."

Otis, when his turn came, materially broadened the base of the discussion. This was characteristic of his style; as critical a commentator as Hutchinson admitted that he "never knew fairer or more noble conduct in a pleader, than Otis; that he always disdained to take advantage of any clerical error, or similar inadvertance, but passed over minor points, and defended his causes solely on their broad and substantial foundations."

130

In opening, Otis took "this opportunity to declare that whether under fee or not, (for in such a cause as this I despise a fee) I will to my dying day oppose with all the powers and faculties God has given me, all such instruments of slavery on the one hand, and villany on the other, as this writ of assistance is."

It was a pleasure, he said, to argue this cause "in opposition to a kind of power, the exercise of which, in former periods of English history, cost one king of England his head, and another his throne. . . . What a scene does this open! Every man, prompted by revenge, ill-humor, or wantonness, to inspect the inside of his neighbor's house, may get a writ of assistance. Others will ask it from self-defense; one arbitrary exertion will provoke another, until society is involved in tumult and blood."

Noting that no locally available law books gave a form for the wording of a general writ and carefully distinguishing between such writs and special writs authorizing the search of places named at the time of issuance, whose validity he acknowledged, Otis pointed out that the general writ ran without a time limit; that a person possessed of such a writ could enter houses and shops at will; and that such a person did not have to be a deputy but could even be his servant. "Now one of the most essential branches of English liberty is the freedom of one's house. A man's house is his castle; and whilst he is quiet, he is as well guarded as a prince in his castle. This writ, if it should be declared legal, would totally annihilate this privilege. . . ."

He developed the thesis that natural rights are above human constitutions and constitutional law above statutes. The natural right of man to life, liberty, and property is infringed by writs such as those under discussion, yet guaranteed by natural law, by the British constitution, and by the charter of Massachusetts. "An act against the constitution is void; an act against natural equity is void; and if an act of Parliament should be made, in the very words of this petition it would be void. The executive Courts must pass such acts into disuse."

Turning to the revenue aspects of the Acts of Trade, Otis declared that citizens of the colony must not be cheated out of their rights by any fiction of being bound by "virtual representation" in the British Parliament. He acknowledged the necessity of the commerce of the empire being under central direction, but stressed that the colony had submitted to the acts of trade as regulatory statutes,

131

not tax measures: "Taxation without representation is tyranny."
Reviewing recent trade restrictions in the light of this distinction, he declared the Sugar Act "to be a revenue law, a taxation
law, made by a foreign legislature, without our consent, and by a
legislature with no feeling for us, and whose interest prompted
them to tax us to the quick."

Otis ended his argument, which held the courtroom silent for
more than four hours, with a peroration deploring the injustice
and illiberality of the mother country toward settlers who were
undertaking the conquest of a continent.

The court recessed.

Chief Justice Hutchinson's account shows that he saw his only
option was to play for time: "some of the judges, not withstanding,
from a doubt whether such writs were still in use in England, seemed
to favour the exception, and, if judgment had been then given, it
is uncertain on which side it would have been. The chief justice
was, therefore, desired, by the first opportunity in his power, to
obtain information on the practice in England and judgment was
suspended."

At the end of term, Hutchinson announced: "The Court has
considered the subject of writs of assistance, and can see no foundation for such a writ; but as the practise in England is not known, it
has been thought best to continue the question until next term, that
in the mean time opportunity may be given to write to England
for information concerning the subject."

Hutchinson wrote the colony's agent in London, William Bollan, son-in-law of former Governor Shirley, "Desiring to know
whether such writs of assistance ever issue from the exchequer, except upon special information, and confined either to particular
houses or to particular goods of which information is made."

On June 13, Bollan sent Hutchinson a copy of a general writ.

Final argument was heard at the November session of the court.
The chief justice produced the model. The other justices concurred
unanimously in the opinion that their court had power to issue such
a document. Next day, court adjourned.

The Boston Gazette of November 23, referring to the merchants'
arguments, commented: "Nothing could have induced one to believe
they were not conclusive but the Judgment of the Court *immediately* given in favor of the Petition" of the customs officers.

On the second of December, the chief justice, after a recital of

133

all the acts justifying his course, issued a writ of assistance to Charles Paxton.

At the next election, Otis entered politics and received a thumping endorsement as one of Boston's representatives in the legislature. On hearing the news, Chief Justice Ruggles of the Worcester Court of Common Pleas growled that "out of this election will arise a d---d faction, which will shake this province to its foundation."

During the 1762 legislative session, Otis actively promoted a bill to restrain the superior court from issuing search warrants except on oath, with the informer, the person owning the alleged uncustomed goods, and the place where the goods were thought to be stored all specified, and with the writ returnable in seven days. Governor Bernard vetoed the measure.

As an expression of its disapproval, the assembly cut the salaries of the justices of the supreme court and dismissed Bollan as the colony's London agent. A member wrote Bollan how "fire-brands set the government into a flame, caused the salaries of the judges of the super'r court to be lessened, endeavored to prevent their having a seat in either house; but failing they were determined to remove you, and for that end privately insinuated to the members of the house that you favour'd the officers of the customs, spent your time in soliciting their affairs in England, and neglected the affairs of the government."

During the next two or three years, serious public tensions were interspersed with administrative comedy at the customs house.

The three-way split of receipts from fines and forfeitures gave ample incentive for the governor and the collectors to work hand in glove. Word got back to London that the governor's hand might not be quite empty of certain uncustomed delicacies.

As a pre-emptive precaution against censure, in October 1763, Bernard sent a letter to Lord Egremont: "There has been an Indulgence time out of mind allowed in a trifling but necessary article, I mean the permitting Lisbon lemons and wine in small quantities to pass as Ships Stores. I have always understood that this was well known in England, and allowed, as being no object of trade, or if it was, no way injurious to that of Great Britain." Lemons, the governor added, are "in this climate not only necessary to the comfort of Life but to health also." In closing his communication, he bespoke "your Lordship's favour that this intimation may not be understood to contain an admission that I myself have been knowingly concerned in or consenting to the aforesaid indulgence."

The next year, the commissioners in London appointed John Temple their surveyor general to inspect the situation along the entire coast. His coming initiated a trial of bureaucratic strength with Governor Bernard.

Temple reached Salem in September. Cockle was still collector there. After a brief review, he dismissed Cockle out of hand: "above all for the Insult offered me by you in the Tender of a Bribe to pass over such your proceedings without punishment." Temple also observed that Cockle was one of the governor's "Most valuable Milch cows."

Bernard wrote London that the surveyor general was possessed of "a most extreme and haughty jealousy of the governor and his office."

Sampson Toovey, Cockle's clerk, gave Temple an affidavit that Bernard shared Cockle's gains.

Bernard dismissed Toovey.

The duel ended with Bernard unsuccessfully trying to get Cockle reinstated and with Temple appointing Toovey customs collector at Cape Ann.

But beneath the merriment, issues were accumulating. Hutchinson by no means accepted the theory of natural rights which Otis had developed in his brief on the writs. By July 1764, the chief justice was affirming that "it is possible for Parliament to pass Acts which may abridge British Subjects of what are generally called natural rights" and declaring himself "willing to go further and suppose that in some cases it is reasonable and necessary, even though such rights should have been strengthened and confirmed by the most solemn sanctions and engagements. The rights of parts and individuals must be given up when the safety of the whole shall depend upon it."

As duties on imports came into increasing use as revenue measures, restiveness under invasions of privacy by enforcement officers merged with restiveness under this form of taxation. Prior to passage of the Stamp Act, Otis prepared a memorial, *The Rights of the British Colonies Asserted and Proved,* that was sent to the colony's new London agent, expanding the argument against taxation without representation. When Massachusetts appointed a delegation to the Stamp Act Congress in October, he headed it.

Incidents accumulated. In August, the house and furniture of

135

one of the Boston collectors was sacked and ransacked by a mob. Next spring, when Captain Shubael Cotton brought John Hancock's brigantine *Harrison* alongside the Long Wharf with news of the repeal of the Stamp Act, a celebrating crowd attacked Hutchinson's residence, demonstrated before the state house and hanged two stuffed figures of customs men on a liberty tree.

That September, the comptroller of customs received information that there was wine in the cellar of Daniel Malcolm's house. Taking a writ of assistance, officers went to see. Malcolm, armed with a brace of pistols and a sword, admitted them to his house, and to part of the cellar, showing what he said were all the goods that belonged to him. He refused to unlock and permit entry to a further storage compartment, declaring that "if any man attempted it, he would blow his Brains out . . . he knew the Laws and that no Body had a right to Come into his House."

Temporarily, the officers retired, returning later in the day with the high sheriff. Malcolm had meanwhile locked the gate to his yard. They remained before it until sunset. By that time, a large crowd had gathered, and though one witness subsequently said in a deposition that "I never saw People that was going to a Funeral behave more Solemn and concerned than they did, not the least noise nor disturbance no more than if Mr. Whitfield had been preaching," their manner appeared sufficiently formidable to cause the officers to leave.

Malcolm announced "I only wanted for the good of the Country to know whether they would break open Houses."

In December, Governor Bernard wrote Lord Shelburne, the secretary of state, that "common talk prevailed among the People that there should be no more seizures in this Town." On reading this, his lordship's private secretary prepared a memo declaring that

If the Rescues made of Contraband Goods when seized in the Province of Massachusetts Bay be indeed as Mr. Bernard affirms a provincial Act and the Effect of Principle and Concert, and that they are generally determined to resist the Acts of Navigation, that Province has doubtless forfeited its charter and Mr. Ottis in my Opinion is guilty of Treason in Consequence of the Declaration He has made on this Subject at a Town Meeting in Boston.

I do not speak rashly when I say that Massachusetts Bay has forfeited its Charter. I have considered the Nature of the Connection between this Country and America, and I have no Doubt to prove that an Obedience to these laws is the necessarily implied Condition of the American Charters, and I have no doubt of the Propriety of trying Mr. Ottis Here upon an Impeachm't of the House of Commons.

A stroke of this Kind will show that England is not to be trifled with in Essentials . . .

In 1767, the Townshend Acts materially increased the classes of goods whose entry was to be monitored. Concurrently, the structure for customs collection was fortified by the establishment of an American board of customs, with headquarters in Boston. Its five members included Charles Paxton, whom *The New-York Journal* charged with having bought this assignment from Townshend by drawing a will which gave Townshend the reversion of a £50,000 estate; John Robinson, lately of the Rhode Island service; and the knowledgeable John Temple, whose views on policy clashed with those of the majority.

The Townshend Acts specifically validated the use of general warrants, but while such writs continued to be granted in New Hampshire and Massachusetts and were inaugurated in New York, the courts of the other colonies evaded their issuance.

At its May term, the Massachusetts assembly elected James Otis speaker, but Governor Bernard refused to allow him to serve.

The next scenes in the developing drama took place along the Boston waterfront.

In February 1768, Daniel Malcolm ordered one of his arriving schooners to anchor five miles out among some islands. He landed her cargo at night, moving it to storage on drays protected by men with clubs. A few days later, he presided over a meeting of Boston merchants to protest the new duties. They passed a nonimportation resolution, and sent it to the other colonies in the form of a *Massachusetts Circular Letter*. It was widely praised. The assembly ignored Lord Hillsborough's order to rescind it.

The Boston merchants' resistance to the new customs board was symbolized by an exchange between John Hancock, probably the wealthiest among them, and the governor. Hancock was captain of a uniformed cadet company, the only regularly drilled military organization in Boston. When Bernard ordered him to supply an honor guard for a street procession welcoming the customs commissioners, he refused. Later, he again refused to allow his company to embellish the governor's election-night dinner, and the city offi-

137

cials declined the use of Faneuil Hall as the place for the dinner, if the commissioners were invited.

Early in April, Hancock's packet *Lydia* arrived with spring goods from London. When she tied up at the wharf, Owen Richards, a tidesman known to have laid numerous informations, came aboard with a companion and said they were there by order of the comptroller. A tidesman's job was to watch unloading. Hancock accepted their presence but warned them not to go below deck.

Next evening, however, about seven o'clock, the pair went down into the steerage and refused to leave. About eleven, Hancock and a party came aboard, demanded to see their orders and their writ of assistance. Richards had no writ. Hancock's men thereupon picked the two up bodily, deposited them on deck, closed the companionways.

The commissioners referred the matter to the attorney general, Jonathan Sewall, with instructions to file a criminal information charge against Hancock for interfering with officers in the performance of their duty. Since the tidesman's job was to stay on deck, the attorney general found no case. The commissioners forwarded the record to the treasury, with the note: "We cannot omit mentioning to your Lordships that Mr. Hancock . . . is one of the Leaders of disaffected in this Town . . . This infatuated man gives out in public that if we Commissioners are not recalled, he will get rid of us before Christmas."

A month later, on May 9, another Hancock ship, *Liberty*, arrived from Madeira; next day her cargo was reported at the customs house as twenty-five casks of wine, and the duty paid on them. At that time, the arrival and unloading appeared routine. Thomas Kirk, the tidesman who with a companion monitored the ship, reported that nothing was disturbed during the night he watched her.

Over the next four weeks, in preparation for an outbound voyage to London, two hundred barrels of whale oil and twenty barrels of tar were put aboard *Liberty*. The procedure followed regular local practice, but the letter of the law required that cargo be bonded and clearance papers obtained before it was put into a ship. So on June 10, about seven in the evening, customs men with both a writ and a written order from the board of commissioners went on board *Liberty*, found the new cargo, declared a seizure of the vessel.

A mob, raised by Daniel Malcolm, quickly formed. The customs officers called for marines from the British warship *Romney*, an-

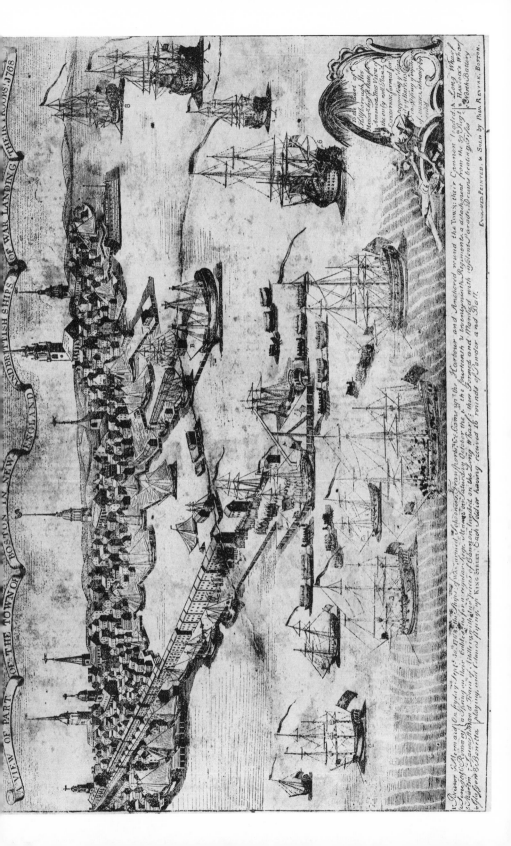

chored in the harbor. In the ensuing scuffle, one of the officers had his sword shattered. The collector and the comptroller of customs were followed to their homes and some windows broken. One of the customs boats was dragged through town and burned on Boston Common. Meanwhile, *Liberty* was towed out and anchored under *Romney's* stern.

The commissioners sent Ben Hallowell, Boston's comptroller, who had ordered the seizure, to England, bearing explanatory documents from Bernard and Hutchinson. He reported to both Lord Hillsborough and the House of Lords.

Immediately after the seizure, Otis moderated a meeting that began in Faneuil Hall but moved to the Old South Meeting House because of the crowd. It voted to address the governor, designated a committee of twenty-one to wait on him, and also chose Hancock, Thomas Cushing, and Sam Adams to consult with committees of correspondence chosen by other Massachusetts towns.

On June 22, *Liberty* was libeled, with the claimants ordered to appear July 7. After a continuance of the case, on August 1 both ship and cargo were declared confiscated "for want of a permit." In due course, Governor Bernard collected his third of the proceeds and Robert Hallowell, a relative of the comptroller, received £650 for refitting *Liberty* as a coast guard vessel—she was used in Narragansett Bay until burned by citizens of Newport.

On October 29, in a surprise action, Attorney General Sewall filed a suit in the Boston admiralty court against Hancock and five others, including Daniel Malcolm, alleging that on May 9, the night *Liberty* came in, they had aided in unloading from her one hundred pipes of wine worth £30 each. Since the Sugar Act permitted suit to be brought for triple the value of uncustomed goods, each man was sued for £9,000. John Adams served as Hancock's attorney; his client's bail was set at £3,000.

The evidence produced was an information by Thomas Kirk, whose recollection of the arrival of the vessel had materially altered. The day before the seizure of *Liberty*, he signed testimony alleging that on the night she came in a Captain Marshall and several other men, none of whom he knew, came aboard about nine in the evening, made propositions to him about unloading her wine, and when he refused to cooperate, forced him below deck and kept him there for several hours. During that time, he heard noises that sounded like tackle hoisting goods out of the hold. After the noises stopped, he said, he was released with a warning not to talk.

His companion tidesman, when questioned, professed no knowledge of the matter, but admitted he may have been asleep; Kirk said he had gone home drunk before the boarding party made its appearance.

In the intervening months, Captain Marshall had died; since Kirk could identify none of the other alleged participants, witnesses were lacking. Various employees and relatives of Hancock were subjected to private interrogation by the attorney general in the judge's chambers; Hancock's office was entered, his desk rifled. Nothing was produced in court.

In November, General Gage, commander of the British forces in North America, wrote Lord Hillsborough an implicit warning with the news that "some Prosecutions were commenced in the Court of Admiralty against two of the most popular Leaders." By return packet, his lordship inquired, on what grounds?

Beginning in September 1768, a day-by-day commentary on events, "A Journal of the Times," was prepared in Boston, published in *The New-York Journal* and widely copied through the colonies.

On the twenty-fifth of March 1769, a second surprise action ended the suit against the merchants as unexpectedly as it had begun: without explanation, the new attorney general came into court and asked that the suit be withdrawn.

Actually, by early 1769, Governor Bernard was on his way to being created a baronet and recalled. Whitehall, while not agreeing with Otis' comment in his *Vindication of the Conduct of the House of Representatives of the Province of Massachusetts Bay* that "Kings were (and plantation Governors should be) made for the good of the people, and not the people for them," nevertheless thought a change of personnel in Boston might be beneficial.

Doubts were likewise circulating in London about the conduct of the American board of commissioners. In January 1770, a Massachusetts grand jury had indicted them for slandering the colony, and Sam Adams and Otis wrote an *Appeal to the World; or a Vindication of the town of Boston, from many false and malicious aspersions.*

Such collaboration as Otis was able to give Adams in the *Vindication* was among his last contributions to public affairs, for in September 1769 he sustained serious and permanent injury in a fight at the British Coffee House near the town house on King Street.

141

The previous day, as a paid advertisement, he had published in *The Boston Gazette* a communication to the commissioners assailing them for their aspersions on him. When he dropped in at the coffee house he found Customs Commissioner John Robinson, other revenue officers, and some military personnel present. An altercation ensued. The others set upon Otis, and drove off a passer-by who came in from the street to aid him.

When the fight was broken up, Otis was seen to have a deep head wound, from knife or sword. The injury removed him from more than sporadic participation in politics thereafter. He did serve in the legislature next session, but where previously he had been excitable, he now became intermittently subject to acute derangement.

Robinson shortly married a Boston merchant's daughter and retired to England. His father-in-law represented him in a damage suit in which the jury awarded Otis £2,000. But when Robinson wrote an apology, saying he "freely confesses that in the assault committed by him . . . in presumptuously attempting to take him, the said James Otis, by the nose, was the first assault which occasioned and brought on all the consequent insults, wounds and other injuries . . . and asks pardon of the said James Otis," Otis declined the proffered payment.

The same year that Otis ceased to be a leader in Massachusetts politics was the year John Hancock first offered himself for election. Initially a Boston delegate to the general court, he became president of the Massachusetts Provincial Congress in 1774 and served successively as chairman of the committee of safety, delegate to the Second Continental Congress, and the elected president of that body through 1777.

During this period, he kept alive the search-and-seizure issue, for though after the repeal of the Townshend Acts fewer attempts were made to use general warrants, at the end of 1772 Boston's committee of twenty-one reiterated that these writs give "full Power and Authority from time to time at their or any of their wills and Pleasures as well by Night as by Day, to enter and go on board any Ship, Boat, or other vessel . . . and also in the daytime to go into any House, Shop, Cellar or any other Place . . . Thus our Houses, and even our Bed Chambers are exposed and ransacked . . . By this we are cut off from that domestic security which renders the Lives of the most unhappy in some measure agreeable."

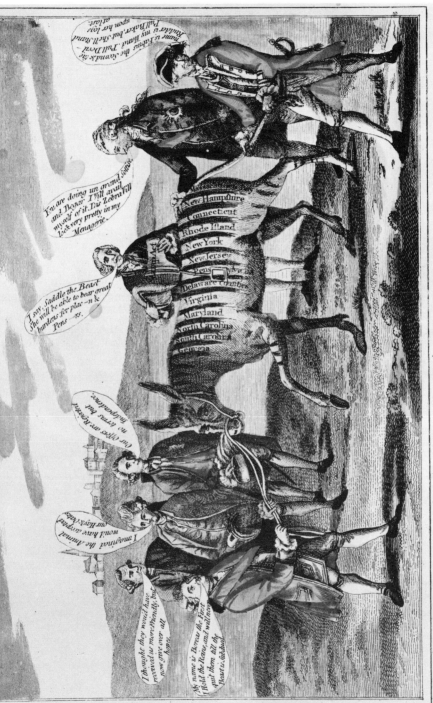

THE CURIOUS ZEBRA.

alive from America! walk in Gem'men and Ladies, walk in!.

London Printed for G. Johnson as the Act directs 3 Sep.r 1778, and Sold at all the Printshops in London & Westminster.

The grievance was still vivid when the time came to form an independent government. In May 1775, the Massachusetts Provincial Congress wrote to the Continental Congress, asking "most explicit advice respecting the taking up and exercising the powers of civil government" and declaring its willingness to "submit to such a general plan as the Congress might direct for the colonies." But the Congress had no plan, beyond suggesting a return to the colonial charter with the substitution of an elected committee for the gubernatorial executive. In September 1776, the Massachusetts assembly appointed a committee to draw up a constitution.

The document submitted to the people in March 1778 failed of acceptance, but eleven months later voters indicated their desire for a second effort. In September 1779, a special convention resolved that a declaration of rights and a constitution be prepared and named a committee of thirty to produce it.

The committee selected James Bowdoin and the two Adamses to do the drafting; actually John Adams did most of it. The Massachusetts Declaration of Rights, like that of Virginia, was substantially the work of one man.

Article XV of his draft, which by the time the document was ratified in 1780 had become Article XIV, read: "Every man has a right to be secure from all unreasonable searches and seizures of his person, his houses, his papers and all his possessions. All warrants, therefore, are contrary to this right, if the cause or foundation of them be not previously supported by oath or affirmation, and if the order in the warrant to a civil officer, to make search in suspected places, or to arrest one or more suspected persons, or to seize their property, be not accompanied with a specific designation of the persons or objects of search, arrest, or seizure; and no warrant ought to be issued but in cases and with the formalties prescribed in the laws."

CHAPTER VI

DUE PROCESS OF LAW

The Bill of Rights: No person shall be . . . deprived of life, liberty, or property, without due process of law . . .

BACKGROUND

No free man shall be taken or imprisoned or dispossessed, or outlawed, or banished, or in any way destroyed, nor will we go upon him, nor send upon him, except . . . by the law of the land." This declaration in Magna Charta shows that by the year 1215, English justice already recognized the right of at least some subjects to enjoy the complex of procedural protections contained in "the law of the land." The phrase by which the eighteenth-century bills of rights most often described them, "due process of law," appears as early as a 1354 statute.

Among the safeguards afforded by due process, habeas corpus, the writ that protects the liberty of the citizen by preventing his imprisonment without cause being known, has been so central to British and American justice as to receive special and often separate treatment in various enumerations of rights—even before a decision was taken to add a bill of rights to the federal Constitution, the drafters of that document embedded in Article I the affirmation that "The privilege of the writ of habeas corpus shall not be suspended, unless when in cases of rebellion or invasion the public safety may require it."

Comparable English affirmations developed in the seventeenth century. Five persons of prominence, resisting Charles I's attempts in the 1620's to extort money by prerogative taxation, refused to pay forced loans to the King and were put in jail. When they applied for a writ of habeas corpus and were brought before the judges of king's bench, they were denied bail and returned to prison uncharged in spite of their counsel's argument that such procedure violated Magna Carta and could result in their perpetual confinement. The grounds given were that these prisoners were in jail by order of the King.

Parliamentary indignation at the Five Knights case was shortly expressed in the Petition of Right of 1628, negotiated on behalf of the commons with lords and King by the skill of Sir Edward Coke and Sir Thomas Wentworth. Charles I was forced to assent to limitations on his sovereignty, including his power of prerogative imprisonment, that confirmed Coke's declaration, "Magna Charta is

146

such a Fellow, that he will have no Sovereign."

Among specified wrongs, Article V of the petition recited: "Nevertheless against the tenor of the said statutes, and other the good laws and statutes of your realm to that end provided, divers of your subjects have of late been imprisoned without any cause shewed; (2) and when for their deliverance they were brought before your justices by your Majesty's writs of *habeas corpus,* there to undergo and receive as the court should order, and their keepers commanded to certify the causes of their detainer, no cause was certified, but that they were detained by your Majesty's special command, signified by the lords of your privy council, and yet were returned back to several prisons, without being charged with any thing to which they might make answer according to the law."

The corresponding list of reforms urged by the petition and acceded to by the King declared: ". . . that no freeman, in any such manner as is before-mentioned, be imprisoned or detained . . . All of which they most humbly pray of your most excellent Majesty as their rights and liberties, according to the laws and statutes of this realm . . ."

Abolition of the court of Star Chamber in 1641 further reduced the occasions on which an executive power to imprison could be exercised. But under the Restoration, repeated political confinements with avoidance or denial of the writ of habeas corpus caused Parliament again to intervene: the Habeas Corpus Act of 1679 reaffirmed the right of prisoners to be brought before a court to hear the reason for their deprivation of liberty and to enjoy a prompt trial thereafter.

The rights of Englishmen comprised in due process under the common law were guarded with similar zeal when that law was brought to America. In South Carolina, in 1773, exercise of legislative prerogative caused the imprisonment of Thomas Powell, a printer, for contempt of the council. He successfully relied on a writ of habeas corpus for his release.

The Powell case drew lasting lines in a previously contented colony. More than the dominant group in any other provincial community, the Charleston gentry of the 1760's were part and parcel of the Whig supremacy in England. Almost without exception, the ranking families spent protracted periods abroad. Some went back to live permanently in the mother country.

147

It was the rule rather than the exception for the sons of the well-to-do to be sent, or more often taken, to England for their higher studies—aside from private tutoring or legal clerkships in the offices of prominent attorneys, means of education were lacking in Charleston once a child had finished dame school. Fledgling lawyers almost invariably went to London—of some 150 Americans at the Middle Temple between 1764 and 1780, 37 came from South Carolina, including all four South Carolina signers of the Declaration of Independence. Intermarriage with English Whig families drew sons and daughters to one side of the Atlantic or the other.

In this compact and colorful cousinry, it was natural that a high proportion of the gentry were repelled by the prospect of a break. Most of them preferred the social ease of like-thinking gentlefolk to the rigors of political controversy. Even as late as 1773, Josiah Quincy, Jr., of Boston, on a visit to South Carolina, noted with puzzlement in his diary the number of evenings when dinner conversation did not include politics: he was unaccustomed to see public affairs subordinated to domestic felicity.

But political talk could cause formidable silences in the drawing room. How formidable can be quickly grasped by comparing the roll of the twenty-nine Charlestonian revolutionaries whom the British, when they occupied the city, forcibly deported to St. Augustine, Florida, for the duration, and the roster of the act of attainder applied to prominent loyalists by the South Carolina assembly after independence. Family connections link the two at almost every name. They are illustrated by the fact that the firebrand Christopher Gadsden's eventual third wife was a close kinswoman of his pre-revolutionary arch opponent, the Tory William Wragge.

During the latter 1760's, Christopher Gadsden persistently broke the rules of this society. From the time he went to New York for the Stamp Act Congress in 1765, he overtly and repeatedly forced the pace of resistance to successive British measures. Older-established Charlestonians such as William Henry Drayton did not appreciate individuals who intruded, asking uncomfortable questions.

Yet only a few years later, Drayton himself was asking an uncomfortable question. In the taking of sides which it made necessary, much of South Carolina's revolutionary leadership was developed.

148

THE CASE

"I cannot in point of good Manners avoid congratulating the Hen-Huffy Kitty . . . on the birth of a son who wrote the letter appearing in the last copy of the Gazette signed 'C. G.' " In January 1770, William Henry Drayton, of Drayton Hall on South Carolina's Ashley River, after delivering this parting shot in a newspaper exchange, quit Charleston for the mother country.

His sweeping gesture of political high dudgeon encompassed two recent events. South Carolina's Commons House had adopted a nonimportation resolution in reply to the Townshend Acts. He disapproved. The same body had contributed from public monies to the fund that sympathizers of John Wilkes were collecting in London. He disapproved still more. With vigor, he had set forth his grounds in a series of blistering communications to *The South Carolina Gazette,* signed "Freeman." Whatever William Henry Drayton felt at a given moment, he felt strongly.

The "C. G." of the above initials, Christopher Gadsden, had been chief advocate of both offending measures. He was a Charleston merchant on his way up the ladder from merchant, to merchant-owner-of-plantations, to planter-who-maintained-a-town-house-in-Charleston, the same ladder that most of the first families had climbed since the foundation of the colony. But he was a rung behind, and both the legislative policies that he initiated and the political mechanism that he created to forward them inside and outside the commons house were causing social discomfort.

Gadsden had been elected to the Commons House in 1757; his 1762 re-election had precipitated a constitutional controversy when Governor Thomas Boone attempted to prevent the house from seating him because he did not like his views. After repeal of the Stamp Act, in meetings around Charleston's liberty tree, he had given coherence to a new type of political organization that was more like a political party than anything South Carolina had previously known.

Freehold suffrage was the electoral basis of the Commons House, and many Charleston tradesmen and mechanics, though custom and class distinction prevented them from offering themselves as candi-

149

dates, were qualified voters. Gadsden organized these men into a constituency.

The sarcasm of William Henry Drayton's communications to the *Gazette* on this development accurately represented the reaction of the established planters. Educated men, he said, did not consult "with men who never were in any way to study, or to advise upon any points, but rules how to cut up a beast in the market . . . cobble an old shoe . . . or build a necessary house. Nature never intended such men should be profound politicians or able statesmen, and unless a man makes a proper use of his reading, he is but on a level with those who never did read . . ."

Tit-for-tatishly, Gadsden replied, "What a pity it is that the Momma of that pretty child which transmitted to you the paper, signed, 'Freeman' published in your last *Gazette* had not now and then whipped it for lying."

The fine flair with which Drayton shook the dust of Charleston from his feet was hardly as dramatic as he tried to make it—he had been away from England only six years, after having lived there for eleven as a schoolboy at Westminster and a student at Oxford.

His earlier stay had been in exceptionally pleasant circumstances. South Carolina's Chief Justice Charles Pinckney, when he was named the colony's agent, moved to London with his wife Eliza Lucas, daughter of the British governor of Antigua. Along with their sons Charles Cotesworth and Thomas, and their daughter, Harriott, they took William Henry Drayton with them. Eliza Lucas was herself highly educated—when she came to Charleston she provided a second staple, along with rice, for South Carolina's economy by demonstrating the fine points of making high quality dye from the indigo plant. Her ambition for her sons' education, started when Charles Cotesworth was four years old. She wrote to London for toys which would enable him to "play himself into learning." Young Peter Manigault visited and described their house beside the Thames: it was not far from David Garrick's villa at Hampton and the Pinckney household "never missed a single play where Garrick was to act."

For his present visit, Drayton would have his own household: in 1764 he had married Dorothy Golightly. Shortly after they arrived, his "Freeman" correspondence was published, and attracted the eye of favor at court. On February 27, 1771, Drayton was received by His Majesty George III and appointed a member of

the council of South Carolina.

Sensible of the honor, he was nevertheless reluctant to leave the congenial London atmosphere: it was April 3, 1772, before he took his seat as councilor to Charles Greville Montagu, the colony's governor since 1766.

The council was composed of four English and six Carolinian members. The former included the attorney general, Sir Edgerton Leigh, a recently created baronet; and Thomas Knox Gordon of Ireland, the new chief justice. The six Carolinians gave the meetings something of the air of a family gathering; four of them were close Drayton relatives.

William Bull, the lieutenant governor, like his father before him, had been in politics all his life. An assemblyman in 1736, he had twice served as speaker of the Commons House. On the council since 1748, he had been acting governor in 1764-66 between royal appointments and again during Governor Montagu's absence from the colony in 1768-71. He was William Henry Drayton's uncle.

William Henry's father, John, was likewise a councilman. His wife was Charlotte Bull, a sister of the lieutenant governor. William Henry's uncle Thomas was both a councilman and a supreme court justice and his wife was Eliza Bull, another sister of the lieutenant governor.

When William Henry took his seat, the governor and the Commons House were dancing a political quadrille over appropriations. Since 1769, no tax bill had been passed. The commons, after Parliament enacted the Stamp Act, had declared: "it is inseparably essential to the freedom of a people and the undoubted right of Englishmen that no taxes be imposed upon them but by their own consent," and the council had thereafter refused to concur in any of its financial proposals. The colony was running out of funds.

The temper of the assemblymen worsened when Montagu, on August 28, issued a writ summoning them for a session to be held at Beaufort, seventy-five miles away. His given reason was lack of a suitable building at the capital, as if the South Carolina currency did not proudly display an engraving of the state house on which some £60,000 had been lavished since the laying of its cornerstone in 1753.

Suspecting that the governor might use failure to attend as a basis for undisclosed projects, thirty-seven members made the journey, though nineteen would have constituted a quorum, only to

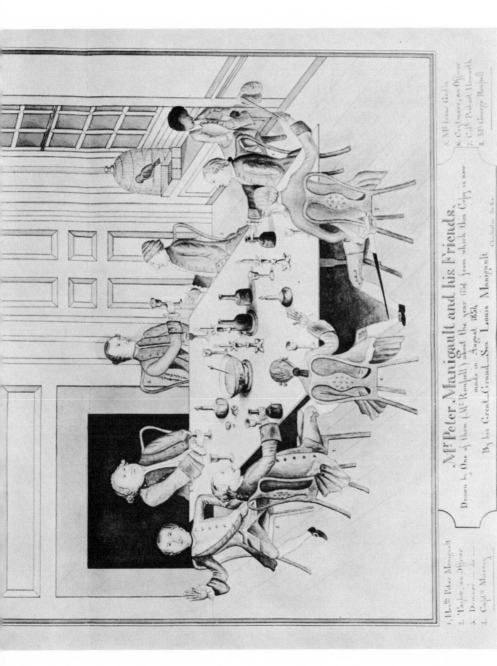

Mr Peter Manigault and his Friends.

Drawn by One of them (Mr Roupell) about the year 1754 from which this Copy is now made in August 1854.

By his Great-Grand-Son Louis Manigault   Charleston So. Ca.

1. Hon.ble Peter Manigault
2. Taylor, an Oyster ———
3. Demere ——do——
4. Capt.n Massey

5. Mr Isaac Godin
6. Coytmore, an Officer
7. Cap.t Richard Howarth
8. Mr George Roupell

be prorogued after two days, with no business accomplished.

At the commons' next session in November, Rawlins Lowndes was chosen speaker, replacing Peter Manigault who had resigned because of ill health. A proposal was introduced for the colony's London agent to make representations to the King regarding the conduct of the governor. While this measure was before it, the house received a summons from the governor to attend him in the council chamber. Correctly suspecting that they were about to be prorogued, members completed their business at hand before complying.

To see what they had been up to, the governor sent for the journal of the house, only to find that Speaker Lowndes had taken the book home with him. Receiving it only after considerable delay, he angrily dissolved the assembly.

During this cotillion, the council, including William Henry Drayton, danced partners with the governor, though among Charlestonians generally, Montagu's treatment attracted sympathy for the commons even among men who had previously disapproved of its contribution to the Wilkes fund.

Hopeful of a turnover in house membership, Governor Montagu called for a new election in mid-December. The same men were voted back in and chose the same speaker. A third reference to the electors, in February, produced an identical result. By that time the governor had had enough of the colony. As a parting good will gesture, he attended a concert of the St. Cecelia Society; on March 8, he sailed away.

Josiah Quincy, Jr., attended that concert; his journal gives an account of the last moments of effective royal rule in the province: "March 3d. The concert-house is a large, inelegant building, situated down a yard, at the entrance of which I was met by a constable with his staff. I offered him my ticket, which was subscribed by the name of the person giving it, and directing admission of me by name. The officer told me to proceed. I did, and was next met by a white waiter who directed me to a third, to whom I delivered my ticket and was conducted in. The music was good; the two bass-viols and French horn was grand. One Abercrombie, a Frenchman just arrived, played the first violin, and a solo incomparably better than any one I ever heard. He cannot speak a word of English, and has a salary of five hundred guineas a year from the St. Cecelia Society. There were upwards to two hundred and fifty ladies present, and it

154

was called no great number. In loftiness of head-dress, those ladies stoop to the daughters of the north; in richness of dress, surpass them; in health and floridity of countenance, vail to them. In taciturnity during the performances, greatly before our ladies; in noise and flirtation after the music is over, pretty much on a par. If our ladies have any advantage, it is in white and red, vivacity and spirit. The gentlemen, many of them dressed with a richness and elegance, uncommon with us; many with swords on. We had two macaronis present, just arrived from London. This character I found real, and not fictitious. 'See the macaroni!' was a common phrase in the hall. One may be styled the bag, the other the queue macaroni. Mr. Deis was very polite, and introduced me to most of the first characters,—among the rest to Lord Charles G. Montague, the Governor, who was to sail next day for London,—to the Chief Justice and two of the assistant judges, and several of the Council."

Governor Montagu's departure left Lieutenant Governor Bull in charge of the colony for a third time. The serious financial situation became his to handle. An even more serious constitutional crisis grew out of it.

The state of the treasury was indeed alarming. The council inspected it, and informed the acting governor that £127,674 was due to be paid out, against reserves of some £10,000, adding in self-protection that its concurrence in any of the tax bills proposed by the house since 1769 would have betrayed the constitution.

Bull resented the council's inspection. The council resented his attitude. The chief justice and William Henry Drayton prepared resolutions declaring it to be the council's duty to inspect the treasury and advise the governor.

Meanwhile, the commons passed a bill making it a felony to counterfeit money: Spanish half-joes of uncertain origin were circulating in some volume. The council deferred action on this bill.

Two of its Drayton members, father and son, convinced that delay was harmful, prepared a formal protest. William Henry Drayton passed a copy of this document to Thomas Powell, printer of *The South Carolina Gazette*. He published it in his issue of August 30.

Two views existed on the nature and functions of the governor's council. According to one, it was merely an advisory body to the governor. According to the other, it was an upper chamber, a miniature House of Lords, and therefore possessed of the privileges and

155

prerogatives of a legislative assembly.

At next day's council session, a majority took the view that Powell's publication of the Drayton protest constituted a breach of legislative privilege. Accordingly, they cited Powell for contempt. He was arrested, brought before council, told he must ask pardon.

He replied that "he had no intention by the publication to offend the honorable body; that, had he known it to be a breach of privilege, he would certainly not have made the publication; that if he had erred, it was owing to his inexperience, and that he was very sorry for it."

On reflection, the council regarded this statement as inadequate. They ordered Powell brought back, in custody of the sergeant-at-arms. He was told to apologize without any *ands* and *ifs* or go to jail.

He replied that, as he did not know he had committed any fault, it was hard to confess himself guilty and be obliged to beg pardon. But if he could be convinced that he had been guilty of a breach of privilege, he should be very willing to ask pardon.

Council took umbrage. This was a most daring disrespect. Such a reply would have been insufficient to satisfy the honor even of a private gentleman.

So a warrant was prepared, duly signed by two of the council's English members, the attorney general and the chief justice, citing Powell as publisher of the *Gazette* "in which paper is printed, part of the proceedings of that House on Thursday the 26th day of August last; which the House hath resolved, to be a high breach of privilege and a contempt of the House; and ordering, that the said Thomas Powell should be therefore committed to the common goal of Charleston, during the pleasure of the House."

Powell was turned over to the custody of Roger Pinckney, sheriff of Charleston, and confined.

The legal maneuvering to get Powell out provided opportunity for the maiden plea of a young member of the Charleston bar.

Edward Rutledge, just back from the Middle Temple, had begun his study of law with his older brother John. John, when he returned from the Middle Temple in 1760, had had a very similar chance to make an immediate name for himself in a previous constitutional struggle: as Christopher Gadsden's attorney in 1762 he had established the right of the Commons House to determine without gubernatorial interference the validity of its members' credentials.

156

When Edward departed for London in 1767, John wrote him a lengthy older-brother's letter setting forth exactly how he could make best use of his time. Edward should learn shorthand, so that when attending His Majesty's courts he could build up a personal casebook preserving the gist of the argument. He should copy out in longhand the major cases that he read, in order to refer to them thereafter. He should attend sessions of Parliament as often as possible, and though he would not be permitted to take notes while there, he should carefully observe both the art of parliamentary maneuver, and the most effective styles of debate.

The Powell case was Edward's first opportunity to show that he had profited by this advice. His line of argument was to persuade the judges that his client had committed no breach of security because the council was not a legislative upper house, but merely a body advisory to the governor. If that were so, its proceedings were not privileged and it could not imprison Powell by the exercise of legislative prerogative.

His first move was to get the matter heard by applying for a writ of habeas corpus. An act of 1712 provided that this writ was returnable before the colony's chief justice or any two of the associate justices. The chief justice was normally, as now, a lawyer from another part of the empire, appointed by the King. The associate justices were usually eminent lay citizens of the colony; the holding of these posts did not preclude other public service, such as membership in the commons. Rawlins Lowndes, speaker of the house, and George Gabriel Powell, member of commons from St. David's Parish, were both associate justices. It was before these two assembly members, in their judicial capacity, that Rutledge presented his plea.

Rutledge started with the affirmation that "The Council was nothing more than a privy council to assist the governor with its advice." He noted that "the power of commitment by the King and Council, it is true, was formerly exercised, but it was held to be so extremely unconstitutional and oppressive that it was checked so early as the reign of the wicked and misguided Charles. I hope that lawlessness will not be tolerated from the hands of plebian authority when it has been plucked up as a weed from the flowers of prerogative." In Powell's case, the judges surely recognized that "Council in this province were not men of such high consequence as to be allowed the power of depriving a free man of his liberty for what they should imagine a breach of privilege, or contempt."

157

In making a decision, the two assemblymen-justices had an obvious conflict of interest: the case pitted house against house. If Powell were freed, two members of one body would be releasing a man committed by two members of the other. Lowndes frankly recognized the situation in his opening paragraphs:

From the rank and station I am in, and from my connection with the Commons' House of Assembly I may be presumed to be under some bias and predisposition in favor of that House and its privileges . . . I confess I am so, but I trust it is no undue bias or prepossession, no propensity to exclude from any other body of men, or any other part of the community, any rights, privileges, or immunities whatever to which they may on a fair inquiry be found to be entitled. It was insisted, however, that I should grant the habeas corpus,—that it was a right,— and it would very ill have become one to have been disobedient to so good and salutary a law . . .

The law of the land provides for the safety of every man's person, his liberty, and his estate. By the great Charter, it is provided, that no freeman shall be taken or imprisoned, but by the lawful judgment of his equals, or by the law of the land. And many subsequent statutes expressly direct that no man shall be taken or imprisoned by suggestion or petition to the King, or his Council, unless it be by legal indictment, or the process of the Common Law. By the petition of rights it is enacted that no freeman shall be imprisoned, or detained, without cause shown; to which, he may answer according to law. And, by the Habeas Corpus Act, of the 31st of Charles II the methods of obtaining that writ, are pointed out . . .

The law of the land not giving the Council the least colour of the right to commit for breach of privilege, or, what they call, contempt of their House; they must found their claim upon the usage, and practice, of the House of Lords in England . . .

But, Lowndes continued, there is a marked difference between an hereditary and an appointed body: "The commitment, therefore, in my opinion, is to be considered merely as the commitment of the Privy Council. And in that case it has no other authority than if done by a private magistrate. The subject has his remedy by habeas corpus in this case, and we are to consider whether the matter is an offense at law, and if an offense, whether it is bailable or not."

With the concurrence of his colleagues, Lowndes then declared: "I am of the opinion that it is no offense at law; that the paper referred to in the commitment, being a protest from two members of the Council against proceedings of that board in a certain matter depending before the Council, and required by its members to be printed by the printer, might lawfully, legally, and warrantably be printed by the prisoner in the way of his profession. The more especially as it was unaccompanied with any remarks, observations, or additions of his own, but simply and literally, as it was received by the prisoner from one of the members of the Council. And it is not clear to me that even the House of Lords would include such a paper under the general idea of proceedings of the House from which they would punish a printer who published it. I am of opinion, therefore, for ordering the prisoner released."

Edward Rutledge's argument had been accepted. Powell was free. The commons thanked its two members for their judicial decision and endorsed their view as to the advisory status of the council. They asked the acting governor to suspend the council members who had voted in favor of Powell's commitment and addressed the throne, requesting permanent removal of these men from that body.

Simultaneously, the council's majority passed a resolution to the effect that William Henry Drayton's protest against the inaction on the counterfeiting bill was false and scandalous, applied to the commons for redress against Lowndes and George Gabriel Powell, and forwarded its own address to the throne.

In receipt of the two conflicting addresses, the colony's agent asked Lord Dartmouth to allow both sides to be presented simultaneously. He was informed that the view that the council was not a true upper house could not be entertained. A further royal determination, announced as forthcoming, never arrived.

The taking of sides on the Powell case greatly strengthened South Carolina's revolutionary leadership. The next July, when a delegation to the First Continental Congress was chosen, Edward Rutledge, with New York's John Jay the youngest of delegates, was included. The others were his brother John, Henry Middleton, Christopher Gadsden, and Thomas Lynch.

Locally, an even greater impact was sustained when the ebullient William Henry Drayton changed sides. Henceforth, the man who had left the colony four and a half years earlier as a disgruntled conservative made enthusiastic common cause with men he had formerly condemned as radicals and held his new views with a vigor quite equal to that with which he had expressed his old ones.

When the Continental Congress met, Drayton issued a pamphlet,

159

To the Deputies of North America, assembled in the High Court of the Congress of Philadelphia, signed "Freeman" even as his 1769 blasts had been, presenting an "American Claim of Rights" that forecast much of the position stated by the congress at its close. Its Item II castigated "The constitution of Council established among them by the Royal Mandamus . . . Seeing they act as a second body of the Legislature, entirely dependent upon the pleasure even of the Governor—that placemen, dependent upon the Crown, being strangers, ignorant of the interests and laws of the colonies, are sent from England to fill seats in the Council, where they often form a majority, as Legislators, determining the most weighty affairs of the new colony, and as chancellors, decreeing in suits relating to the most valuable property of the subject."

Shortly thereafter, when one of the associate justices died, Drayton volunteered to serve in his place until London announced a new appointment. Acting Governor Bull was agreeable—it would get him out of town. At the opening of the November term of court, Drayton set forth on the northern circuit.

In the course of his tour, his charges to the grand juries of Georgetown, Camden, and Cheraws included rousing affirmations of the rights of Americans as British subjects. At Cheraws, the grand jury responded with a declaration that "The right of being exempted from all laws but those enacted with the consent of representatives of their own election we deem so essential to our freedom and so engrafted in our constitution that we are determined to defend it at the hazard of our lives and fortunes."

Christopher Gadsden and others whom Drayton had tongue-lashed for holding similar ideas five years earlier may well have been amused at his current fervor. His fellow judges in Charleston, however, were not amused at all. A quadrille of robes and wigs ensued: as soon as Drayton's pamphlet appeared, Chief Justice Gordon and Associate Justice Charles Matthews Cosslett issued a remonstrance. Drayton replied to the remonstrance. The judges published a rebuttal to his reply. The rebuttal contained a disclaimer that witnessed Drayton's growing popularity: "We shall not, in imitation of him, endeavor to amuse the fancy or mislead the judgment by attempting a display of wit and humor."

The quadrille was halted by arrival from England of the official replacement for the deceased justice. A messenger with a supersedeas was dispatched in pursuit of Drayton, relieving Acting Gov-

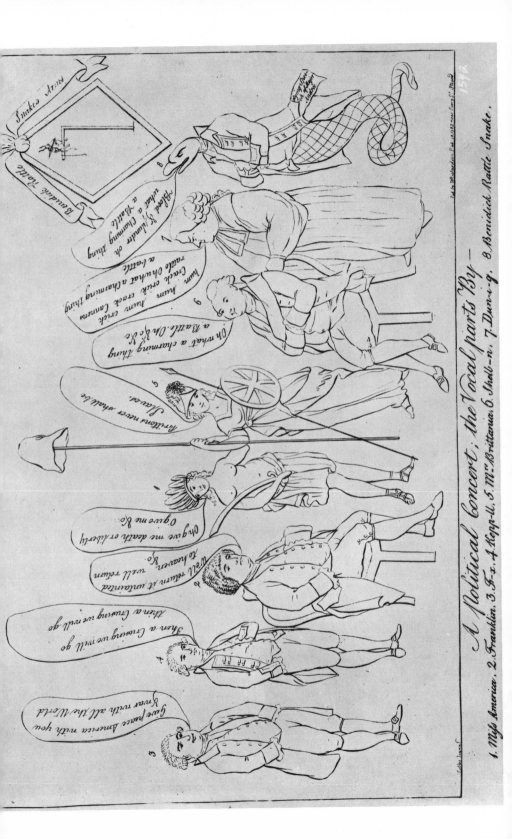

A Political Concert; the Vocal parts By:–

1. Miss America. 2. Franklin. 3. F–x. 4. Keppell. 5. Mr. Brittania. 6. Shell–n. 7. Dun–g. 8. Benedick Rattle Snake.

ernor Bull of the necessity of facing the judges' request that he deal with his nephew. The nephew emerged from the affair with ammunition left over: his papers include a "Rejoinder Intended To Have Been Delivered."

But the acting governor did have to face the wrath of council members regarding the ideas expressed by "Freeman." "By entering captious and frivolous Protests against the proceedings of the House," a council committee declared, Drayton had been "industriously endeavoring to destroy all confidence of the people in this House and to bring it into contempt . . ." As to the pamphlet, the committee "submit to his Honor's consideration, whether the author thereof is a proper person to be longer continued a Member of his Majesty's Council in this Province." On March 1, 1775, the uncle suspended the nephew from the council.

Unabashed, by April 25, Drayton and seven others had formed a new body, "the Committee of Intelligence, set up to correspond with the back parts of this colony." Fourteen months later, he was chief justice of the new state of South Carolina.

The last assembly under royal rule was prorogued in September 1775. The following March, the South Carolina legislature met under its own auspices and adopted a brief constitution intended, as stated in its text, to keep government running during "accommodation of the differences" with England. By 1778, when the possibility of accommodation had clearly ceased to exist, a much fuller document replaced it.

Article IX of the 1778 constitution, in setting up an advisory body of nine under the lieutenant governor, gave lasting force to Edward Rutledge's brief on the nature of the governor's council. It stipulated that "the Privy Council is to advice the Governor and Commander in Chief, when required, but he shall not be bound to consult them unless directed by Law."

The Powell case was further recalled by Article XLI, that guaranteed the enjoyment of due process in wording very similar to Magna Carta, wording that was carried over verbatim when a declaration of rights was incorporated in the definitive version of the South Carolina constitution adopted in 1790: "No Freeman of this State shall be taken, or imprisoned or disseised of his Freehold, Liberties, or Privileges, or outlawed, or exiled, or in any Manner destroyed, or deprived of his Life, Liberty or Property, but by the Judgment of his Peers, or by the Law of the Land . . ."

162

CHAPTER VII

TRIAL IN THE VICINAGE

The Bill of Rights: In all criminal prosecutions, the accused shall enjoy the right to a speedy and public trial, by an impartial jury of the state and district wherein the crime shall have been committed . . .

BACKGROUND

The free man's right to "the legal judgment of his peers" was one of the major guarantees of Magna Carta. Early interpreted as trial by a jury drawn from the locality where the alleged offense took place, it has been recognized down the centuries as an essential element in due process of law. But in the course of English history, it was subject to exceptions, and these in turn had counterparts in America.

Particularly where the charge was treason, early statutes gave the Crown latitude in respect to the place where trials could take place. In 1351, the Treason Act of Edward III warned that treason might be committed both "in the realm, or elsewhere." Henry VIII, well aware of the intrigues carried on elsewhere by his Catholic subjects, especially in France, caused Parliament, by the Act of 1543, to clear up all doubt that treasons committed abroad "may by the common law of this realm be enquired of, heard, and determined within this his said realm of England."

In the third quarter of the eighteenth century, new legislation, some of it based on these old statutes, threatened to deprive American colonists charged with certain offenses of trial by a jury of the vicinage.

From the standpoint of colonial administration, the choice between use of common law courts and use of administrative courts presented something of a dilemma to policy-makers. Enjoyment of the traditional rights of Englishmen comprised in the common law on an equal basis in the colonies and in Britain was a great unifying influence binding the empire together. Yet in cases that dramatized differences between the colonies and the mother country, convictions before colonial juries were difficult to obtain.

As differences sharpened, means of getting such cases away from the local common law courts were increasingly devised. A ready instrument at hand were His Majesty's courts of admiralty. They sat without juries, and the seat of their American headquarters was Halifax, Nova Scotia. During the 1760's, their administrative jurisdiction was specifically enlarged when enforcement proceedings under the Sugar Act of 1764 and the Stamp Act of 1765 were vested

164

in them. John Adams, in his *Instructions to the Town of Braintree, Massachusetts, on the Stamp Act,* exclaimed: "But the most grievous innovation of all, is the alarming expansion of the power of the courts of admiralty. In these courts, one judge presides alone! No juries have any concern there! The law and the fact are both to be decided by the same single judge, whose commission is only during pleasure, and with whom, as we are told, the most mischievous of all customs become established, that of taking commissions on all condemnations; so that he is under a pecuniary temptation always against the subject . . ."

Then in the summer of 1768, a still more serious danger became manifest. After the rioting that followed seizure in Boston harbor of John Hancock's sloop *Liberty,* Lord Hillsborough inquired "If any person had committed any acts which, under the statute of Henry VIII against treason committed abroad, might justify their being brought to England for trial."

At the time, doubt existed as to the applicability of this statute to the New World. It had been passed prior to the establishment of British colonies in America, and it had long been obsolescent in England. But all doubt was abruptly removed in the spring of 1769 when Parliament, over the opposition of Burke and a number of other powerful leaders, specifically extended coverage of the act to North America.

Up and down the coast, shock followed this news. In November, the North Carolina Assembly resolved: "that trials for treason, committed in the colonies, ought to be had here; and removing suspected persons, to be tried beyond the sea, is derogatory to the rights of a British subject."

Then in 1772, the Dockyards Act specified that persons charged with destroying His Majesty's ships or naval stores should receive a death sentence on conviction and might be tried either where the offense was committed or elsewhere in the realm. This act, to which royal assent was given in April, almost immediately became pertinent to a ship-burning in Rhode Island.

Where its waters flow out into Block Island Sound at the end of the Newport peninsula, Narragansett Bay is only three miles wide. A watch kept at The Narrows stoppered the neck of a bottle whose dimple lay thirty miles upwater. It closed the alternative routes inside the bay around large and small islands, across points, and over shoals that would otherwise have been enjoyed by captains from

165

Bristol, Warwick, Pawtuxent, and Providence as well as Newport. Adoption of a policy of stricter enforcement of the Navigation Acts in the mid-sixties, along with passage of the Sugar and Stamp acts, increased pressure on the stopper.

Irregularities were committed by both merchantmen and the royal navy. Skillful seamen of the Rhode Island and Providence plantations prosperously practiced smuggling—and on occasion piracy—along with their legitimate trade. British men-of-war monitoring their proceedings not only impounded cargoes but from time to time replenished their crews by impressment from merchant vessels.

After the captain of H.M.S.'s *Maidstone* impressed the entire crew of a brig newly arrived from Africa, a mob of some five hundred Rhode Islanders took one of her longboats from its moorings at a landing stage, dragged it through the Newport streets, and burnt it on the common in front of the colony house.

Lieutenant William Dudingston reported to Admiral John Montagu, at anchor off Boston, that he had sent a captured sloop with a cargo of rum up to Massachusetts. He did not believe the cargo could be safely kept if it were put ashore at Newport.

By 1772, tempers on both sides had reached a point where a major incident was close to inevitable.

The situation was profoundly affected by the fact that during the troubles under Sir Edmund Andros, Rhode Island had succeeded in retaining its early charter. As a result, its officials were elected by the voters of the province: from governor to chief justice, they were the people's choice rather than appointees of the King. Their frame of government .was related to England only through the Crown.

Their loyalty was thus far more a matter of conviction and sentiment than if they had been serving at the royal pleasure and subject to peremptory recall. The absence, ashore, of a focal point of British official responsibility designated by London created an exceptional atmosphere such as existed in no other colony but Connecticut.

THE CASE

"I do not receive instructions for the administration of my government, from the King's Admiral, stationed in America," wrote Governor Joseph Wanton of Rhode Island to Admiral John Montagu on May 8, 1772. By packet at the same time, he complained to the colonial secretary, Lord Hillsborough, about the admiral's attitude and, more particularly, about the activities of two of H.B.M.'s eight-gun schooners, *Gaspee* and *Beaver,* then operating in Narragansett Bay.

He took these steps more as an assertion of his own position than from any sense of crisis. Over the past forty years, beginning with his father, William, four successive Wantons had been chosen by Rhode Island voters to serve in the colony's elective governorship. It was under his uncle, John, that Richard Munday, the builder who designed much of what was most beautiful in Newport, completed the colony house on the parade in which he now officiated. It was during his uncle Gideon's administration that former Governor Jonathan Nichols, Jr., built the imposing house on the street overlooking the waterfront in which he himself lived. This fourth Governor Wanton felt born to the amenities and enjoyed them, from the rich velvet and brocade of his dress to his well-supplied table. The latter accounted for his portliness and added significance to the carving of his entrance doorway, where the traditional symbol of hospitality was expressed not by one plump pineapple, but by three. Wanton was wholeheartedly devoted to his King, but he liked proper deference from his King's subordinate officers.

The chief justice of Rhode Island's Superior Court, Stephen Hopkins, had found "that no commander of any vessel has a right to use any authority in the body of the colony without previously applying to the governor, and showing his warrant for so doing, and also being sworn to a due exercise of his office." Yet when the governor had sent a high sheriff on board *Gaspee,* asking Lieutenant William Dudingston, her commander, for his commission and instructions, the lieutenant had sent a lofty reply back by a junior officer. When Wanton repeated his demand, Dudingston had forwarded the whole correspondence to Admiral Montagu, and the

167

admiral had used the occasion to ridicule Wanton's conduct and declare that, in case any rescue should be attempted of shipping taken into custody as prizes, he would "hang as pirates" those making the attempt.

Looking out of his waterfront windows of an evening, Wanton was therefore dissatisfied with what he saw, and so were many of his associates among the merchant-traders of the area. Lieutenant Dudingston's zeal in following all shipping in the bay extended even to coastwise barges. *The New-York Gazette* of November 23 and *The Pennsylvania Gazette* of November 25, 1772, both published a communication from Newport referring to "the ill behavior of some few of his [the King's] servants, who, when abroad among an unarmed People, are more imperious and haughty than the Grand Turk himself."

The merchants' stakes were high. The Brown family of Providence differed from its neighbors only in the extent of its commerce. The Browns' local business consisted in distilling rum and manufacturing the spermaceti candles introduced in 1740 by Jacob Rodriguez Rivera of Newport. When bringing molasses for the rum from the West Indies, their ships also imported finished goods.

In the 1630's, Chad Brown, their ancestor, had been one of Roger Williams' handful of companions settling the port in the wilderness to which Providence had led them after Massachusetts Bay refused further harbor. The eighteenth-century members of the family included James Brown, who died in 1739, and the four sons he left to be brought up in the family business by their uncle Obediah. The boys' names were Nicholas, Joseph, John, and Moses; among their fleet, plying from Providence to the Barbados, was the sloop *Four Brothers*.

In shipping families, successful boys began as seamen, became captains, retired from the sea as merchants, to build houses topped by captain's walks overlooking the harbor. Young John Brown's shipping list, when he took the sloop *Mary* to Philadelphia in 1757, included "1 seet chaney" for Mrs. Angell, an "allebaster babe" for an undesignated client, and Franklin's *Electricity* for himself. In 1762, he helped found *The Providence Gazette* as a more popular contrast to *The Newport Mercury*. He laid the cornerstone when Rhode Island College, founded in 1764, moved from Warren to Providence in 1770; for a generation he served as trustee. (Later the college became Brown University in recognition of a benefaction by John's nephew.) In the 1780's, he built a house from plans drawn by his brother Joseph that John Quincy Adams regarded as one of the country's finest. Its address was both a fact and a symbol: the corner of Power and Benefit streets.

Among the Browns' neighbors were the Hopkins, likewise descended from one of Roger Williams' associates. Stephen Hopkins, currently chief justice of Rhode Island, was an elder statesman who earlier had repeatedly served as the colony's elected governor—dueling for it in alternate terms with Newport's Samuel Ward. He had been the first chancellor of Rhode Island College. In 1776, he and William Ellery of Newport were Rhode Island's signers of the Declaration of Independence. Of his five sons, four followed the sea and three became masters of vessels.

These were only two of the Providence families involved in what was easily the most serious of all the incidents between sea captains and customs officers in Narragansett Bay. It occurred on the night of June 9-10, 1772.

On the eighth, the sloop *Hannah,* captained by Benjamin Lindsey, reached Newport from New York. Her skipper reported his arrival at the customs house. Next day, he started upriver toward Providence. Lieutenant Dudingston, aboard *Gaspee,* gave chase.

Below Pawtuxent, Namquit Point extends out into the water in subsurface shoals whose depth varies with the tide. The experienced Captain Lindsey rounded this point at a distance adequate to *Hannah's* draft, but insufficient for *Gaspee's.*

Heavily, the Navy sloop jarred aground, and stuck.

Hannah reached Providence by sundown.

At No. 124 Planet Street in Providence, James Sabin kept an inn. Around nine o'clock, drums in the street summoned whom it might concern to meet there. An expedition was preparing. Its object: destruction of *Gaspee.*

Across the way, at Fenner's Wharf, eight longboats provided by John Brown waited with muffled oars.

As they pushed off, each was handled by an experienced captain. Abraham Whipple, master of *Four Brothers,* was at one tiller; during the French and Indian War, in *Game Cock,* he had hung up a record, taking twenty-three prizes in a single cruise. Namquit Point lay in Kent County—he was sheriff there. Another skipper was John B. Hopkins, nephew of the chief justice. Altogether, counting old salts and young bucks, some forty to fifty men were in the boats.

169

As they rowed down the bay, they were joined by others from Bristol.

Around midnight, they approached *Gaspee;* until they were very close, the moonless dark prevented their being noticed. According to Ephriam Bowen's account in his old age, *Gaspee's* lookout hailed them twice before Captain Whipple answered: "I am sheriff of the county of Kent, G-d D--n you. I have got a warrant to apprehend you, G-d d--n you. So surrender, G-d d--n you."

Lieutenant Dudingston jumped to *Gaspee's* gunwale.

Joseph Bucklin, a Providence innkeeper, was standing on the main thwart of Whipple's boat near the larboard rowlock. Young Bowen pulled that oar, with his father's gun beside him. Bucklin whispered:

"Ephe, reach me your gun and I can kill that fellow."

His shot hit Dudingston in the arm, passed through it, and entered the groin about five inches below the navel. Dudingston fell to the deck.

Quickly the attackers boarded the schooner, drove the crew below, pinioned and bound them there with tarred ropes. Dudingston, taken to his bunk, was tended by Dr. John Mawney, a learned member of the expedition knowledgeable in surgery as well as Latin and Greek; he closed the abdominal wound so skillfully—later setting down a meticulous account of his procedure—that Dudingston recovered.

Gaspee's company was then put into the boats. When all were clear, the boarding party set fire to the schooner. Blazing against the night, she burnt to the water's edge.

The rowers landed her crew at Old Still House Wharf at Pawtuxent, carried her captain to be cared for at the home of Joseph Rhodes. Then they disappeared into the darkness upriver.

Next morning, everyone realized that a serious situation existed. Reporting to Admiral Montagu, Midshipman Dickenson of *Gaspee* stated that some hundred and fifty men had engaged in the attack, maltreated the commanding officer, "robbed his servant of several silver spoons and throwed his linen and apparel overboard."

Queried the admiral: "Did any of the people that boarded you, appear like gentlemen?"

Replied the midshipman: "Yes, many of them appeared like men of credit and tradesmen; and a few like common men."

The admiral turned upon the governor.

Anticipating his reaction, the lieutenant governor, Darius Sessions, who lived in Providence, had gone to Pawtuxent, collected the British seamen, given them food and lodging and transportation to H.B.M.'s other schooner, *Beaver*. He offered Dudingston surgeons and any other aid he might require, and attempted to get a deposition from him as to what had happened. The lieutenant gloomily replied that if he lived he would give his account at the court-martial to which he would be subjected for losing his ship, and if he died the information would die with him.

Sessions consulted with the chief justice, who "highly disapproved of the riot," and wrote the governor in Newport to offer a reward for information as to the culprits, adding that substantial citizens supported the effort to find them.

On June 12, Governor Wanton proclaimed a reward of £100 sterling for information sufficient to convict. He likewise wrote Lord Hillsborough that "This transaction gives me the utmost uneasiness; and Your Lordship may be assured, that the utmost vigilance of the civil authority will not be wanting, to bring the perpetrators to exemplary and condign punishment; and in justice to the inhabitants of the colony, I must not omit mentioning, that the conduct of those who committed this outrage, is, by them, universally condemned."

But Charles Dudley, an American loyalist, wrote a friend: "The attack upon the Gaspee was not the effect of sudden passion and resentment but of cool deliberation and fore-thought. It had long been determined she should be destroyed."

In London, the case was regarded with even greater gravity. On September 4, Lord Dartmouth wrote Governor Wanton: ". . . in the obvious view of the whole transaction, and taking all the circumstances together, the offense is, in the opinion of the law servants of the crown who have been consulted upon the question, of a much deeper dye, and is considered in no other light, than as an act of high treason, viz.: levying war against the King."

This official designation of the incident as a case of treason gave sudden reality to the legal danger than had been latent for four years: the *Gaspee* incident supplied an occasion for the application of the statute of 1769 permitting persons accused of treason in North America to be brought to England for trial.

To Lord Dartmouth's annoyance, Governor Wanton showed his letter to the assembly, which ordered it printed; excerpts were published in the newspapers. Accompanying it was a proclamation in which George III offered rewards of £1,000 for the arrest and conviction of the expedition's two leaders, £500 for any other of its members, and a free pardon for any one other than the two chiefs who would give evidence.

At the same time, London named a special commission of inquiry to sit at Newport and take evidence. Its membership was calculated to bring this case to the attention of all of the chief trading colonies. Designated, in addition to Governor Wanton, were Robert Auchmuty, judge of vice-admiralty at Boston, and three chief justices: Daniel Horsmanden of New York, Frederick Smythe of New Jersey, Peter Oliver of Massachusetts. These, or any three of them, were to find the facts of the case and report them to London: "We," ran the King's instructions, "being desirous to be perfectly informed how so daring an attempt could be concerted, prepared and carried into execution in the chief town of our said colony. . . ."

Because the commissions for this group were sent, not to Rhode Island, but to Admiral Montagu in Boston, rumors spread that military investiture of Rhode Island was in the offing. Boston buzzed with them. On December 3, John Allen preached a sermon at the Second Baptist Church on "The Beauties of Liberty, or the Essential Rights of Americans." The Providence and Newport papers vied with each other in inflammatory speculation. *The Pennsylvania Gazette* of December 16 printed a communication from Boston that a man of war was being fitted to go to Newport. *The New-York Gazette* of the twenty-first ran a similar story and, on December 28, after reporting the arrival of the official dispatches establishing the commission, added that "Admiral Montagu is ordered to hoist his flag in Newport Harbour."

Actually, the admiral transmitted the dispatches to Governor Wanton, who in turn notified the other commissioners and, on December 31, informed the admiral that the court of inquiry would sit in about a week's time.

On January 5, 1773, the four judges and the governor met at the Newport Colony House, took their oaths, subscribed to the test act, and prepared to receive depositions.

The third article of their instructions was greatly on their minds: they were to identify the persons involved in the incident, "to the end that they may be accordingly arrested and delivered to the custody of the commander in chief of our ships and vessels in North America, pursuant to such directions as we have thought fit to give

173

for that purpose." The meaning of the words seemed quite as clear as if they had been wholly specific: the accused were to be transported overseas for trial.

Nevertheless, the commission made diligent inquiry. During mid-December, the King's proclamation had been widely posted by sheriffs throughout the colony. On arrival, the commissioners advertised in *The Newport Mercury* their presence and readiness to hear testimony, daily except Sunday: "Wherefore, all persons who can give any information to the said commissioners, relative to the assembling, arming and leading on the persons who made the attack, and the directing and preparing the same, are requested forthwith to give information thereof, to the said commissioners at the above mentioned place."

Nothing happened. The court's first days were spent taking depositions from the *Gaspee* ship's company, establishing facts already familiar. Unsurprisingly, the British sailors were unable to name members of the boarding party. Midshipman Dickenson's account indeed seemed to offer a basis for exonerating participants who might be detected: "In going ashore, one of the mob that rowed the boat, said, that he and several more, would not have been there, but that they were taken out of a house by force, and compelled to go; that they beat a drum round the town of Providence, in the evening to raise a mob."

Among Rhode Islanders, however, the names of the chief participants were common knowledge—a number of the young bucks in the expedition, exhilarated by their clandestine nocturnal adventure, had returned to Providence dazzled by the glitter of their dagger and careless of the cover of their cloak. The King's proclamation itself had indicated that the ringleaders were two in number. Yet when it came to giving evidence, it was as if every clam along the entire tortuous shore line of Narragansett Bay had closed its shell.

The safety of many men depended on that unanimous silence; if one clam opened, indictments would be unavoidable; and there was leverage in the princely dimensions of the rewards.

The previous July, a suggestion of an opening had occurred when Admiral Montagu supplied Governor Wanton with a deposition, taken by Captain Linzee on board *Beaver*, from a runaway mulatto indentured servant named Aaron Briggs. According to Briggs, as he was rowing a boat belonging to his master around

Prudence Island that night, he crossed the way of a boat coming from Bristol occupied by Simeon Potter and eight armed men. Potter ordered Briggs to row along with them and later required Briggs to transfer to his boat. They met up with seventeen other boats from Providence. In these, he identified John and Joseph Brown, a Mr. Richmond, and Dr. Weeks of Warwick, who he said was the surgeon who dressed Dudingston's wound. He himself pulled bow oar in the boat that took the British lieutenant ashore after the raid; the boat was steered by John Brown.

On receipt of this deposition, Governor Wanton sent Captain Linzee an order to bring Briggs ashore; Linzee refused. Wanton complained to the admiral, but received no satisfaction. The admiral replied that he had seen Briggs, and that "it is clear to me, from many corroborating circumstances, that he is no imposter." Briggs' testimony therefore remained unfinished business which the court of inquiry would have to consider.

Then on January 12, the court received testimony from a laborer named Stephen Gulley. He swore that Captain William Thayer, innkeeper of Mendon, had told him that Saul Ramsdale, shoemaker, of Providence, knew who the raiders were and that Ramsdale had admitted to him that he did know, but "though picked for one of the gang," he being fainthearted, had not joined them. He thought the Browns were in it and estimated the total number in the expedition as upward of three hundred. He begged Gulley not to discover him to the court.

Gulley further said that on the night of January 5, he had some drinks at the public house by the ferry and then ordered supper. The landlord and another fellow came and sat down with him and warned him that twenty armed men, one of whom carried two brass pistols, were lying in wait outside to take him, dead or alive, back to Providence. The landlord then showed him a back way out to the road to Newport, and he went there and took refuge on H.M.S. *Lizard* out of fear for his personal safety.

The innkeeper in question, Joseph Borden of Portsmouth, gave a very different version of the evening: Gulley, drunk, had arrived at the inn and gone out before supper with Thomas Aylesbury. Since both were using foul language, Borden barred the doors to prevent their coming back, but later readmitted Gulley and gave him supper. Aylesbury likewise returned and said to Gulley that he believed him to be "upon some bad design," and inquired if he was going to Newport to give evidence. Gulley retorted that "It was nobody's business but my own."

Aylesbury then assured Gulley that there were a number of "Indians, with brass pistols, in the road, who would take care of him," and left. Borden proposed to Gulley that if he would pay up and get out, he would show him a back road.

Borden ended his testimony with the comment that while he was in the kitchen, soon after Gulley came to his house and before Aylesbury had accused Gulley of being upon some bad design, "he heard a person reading the King's proclamation for discovering the persons who burnt the Gaspee schooner; upon which, Gulley said it was a fine reward and he intended to have it. . . ."

The court turned to Captain Thayer. Via Deputy Governor Sessions, he sent down a deposition giving as his reason for not coming in person: "he is near seventy years of age, grievously afflicted with the rheumatism, attended with many symptoms of paralysis; and that riding yesterday in the cold, stormy weather has revived and so much increased his disorder, that he was unable to proceed to Newport." Thayer both derogated and confirmed Gulley's statements: "if the gentlemen . . . had any idea of the villainy of the fellows who informed them, neither he, nor any one else, he believes, had been troubled by them." But he did admit to having heard mention of the names of "Potter and Brown or Browns . . . only some rumor which I heard among the people in my house, it being a public one." The commissioners did not extend summonses on the basis of this evidence.

On January 14, Admiral Montagu, who had been reluctant to come to Newport because of the bad winter weather, arrived and made *Lizard* his temporary flagship. He ordered Aaron Briggs brought before the commissioners.

In repeating substantially the same story that had been in his deposition, Briggs emphasized the circumstances in which his testimony had been obtained. He said he had determined to run away from his master and went on board *Beaver* as part of that plan. But Captain Linzee first ordered him put in irons and the next day had him tied to the mast preparatory to flogging him. One of the crew then identified him as having been with the boarding party. The captain said: "My lad, you see this man has declared you was there; and if you don't tell who was there with you, I will hang

176

you at the yardarm immediately; and if you do, you shall not be hurt."

Patrick Earle, mariner on *Gaspee*, likewise identified Briggs. He said Briggs had given him a chew of tobacco in the boat in which he was rowed ashore and allowed him to row for a time to warm up in the night chill. Earle said the captain "gave directions . . . to get some spun yarn, to tie up the negro, and give him two or three dozen to find out what he came on board for, or if he knew anything concerning the burning of the schooner."

The court turned Briggs' deposition over to the justices of the Rhode Island Superior Court for examination.

On the eighteenth, Admiral Montagu asked the court to summon James Sabin, the Providence innkeeper on whose premises the plan for the attack was said to have been made; Arthur Fenner, from whose wharf the longboats had departed; and a number of members of bench and bar known to have been at Sabin's inn on the night of the incident.

In courteous replies, giving a wide variety of reasons, these gentlemen all announced themselves unable to attend:

JAMES SABIN: In the first place, I am an insolvent debtor; and therefore my person would be subject to an arrest by some one or other of my creditors; and my health has been on the decline these two months past, and it would be dangerous should I leave my house.

And further, were I to attend, I could give no information relative to the assembling, training, and leading on the people concerned in destroying the schooner Gaspee.

GEORGE BROWN (*detained because the court of common pleas was sitting in Kent*): it has long been a custom for the attorneys, upon the concluding evening of filing pleas to the court, to meet together, to spend the evening.

That night, the said schooner was burnt, happening to be the concluding evening . . . accordingly, the gentlemen of the bar, together with myself met at the house of James Sabin . . .

Some time after, I being there, heard a drum beat; I asked the reason of said drum beating; I was assured by some of the company that there was a number of boys met together, they supposed, to divert themselves. . . .

JOHN ANDREWS (*judge of vice-admiralty*): should have cheerfully obeyed said summons, had my health permitted; but I have been

177

confined for a week past, with a swelling in my hand, which hath rendered me unable to stir out of doors.

But as soon as I am able, I shall wait upon Your Honors, and inform you of all I know, relating to that matter, which your Honors will judge just nothing at all to the purpose.

JOHN COLE: I pulled back the shutters of one of the windows next the street and saw several people collected together, but did not know any of them; upon which I made inquiry of the gentlemen in the room if they knew the occasion.

And was answered by some of the company, but by whom I cannot particularly recollect, that he hoped they were not designed for mischief.

To which I replied, I believed not; if they were, they would not be so public.

DANIEL HITCHCOCK: We met at Mr. Sabin's, by ourselves; and about six o'clock, I went to the door, or finally, kitchen, and saw a number of people in the street, but paid no attention to them, as that place was a place of public resort.

ARTHUR FENNER (*from whose wharf the longboats had departed*): I am a man of seventy-four years of age, and very infirm; and at the time the said schooner was taken and plundered, I was in bed, and I knew nothing of it until the next day.

For the time being, the court had had enough. On January 25, they wrote Lord Dartmouth announcing their adjournment until the end of May, citing bad weather as an obstacle to obtaining witnesses.

When they reconvened, the superior court reported that it found the deposition of Aaron Briggs invalid on two counts. Daniel Tompkins of Prudence Island, to whom Briggs was indentured, had given evidence, supported by testimony of two other indentured Negroes, that he had seen Briggs about 9:00 P.M. on the night *Gaspee* was burnt and that Briggs was likewise on hand to bring up the cows very early the following morning. Further, the only boat available that night was in too bad condition for Briggs to leave the island.

The other count notes that Briggs' deposition was obtained under duress: "Another circumstance which renders the said Aaron's testimony extremely suspicious is Capt. Linzee's absolutely refusing to deliver him up to be examined by one of the justices of the Superior Court, when legally demanded."

So this clam shell was empty, after all.

By June 22, the court of inquiry was ready to announce its failure. A Newport dispatch printed in *The New-York Gazette* of Monday, July 5, stated: "The Court of Inquiry is broke up, having made no material discoveries that we can learn." Said the court: "the whole was conducted suddenly and secretly . . . after our utmost efforts, we are not able to discover any evidence."

Because no one was identified at Newport in 1773, neither Admiral Montagu's intention of hanging as pirates those who obstructed enforcement of the Navigation Acts nor the royal instructions to the court of inquiry to turn indicted persons over to him for transportation to trial outside the colony went into effect. But the Newport hearings had witnessed a clear and present danger; it was recognized up and down the coast.

The most important passages in Lord Dartmouth's letter to Governor Wanton of the previous September were sent to Samuel Adams in Boston by Lieutenant Governor Sessions, Chief Justice Hopkins, Assemblyman John Cole, and Moses Brown. *The Massachusetts Spy and The Boston Gazette* republished them.

The Providence Gazette had drawn maximum conclusions as to their meaning: "In this situation of affairs, every friend of our violated constitution, cannot but be greatly alarmed. The idea of seizing a number of persons, under the points of bayonets, and transporting them three thousand miles for trial, where, whether guilty or innocent, they must unavoidably fall victims alike to revenge or prejudice, is shocking to humanity, repugnant to every dictate of reason, liberty and justice; and in which, Americans and freemen ought never to acquiesce."

Taproom ballads spread these sentiments: a long ditty ascribed to a Bristol sea captain runs in part:

> Twas in the reign of George the Third,
> Our public peace was much disturbed
> By ships of war, that came and laid
> Within our ports, to stop our trade. . . .
> Now for to find these people out,
> King George has offered very stout;
> One thousand pounds to find out one
> That wounded William Dudingston.
> One thousand more, he says he'll spare,
> For those who say the sheriffs were;

One thousand more, there doth remain
For to find out the leader's name;
Likewise, five hundred pounds per man
For any one of all the clan.
But let him try his utmost skill,
I'm apt to think he never will
Find out any of those hearts of gold,
Though he should offer fifty-fold.

Private letters circulated views ranging from one extreme to another: in Boston, loyalist Governor Hutchinson, at the end of August 1772, wrote to one correspondent that if the affair is "passed over without a full inquiry and due resentment, our liberty people will think they may with impunity commit any acts of violence." In early September, he assured another that "so daring an insult, as the burning of the King's schooner, by people who are as well known as any who are concerned in this last rebellion [the Hancock affair] and yet cannot be prosecuted, will certainly rouse the British lion, which has been asleep for four or five years."

Shortly, Boston correspondents of opposite sympathies were imaginatively warning friends in Newport that the admiral was readying ships for "an expedition which promises to gratify his rancor against your colony;" that three regiments are preparing to converge on Rhode Island, and that "unless you exhibit a *quantum sufficit* of passive obedience and nonresistance, the same tragedy may be enacted in Newport and Providence, which makes the 5th of March [the date of the "Boston Massacre" of 1770] so memorable in Boston."

Various Massachusetts town meetings passed resolves urging vigilance. That of Dorchester expressed alarm at "a new and unheard of grievance, in a late act passed by the British Parliament, whereby the crown is empowered, so that persons supposed to be guilty of certain crimes, may be hurried away from any county in North America, where such crime may be supposed to have been committed, to be tried in any county in England, where His Majesty or his successors shall judge proper. . . ."

At Boston's October town meeting, Samuel Adams moved the appointment of a committee of correspondence, "to state the rights of the colonists of this province in particular, as men and Christians and as subjects; and to communicate and publish the same to the

The able Doctor or America Swallowing the Bitter Draught

several towns and to the world as the sense of this town; with the infringements and violations thereof that have been, or from time to time may be, made."

By year's end, over eighty Massachusetts towns had set up such committees. The following April, Adams wrote Richard Henry Lee of Virginia suggesting the usefulness of a structure of this sort in every colony, only to find that the spring meeting of the Virginia House of Burgesses had already acted along those very lines, with members of the committee specifically "instructed to inform themselves particularly of the principles and authority on which was constituted a court of inquiry, said to have been lately held in Rhode Island with power to transport persons accused of offences committed in America, to places beyond the sea, to be tried."

At its spring session, the Rhode Island Assembly named a committee of correspondences, including Chief Justice Hopkins, Moses Brown, and John Cole.

It was on the basis of the *Gaspee* incident that the First Continental Congress, when it issued its Declaration and Resolves in the fall of 1774, including among specific grievances Whitehall's establishment of a board of commissioners "with unconstitutional powers" and Parliament's determination "that by force of a statute, made in the thirty-fifth year of the reign of King Henry the Eighth, colonists may be transported to England, and tried there upon accusations for treasons and misprisions, or concealment of treasons committed in the colonies, and by a late statute, such trials have been directed in cases therein mentioned." Likewise listed was the statute itself, "which declares a new offence in America, and deprives the American subject of a constitutional trial by jury in the vicinage, by authorizing the trial of any person, charged with the committing any offence described in said act, out of the realm, to be indicted and tried for the same in any shire or county within the realm."

In July 1775, the second Congress, in its Declaration setting forth the Causes and Necessity of their Taking up Arms, cited among enumerated rights that had been impaired "the accustomed and inestimable privilege of trial by jury . . . It has also been resolved in parliament, that colonists charged with committing certain offences, shall be transported to England to be tried."

Next year, the third Congress, in the itemized charges of the Declaration of Independence, again cited the legislation "For transporting us beyond Seas to be tried for pretended offences."

When the break with the mother country came, Rhode Island and Connecticut, alone among the colonies, still enjoyed the broad powers of self-government extended by their seventeenth-century charters—elsewhere, the early documents had been revoked and replaced with much more limited allowances of self-government. In these two new states, therefore, brief resolutions deleting references to the King from their constitutions were all that was required to provide them with independent frames of government.

Indeed, New York's Chief Justice Horsmanden, writing to Lord Dartmouth from Newport during the sitting of the court of inquiry, had said of the Rhode Island constitution:

> My lord, as to the Government (if it deserves that name), it is a downright democracy; the Governor is a mere nominal one, and therefore a cipher, without power or authority; entirely controlled by the populace, elected annually, as all other magistrates and officers whatsoever . . .
>
> Though by their charter, they are inhibited from passing laws contrary to those of England, but to be as near as may be, agreeable to them, yet they seem to have paid little regard to that injunction, as may appear upon inspection of the printed book of them; they have never transmitted them for the royal approbation, nor indeed, by their charter were they obliged to do so.
>
> Under these circumstances, Your Lordship will not wonder that they are in a state of anarchy; and I assure Your Lordship, that their sister colony of Connecticut is in the same condition in all respects; justice had long since fled that country . . .

Rhode Island lived under its Charter of 1663 until 1822. That year the state adopted a ten-section bill of rights, plus a separate statute on religious freedom, Rhode Island's early specialty. In wording almost identical with the Seventh Amendment of the federal Constitution, the right to trial by a jury of the vicinage was then affirmed.

CHAPTER VIII

THE RIGHT TO A JURY

The Bill of Rights: In suits at common law, where the value in controversy shall exceed twenty dollars, the right of trial by jury shall be preserved, and no fact tried by a jury shall be otherwise re-examined in any court of the United States than according to the rules of the common law.

BACKGROUND

From the foundation of the colonies, appeals to London from colonial courts had been allowed in certain instances. Sometimes the basis for such appeals was set forth in a colony's charter; more often, the instructions issued to colonial governors indicated the circumstances in which cases could be forwarded to Whitehall for review.

Over the years, the concept of the nature of an appeal evolved and altered. A distinction was made between procedures for legal review and requests for clemency or pardon in which a plaintiff threw himself on the mercy of his prince in the exercise of the inherent right of the subject to petition the Crown.

In 1664, when Charles II granted New York to James, Duke of York, his brother and successor, he gave him "full and absolute power and authority to Correct punish Pardon Governe and Rule . . . as well in all Causes and matters Capitall and Criminall as Civill both Marine and others SOE ALWAYES as the said Statutes Ordinances and Proceedings bee not contrary to but as neare as conveniently may bee agreeable to the Lawes Statutes and Government of this our Realme of England. . . ."

But he specifically retained blanket powers in respect to appeals. The charter continues "AND SAVEING and reserving to us our heirs and Successors the receiveing heareing and determineing of the Appeale and Appeales of all or any Person or Persons of in or belonging to the Territories or Islands aforesaid in or touching any Judgment or Sentence to bee there made or given."

But after the board of trade and plantations was set up in 1696, an order in council directed the formation of a committee of at least three privy councillors to consider colonial appeals, with their findings referred to the privy council as a whole for the rendering of a final decision. American cases sent up for review henceforth received this committee's attention, and the procedures for forwarding cases became increasingly precise. In criminal trials concerning murder, treason, and fines in excess of £200, recourse was allowed directly from the trial court to the Crown; the governor merely granted the necessary reprieve or stay and sent the record forward.

186

By contrast, in civil cases appeal initially was to the governor in council and consisted of review for possible error in the handling of the case.

The commission of Governor Thomas Dongan, under whom representative institutions were set up in New York, authorized appeals "in cases of error from our courts of New York unto the Governor and Council in civil causes," provided the values appealed for exceeded £100; appeals to the King in council, after examination by the governor in council, were allowed when the sum at issue exceeded £300.

Subsequent gubernatorial commissions repeated these provisions until the appointment of Sir Robert Monckton in 1753. For reasons of which no record could subsequently be found, a slight variance occurred in article 32 of his instructions: it specified issuance of "writs in the usual manner" without specifically limiting consideration to "appeals in cases of error."

This variance became the basis of a substantial dispute between the acting governor and members of the council and the supreme court of New York. Cases initiated before the supreme court were tried with a jury. Appeals to the governor in council, brought because of alleged error in its proceedings, consisted of examinations of the record to see if due process had been followed and the law correctly applied. They did not include reopening of a jury verdict rendered without error. Since appellate courts do not use juries, power in the council to revise a jury verdict in the absence of error would be tantamount to trying a case *de novo* without a jury. Transmission of a case for overall reconsideration by the committee of the privy council would do the same thing. Either would nullify the right to a definitive judgment by one's peers.

In the case of *Forsey* v. *Cunningham* in the 1760's, New York's council members, judges and lawyers stood unanimously against the propriety of such appellate jurisdiction, and the Crown's lawyers eventually supported them. When the case was finally closed, the principle that no fact properly tried by a jury could be retried on review had been established in New York.

THE CASE

On the twenty-ninth of July, 1763, two New York merchants jarred their way into the public prints when Waddell Cunningham attacked Thomas Forsey in the street. Drawing a concealed sword, Cunningham proceeded to "beat Thrust Stab wound and evilly treat Forsey" so grievously that his victim was laid up for eighty-two days.

Cunningham was a merchant of some consequence and well-connected in London. During the ensuing autumn, his firm, Greg, Cunningham & Co., took advantage of *The New-York Gazette's* offer to insert "an Advertisement of a Moderate Length" for four consecutive weeks for a total price of five shillings and announced itself ready to supply the public with the following merchandise, just imported by Captain Chambers in *Snow:* "Bohea, Congo, Suthong, plain Green, and Hyfon Teas: Ruffia Hemp. a few Tons of best Swedes Iron, a large Assortment of Irish linens, Callicoes, & Chints; & a few Casks of best London Porter in Bottles.—They have also for Sale, Irish Butter & Salmon in Firkins, French and striped Blankets, green and spotted Rugs, English Sail Cloth, No. 1 to 8; long middling & short Pipes; Kegs of Capers, best British bottled Beer, Glo'ster & Cheshire Cheese, empty Bottles in Hampers, plate Copper of all Dimensions; 8d, 10d, 12d, & 20d Nails; Castile Soap; Madeira, Fyal, Sherry & Lisbon Wines: Claret, British & French Brandy, Jamaica Rum, Geneva in Cases & Hogshead."

Cunningham's specific animus against Forsey is not a matter of record, but general irritability on his part is easy to understand. During the active years of the French and Indian War—the Treaty of Paris, terminating it, had been signed only in February—trading with the enemy had been extensively practiced by New York merchants. Four years previously, an impecunious informer, George Spencer, had turned in the names of sixteen of them, Cunningham's included. The merchants decided to get rid of Spencer. On November 2, 1759, they instigated a riot.

Their hatchet men, having obtained a bond posted to secure one of Spencer's numerous unpaid obligations, appeared in the mayor's court and got a process server dispatched to Spencer's home. Arrested and conducted to a private house, Spencer was seized by a prearranged mob of some hundred lusty sailors. They commandeered the use of a cart, dragged him at its tail gate through the streets, "showered with filth and offal, much to the disgrace and annoyance of the said George Spencer and the peace and quiet of the inhabitants." The carting ended at a public pump, where they proceeded to "pump George Spencer."

Immediate court proceedings against the sponsors of the riot, again including Cunningham, were supplemented in May 1762 by the vice-admiralty court's sequestration of several ships and their cargoes, among them one of Cunningham's, on the basis of a report on illegal trade presented to the council late in 1760. In April 1763, the supreme court found him guilty of trading with the enemy.

At the time he beat up Thomas Forsey he was still unsure whether his vessel and its cargo would be confiscated and a further fine assessed—it was—and whether he would be additionally prosecuted and fined for violating the Provision Act by not giving security before putting the cargo on board—he was. His complaint that this was double jeopardy was repudiated by the court, which declared him to have committed two offenses. Clearly, when he met Forsey on the street, Cunningham had much on his mind. Having been run through by a sword, Forsey seemed entirely likely to die as a result of the encounter. In that case, Cunningham would be charged with murder. A ship that made an exceptionally fast voyage conveyed the news to Whitehall. On September 3, the Earl of Halifax dispatched a return letter, addressed to the governor, the lieutenant governor, or the commander in chief, depending on who was momentarily in charge: "It having been represented to The King, that on the 29th Day of July last, a Quarrel happened in the Province of New York between Mr. Forcey, and Mr. Waddell Cunningham two Merchants of that Place, and that Mr. Forcey having first struck Mr. Cunningham he thereupon drew his Sword and stabbed Mr. Forcey; and for which Mr. Cunningham will consequently take his Trial there, if Mr. Forcey should dye of his Wounds; I am commanded to signify to you His Majesty's Pleasure that you cause a Report to be made to His Majesty of Mr. Cunningham's Trial, in case he should be convicted, and that you do in the meantime cause his Judgment and Execution to be respited till His Majesty's Pleasure shall be known thereupon."

The letter came to seventy-six-year-old Lieutenant Governor Cadwallader Colden. Had Forsey died, the procedure indicated

189

would have been the suitable one. But Forsey recovered.

When the supreme court met for its October term in 1763, therefore, the two suits filed against Cunningham on behalf of Forsey were only a criminal suit on the mild charge of assault and battery and a civil suit in which the plaintiff asked £5,000 damages.

Next January, Cunningham emerged from the criminal suit with a fine of a mere £30. But when the civil suit was tried the following October, a sympathetic jury awarded Forsey damages of £1,500. Cunningham's attorney protested. He moved the court to set aside the verdict and grant a new trial. The court refused either to mitigate the damages or hear the suit over again.

Cunningham's demand for a new trial was based on the new wording contained in article 32 of the general instruction transmitted to General Sir Robert Monckton when he was named governor of New York, specifying issuance of "writs in the usual manner" to bring a case before the council without limiting the council's consideration to "appeal in cases of error."

His contention was that the broadened instruction authorized the council to rehear his entire case, and in so doing to reconsider the jury's award. What he proposed was thus not a review of the proceedings of a court, but a reopening of the verdict of a jury.

Monckton, after absenting himself from the colony to campaign in the West Indies, had returned to England to regain his health. As a result, Colden became acting governor. As soon as it was learned that the acting governor shared Cunningham's interpretation of article 32, the Forsey-Cunningham case rose from obscurity to present a highly visible public issue.

The forces which engaged in a political struggle over the affair were essentially the same as those which had opposed each other in the Zenger case a generation earlier. Colden's main opponents in the months of the Cunningham plea were William Livingston, one of the current generation of that numerous family, who had recently completed his law training at London's Middle Temple; William Smith, Jr., son of a councilman and Livingston's law partner; and John Morin Scott, a ranking attorney, whose reputation was substantiated by his filing of 114 cases before a single term of court in 1767. These three, all skilled with pen as well as in verbal argument, were popularly known as "the triumvirate."

The relations of the acting governor with the colony's bench and bar and the attitude of the supreme court in this dispute were

affected specifically by some recent decisions with regard to judicial appointments and the basis for judicial tenure.

On the death of Chief Justice DeLancey, his political faction had supported the advancement to the chief justiceship of either of two associate justices close to their way of thinking, Daniel Horsmanden and John Chambers. The Livingstons had advanced as their candidates William Smith, Sr., and Richard H. Morris.

While the appointment was pending, the death of George II made all commissions renewable. In 1744, Governor George Clinton had given Chief Justice DeLancey a commission that provided the independence of life tenure by designating him "during good behavior" rather than only "during the King's pleasure." All the justices eagerly desired their renewed writs to provide tenure "during good behavior"; factional lines within the court disappeared in a common cause.

But Acting Governor Colden took the view that service should be "during the King's pleasure only," and the board of trade in London not only upheld him but ignored both sets of applicants as well by naming Benjamin Pratt of Boston to serve as New York's chief justice "during pleasure." Associate Justice John Chambers resigned rather than accept a commission so worded. The court's two other members, Associate Justices Horsmanden and Jones, submitted, though the former did so with reluctance.

The venerable Mr. Pratt found the New York atmosphere so hostile that he resigned after only six months and returned to Boston, observing in a letter to Thomas Pownall that "The Granting Commissions as they were before, that is During good Behavior, is now the Popular Demand & made the inflaming Topic but at Bottom the Point of View is to compel the Crown to appoint one of Themselves Ch: Justice."

After Pratt's departure, Daniel Horsmanden was advanced to the chief justiceship and William Smith, Sr., and Robert R. Livingston named to the two vacancies. Against this background and with this membership, the court was inclined to a narrow construction in the Forsey-Cunningham affair. The judges held that there was no basis —indeed, none was alleged—for sending the case to the council on a writ of error and that no other proper writ existed. They declined to provide Cunningham's representatives with the official minutes of the previous trial. (Cunningham's people had rather full notes of their own, taken because Cunningham himself was in England during much of this affair, but they lacked legal standing.)

Originally, the case had appeared so entirely routine, so wholly lacking in political overtones, that the triumvirate had taken briefs as opposing counsel. John Morin Scott had represented Forsey; the firm of Livingston and Smith, Cunningham. But Cunningham's attempt to appeal caused all lawyers to take another look. Thinking Colden confused and the justices right in their refusal to refer the case, Livingston and Smith withdrew from it, and solidarity among the members of the bar made it impossible for Cunningham to get new advocates. George Harrison, a notary, and Robert Waddell, a business partner, became his representatives.

Colden asked the attorney general, John Tabor Kempe, to review their application. Reporting on October 31, 1764, Kempe said: "I understood from your Honor that Mr. Waddel expects in Consequence of his Application, not only that the Record and the Judgment should be removed before you in Council, but also the Evidence given in the Cause, and contends that it is the Sense and meaning of the Instruction, that your Honor and the Council are on such Appeals to determine the Merits of the Case on the Matters of Fact, as well as on the Points of law . . . I do not see that it must be concluded his Majesty intended to constitute the Governor and Council a Court to try any Case de novo as far as relates to the finding of Facts."

In substantiation of his opinion, Kempe reminded Colden:

1. that it is the "function of the judges to judge law, of juries to judge facts";

2. that since the courts of common law examine witnesses viva voce, with no records kept, no evidence can be returned to the governor in council and the same witnesses are often not available;

3. a writ of error applies to matters of law only;

4. the royal instructions stipulate that the judges of the court from which an appeal comes who are also members of the council may give the council their reasons for their decision but not vote anew;

5. the judges of the supreme court said during an earlier term that only a writ of error was applicable to such cases.

Colden found this advice inacceptable. He had been ordered to forward an appeal to London if the charge was murder, and he was strongly inclined to permit one locally in lesser circumstances.

193

The old man's stubbornness was doubtless exacerbated by aware-
ness of the contempt in which the legal fraternity held his lack of
legal learning: William Smith, Jr., said that "vain and ambitious
of power he had always found himself in Council of less consequence
than some other law-members, for his opinions wanted weight, because he himself wanted information." A little later, the barbs the
triumvirate kept ready for accurate placement were displayed in
The New-York Gazette, when their column, signed "The Sentinel,"
proposed publishing an *Analogy between Physic and Law: or, An
Argument Proving That Every Doctor as Such Is An Able Lawyer.*
Colden's sensitivity is plain from a statement to the council that
combined defensiveness with desire to get a bit of his own back:

> The Law has not been my Study, but as, in my present situation, I
> am under necessity of Judgeing on a matter of Law of great importance,
> I have thought it my Duty to inform my self, in the best manner I have
> been able, that I may Judge by my own understanding, not by faith in
> others.

> If I cannot deliver my conceptions without a multiplicity of per-
> plexed Arguments & Verbose harangs, you will have just reason to think,
> that my Conceptions of the matter are not clear: for a Multiplicity of
> Words generally arises either from a perplexed imagination, or from
> a view to perplex others.

Week after week, at sessions from mid-November until mid-
January, the acting governor attempted to get the council to agree
to the propriety of Cunningham's appeal.

On November 19, he ordered the supreme court justices to appear before council, and there demanded that they permit it. Chief
Justice Horsmanden's written presentation of the court's thinking
spread the reasons for refusal on the record.

First, in order to show that due process had been fully observed
and that no basis for issuance of a writ of error existed, he carefully
reviewed the procedure by which the contested verdict was reached.
The case came before the supreme court in an action of trespass
for assault, battery, and wounding. Forsey asked for damages of
£5,000. Cunningham entered a plea of not guilty. The trial lasted
for twelve hours. No one on the special jury of freeholders was
struck at the defendant's request. As counsel, the plaintiff had the
services of three, the defendant of four, gentlemen. In such circumstances, the chief justice affirmed, "The Barr and Country must

unanimously declare that the Trial was Regular and Solemn; and conducted with the utmost fairness and Deliberation."

On the last day of the court term, Horsmanden continued, counsel for the defendant asked for a new trial. Since no complaint was offered except that the damages were excessive, "which did not appear to the Court to be well founded; and the Trespass being very atrocious, and the Proofs clear, the Court over-ruled the Motion." No writ of error was offered, so "the Verdict of the Jury must therefore be the sole cause of Complaint, and Relief against that is now Expected from your Honours."

The chief justice then affirmed that he regarded it as a misreading of Monckton's thirty-second instruction to conclude that it would admit the appeal; such a construction "supposes the Royal Order to Aim at altering the Ancient, and wholsome Laws of the Land." The common law of England recognizes that the finding of fact should be by the jury, the declaring of law by the judges. Errors of judges may be corrected, "But in all these Removes, the Verdict of the Jurors suffers no Re-Examination." All previous appeals have been in cases of error. Since the evidence given in the court of first instance was viva voce, "the Court above remains then uninformed of the Facts upon which the Verdict was given."

Adoption of a procedure permitting appeals of the sort now sought would in effect invalidate all initial verdicts for any substantial amount; it would open the floodgates to perjury and the discrediting of the testimony of previous witnesses; it would encourage litigiousness and result in intolerable expense; it would fully occupy the governor and council to the harm of other business.

None of his predecessors, Horsmanden concluded, had ever accepted a basis for an appeal like the present one. Therefore, he must refuse to support the defendant's application.

The acting governor stated that he disagreed.

Colden then asked George Harrison to summarize the notes he made when he accompanied Robert Waddell to Fort George on October 30 to present papers on behalf of Cunningham to the governor. Harrison reported that when they arrived the governor was urging Attorney General Kempe to find a means of bringing the case to council, with Kempe replying that he knew of no suitable writ. The acting governor then asked Kempe to explain the writ of inhibition or injunction. Kempe said that while the writ was acceptable in civil law courts, it did not exist in courts of common law. Colden then turned to his visitors and told them to attend him on the morrow. Harrison recalled him as saying "that for your part you was determined to do what you thought right, without regard to any Man."

Each of the other justices thereafter filed a brief corroborating his agreement with the chief justice's position. Justice Jones reiterated that a writ of certiorari cannot be used to re-open a jury's verdict. Justice Livingston's third point emphasized that: "Your Honours are incompetent judges of the merits of the verdict, because it is impossible to inform you of the grounds on which the jury founded it, since they sometimes are guided by what they know of their own knowledge; especially in what relates to the characters of the witnesses, of which they coming from the neighborhood, are the most proper judges."

On January 11, when those present were Colden, Watts, Walton, DeLancey, Reade, Morris, and the "earl of Stirling" (the son of James Alexander so styled himself during his prolonged effort to be recognized as the rightful heir to this title), the council voted against hearing the appeal. This time, the acting governor not only registered his dissent, but declared he would forward his objections to His Majesty's ministers.

Colden then developed a new basis for the council's jurisdiction —according to him, the council could and should act, not as an appellate tribunal, but as an avenue of access for a subject to his King. It was essential to the prerogative that appeals lie to the King. When the King in council, he argued, entertains a subject's request for redress of grievances, the entire situation is considered in all its aspects. If the King is willing to hear this type of cause, by what right were a colonial court and a colonial council blocking the path up which appeals go to the Crown?

On January 3, at the request of council members, Colden distributed copies of a long memorandum that he had read aloud to them in the previous day's session developing this view. The first question considered was: "Whether the King by the 32d. Article of his Instruction to his Captain General hath given an appeal in all Civil Courses from the Courts of Common Law to his Governor and Council and whether his Majesty has by his said Instruction constituted his Governor and Council a Court for the hearing and determining of such appeals?"

Arguing that this question required an affirmative answer, Colden

197

noted that the right of appeal to the King is specifically assured in the charters of some colonies—Massachusetts and Pennsylvania, among others—and that elsewhere—in Connecticut, for instance—it is assured by practice. In such instances, the whole case is considered. "The King has not given Authority to the Governer & Council of this Province to hear & determine on Writs of Error But has given them Authority to hear & determine on appeals their authority is therefor clearly confined to appeals by which the whole cause is brought before them in order that, if need be, it may be transmitted by further Appeal to the King in his Privy Council . . . The Laws of England abhor all arbitrary powers, & therefor the King has given his Subjects in the Colonies a Right to Appeal from every iniquitious verdict without depending on the good will or pleasure of any Judge. If no appeals were to be allowed from the Supreme Court of New York, the Court must become uncontroulable. However agreable this may be to Judges fond of Power, it must become terrible to the People under their jurisdiction."

Cunningham's representatives were quick on the cue. At the January 23 council meeting, they came in with a new request: "Your petitioner most humbly prays your honours will be pleased to allow an appeal to his Majesty in his privy Council."

The councilmen's reply was firm: "The Council apprehend the lieutenant governor and Council unauthorized to direct further upon the prayer of this petition."

For the third time, the acting governor signified his dissent, and wrote Whitehall suggesting that Horsmanden, Livingston, and Kempe be removed from office.

In mid-summer, though without authority, Cunningham's representatives dispatched a petition for a hearing directly to the King.

Through the next months, Colden awaited replies to his requests for guidance and Cunningham nursed hopes.

During the interval, the case was thoroughly canvassed in the public prints. Chief Justice Horsmanden's statement was published and circulated in various forms, both alone and accompanied by fervent commentary.

Week after week, the make-up of *The New-York Gazette* varied little. Page one steadily featured the Cunningham case, serializing Chief Justice Horsmanden's opinion, reproducing the briefs of other justices, providing accounts of council meetings. The Livingston-Smith-Scott triumvirate's column appeared frequently; on June 27, it inquired, "What can concern men so much, as whether they shall be happy, or miserable; free, or in chains?" Colden grumbled repeatedly about the "licentious abusive weekly printed paper."

Page two was as steadily devoted to the Stamp Act controversy. When this eventually pushed the Cunningham case off the front page, it was to stress the absence of trial by jury in cases of persons accused under this act and brought before the admiralty court at Halifax, Nova Scotia.

In October, the New York Assembly bracketed the colony's two grievances. It named a committee of correspondence and approved the call for the Stamp Act Congress. At the same time, it resolved that "an illegal attempt had been made, during the late Recess, to deprive the Inhabitants of this Colony of their antient and undoubted Right of Trials by their Peers, by bringing an Appeal from the Verdict of a Jury, in a cause between Forsey and Cunningham" and appointed a committee to consider what could be done.

While the assembly was in session, representatives from nine of the colonies arrived to take part in the congress at the town hall on Wall Street. The *Gazette* sported an elaborate new masthead beneath which a banner strip announced: "The United Voice of all His Majesty's *free* and *loyal* Subjects in America,—Liberty and Property, and No Stamps."

At its concluding session, the congress, after eloquent urging by Christopher Gadsden of South Carolina to "stand on the broad and common ground of natural and inherent rights," issued a declaration of rights of which the seventh and eighth articles read:

That trial by jury, is the inherent and invaluable right of every British subject in these colonies.

That the late act of Parliament entitled, an act for granting and applying certain stamp duties, and other duties, in the British colonies and plantations in America, &c., by imposing taxes on the inhabitants of these colonies, and the said act, and several other acts, by extending the jurisdiction of the courts of admiralty beyond its ancient limits, have a manifest tendency, to subvert the rights and liberties of the colonists.

The Stamp Act was scheduled to come into force on November 1. Governor Colden had indicated his willingness to receive New York's allotment of stamps and had appointed one James McEvers to distribute them. But sensing the mood of the community, McEvers appeared before council on August 30 and declined the appointment: "I find it will be attended with the greatest Risque of my Person and Fortune, to Attempt, & indeed impossible for me to execute the Office."

In the midst of these events, on October 9, Colden convened his council and informed members that word had come from London that they were to hear Cunningham's appeal. He sent a communication to Chief Justice Horsmanden that "all further proceedings be stay'd on the Verdict against Waddel Cunningham in Trespass and assault . . . until the merits be heard before the Governor in Council on the appeal," and instructed him that "all proceedings whereon the said Verdict was obtained to be brought before the Governor and Council." He also asked for assignment of counsel to the case.

On October 22, Waddell appeared before the court with Cunningham's petition. The justices called on him to show his authority to bring it. He offered a power of attorney. They held it to be insufficient. They informed Colden that ". . . this Court cannot comply with the prayer of the petitioner because no proper Writ to Authorize their sending up the Record has been brought, nor do they know of any Power they have to Assign Counsel to Transact business in a Court where they have no jurisdiction." Once more, the Cunningham case was at a standstill.

This last try added fuel to a bonfire that was already in preparation. The very day that the above exchange took place, the ship *Edward Davis,* with the stamps on board, hove in sight off New York harbor. Some twenty-five hundred expectant and indignant people descended to mill about the battery. The stamps were landed secretly under armed escort. The ship anchored for safety under cover of the cannons of Fort George.

In a carnival spirit, the night the Stamp Act became effective, the New York Sons of Liberty staged an elaborate riot. They stormed about the gate of Fort George, where Colden had taken refuge—his wife and children were given protection aboard a warship in the harbor. They wrecked the furnishings of the acting governor's town house and that of the commandant of troops for the New York area. They held a parade and burned an effigy of Colden accompanied by the devil.

The artist Montresor said of the effigy, "The Figure was made much to resemble the Person in was intended to represent. In his Hand was a stamped Paper, which he seemed to constrain the People

200

The RECONCILIATION between BRITANIA and her daughter AMERICA, 1782

to receive . . . By his Side hung, with a Boot in his Hand, the grand Deceiver of Mankind, seeming to urge him to Perseverance in the Course of Slavery."

Three weeks later, Sir Henry Moore arrived to take up the governorship, and Lieutenant Governor Colden ceased to be in a position to press his views. The common council of New York, in welcoming Moore, let it be known that "it affords us no small Pleasure, that by your Accession to the Government, we again have the Prospect, that the true State and Fidelity of his Subjects in this Colony, will be faithfully represented to the Throne."

At the same time, London's position on the Cunningham appeal was reversed. The board of trade sent dispatches to the new governor, dated November 26, informing him that after due consultation with lawyers of the Crown, they had reached the conclusion that appeals must be limited to examination of trial records for judicial error. They inclosed an altered form of the general instructions issued to Governor Monckton "restoring that Article to the same Words and Form, in which it stood in Your Predecessors in Government. . . ."

In December, the New York Assembly denounced Colden, complimented the supreme court and council members, and found the attempt to appeal a jury verdict "illegal, an attack upon the right of the subject, and a most dangerous and mischievous innovation, tending to encourage litigiousness and delay, promote perjury, prevent justice, subject the people to arbitrary power, and ruin the colony."

Up and down the coast, the history of New York's street-corner foray had over two and a half years notably reinforced existing convictions about the importance of judgment by one's peers. Very few of the bills of rights adopted by the new states failed to mention trial by jury.

New York's emergency first constitution was so hasty and incomplete that it did not include a bill of rights, but when a complete and systematic frame of government was provided for the state in 1821, Article 7, Section 2, read: "The trial by jury, in all cases in which it has been heretofore used, shall remain inviolable for ever. . . ."

CHAPTER IX

FREEDOM FROM EXTORTION

*The Bill of Rights: Excessive bail shall not be re-
quired, nor excessive fines imposed . . .*

BACKGROUND

The tenth section of the English Bill of Rights of 1689, from which these words were transferred to various American bills and eventually inserted in the federal Constitution as the Eighth Amendment, was part of a document warning the new monarchs, William and Mary, against repetition of the combination of administrative and judicial abuse that had disgraced the Restoration.

The articles of impeachment presented in the successive arraignments for high treason of the Earl of Clarendon, Charles II's lord chancellor, in 1663 and 1667, and Sir William Scroggs, his chief justice of King's bench in 1680, particularize the malfeasance of Stuart courtiers and courts. Lord Jeffreys of the Bloody Assizes, who subsequently enjoyed both of these offices under James II, did not come to trial only because he died in the Tower after arrest while attempting to flee the country in the wake of the King.

The accusations against Clarendon explain why Parliament determined to enact the Habeas Corpus Act of 1679. In various cases of the arrest of a political prisoner whose continued incarceration was desired by the court party, Clarendon's frequent violation of the right of the subject to be charged and to offer bail had made the Petition of Right an insufficient instrument. The lord chancellor was accused of having "procured divers of his majesty's subjects to be imprisoned against law, in remote lands, garrisons, and other places, thereby to prevent them from the benefit of the law, and to produce precedents for the imprisoning any other of his majesty's subjects in like manner."

Continuance of such abuse is documented in an exchange between counsel for Francis Jenkes, arrested in 1676 for having made a speech at the Guildhall deploring the recent decline of trade, and the Westminster court of quarter sessions. The court declined to grant Jenkes bail:

THE COURT: He is committed by a superior court, and we, who are an inferior one, cannot bail him.
COUNSEL: It is not the Court that commits, but the fact for which the party is committed, ought to direct you in bail. The

statute of H 7, hath no such exception in it; nor hath any other since put any such instrument upon you.

THE COURT: Would you have us bail him, after the lord chancellor and the lord chief justice have refused to grant a habeas corpus?

With regard to Scroggs's excesses, the committee of the House of Commons appointed to examine them listed the cases of bailable offences in which the lord chief justice had refused bail and "Resolved, . . . that the refusing of sufficient bail in these cases, wherein the persons committed were bailable by law, was illegal, and a high breach of the liberty of the subject."

Prolonged confinement in prison was a means of financial ruin practiced by Scroggs upon merchants and booksellers of whose views he disapproved. When Francis Smith, a bookseller, "tendered three sufficient citizens of London for his bail, alledging, inprisonment in his circumstances would be his utter ruin," the chief justice replied, "the citizens looked like sufficient persons, but he would take no bail."

To the friends of Jane Curtis, apprehended for selling *A Satire against Injustice,* which Scroggs took to be a libel on him, "tendering sufficient bail, and desiring him to have mercy upon her poverty and condition, he swore by the name of God she should go to prison, and he would shew her no more mercy, than they could expect from a wolf that came to devour them."

It was likewise charged that Scroggs, "together with the other judges of the said court, most notoriously departed from all rules of justice and equality, in the imposition of fines upon persons convicted of misdemeanors" and particularly, "in Term of Easter last past, did openly declare in the said court, in the case of one Jessup, who was convicted of publishing false news, and was then to be fined, That he would have regard to persons and their principles in imposing fines, and would set a fine of 500 £ on one person for the same offense for which he would not fine another 100 £ . . . Nor hath the said sir William Scroggs . . . had any regard to the nature of the offences, or the ability of the persons, in the imposing of fines; but have been manifestly partial and favorable to papists . . . and at the same time have most severely and grievously oppressed his majesty's protestant subjects, as would appear upon view of the several records of fines set in the said court."

Licentious Restoration administration, with courtier-courts con-niving, was clothed in majesty. In the 1760's, the North Carolina upcountry exhibited a homespun equivalent.

Orange County, North Carolina, was far upcountry indeed. By the flight of a knowledgeable crow, the county seat at Hillsborough was some 140 miles inland from the colonial capital at New Bern. A surefooted horse took more than a week to get there, in favorable weather.

The people who lived in this region between the Eno and Yadkin rivers below the Virginia line were mostly sturdy Scotch-Irish and Germans who had migrated south from their port of entry at Phila-delphia along the inland valleys. They knew next to nothing of the English planters of the coast. Even in religion the upcountry was different: on the coast, the Establishment was taken for granted; in the Piedmont, there was much dissent.

The livelihood of the upcountry folk was home grown, on the very edge of the money economy. A man was hard put to find the necessary money even to register the deed to his land; he was vulner-able to court judgments because that land was his sole means of livelihood. If something went wrong and he had to tide himself over by putting up this precarious patrimony as security for scarce and high-priced credit, he rarely extricated himself from the ensuing debt.

To the people of the red hills, the government was an alien force away on the seacoast—that part of it which lay overseas was in very truth beyond the horizon. Next to no sense of common pur-pose existed between the traders in the coastal communities, who in 1765-66 were engaged in an active, at times armed, and in the end successful struggle with the royal governor to prevent enforcement of the Stamp Act, and the subsistence farmers of the back country. The latter knew the coastal families as kin to men close to the governor and as over-represented electors whose assemblymen out-voted those of the hill people in making laws and laying taxes. From their kind of folk came both the officials who staffed the Piedmont courthouses and the judges and lawyers who applied the low-country law to the hill people's cases.

North Carolina's county officials, like those of other colonies, were unsalaried. They were paid under a fee system, receiving so much for each service performed. The legislature set the rates to be charged. But the legislature was far away, and from time to time it changed the schedules. In the upcountry, schooling was rare, and few among those who could read found the law intelligible. The situation was ripe for abuse, and most local officers plucked the ripeness while judges were tolerant. In 1769, ninety-nine signatories to a complaint against a county clerk specified: "his extortions are burdensome to all that fall in his power, as he takes double and sometimes treble his due. . . . And tho' it is true he purchased his office from Col. Frohock and gave to the amount of one hundred and fifty pounds for it yet it's unreasonable we should bear the expense by way of extortion."

Repeatedly, Whitehall instructed governors to restrain the exaction of exhorbitant fees. In 1764, Governor Arthur Dobbs ordered the legal rates to be posted in public offices. His successor, Governor William Tryon, reported to the Earl of Shelburne in 1767, "The sheriffs have embezzled more than half of the public money ordered to be raised and collected by them," and issued a proclamation against malpractice. But proclamations were not followed by prosecutions in court.

In the Regulator Movement, upcountry citizens attempted to take matters into their own hands.

EDMUND FANNING.

THE CASE

> When Fanning first to Orange came
> He looked both pale and wan
> An old patched coat upon his back,
> An old mare he rode on.
>
> Both man and mare warn't worth five pounds
> As I've been told;
> But by his civil robberies
> He's laced his coat with gold.

Colonel Edmund Fanning, clerk of Orange County, North Carolina, had indeed done himself very well. Born on Long Island and educated at Yale, he held office simultaneously in North Carolina and as His Majesty's surveyor general for New York. The last line of the ditty about this young-man-on-the-make was accurate: his order on a Philadelphia merchant for lace for a jacket and "some double Gold lace for a Hat" still exists.

The term "Regulators" was first used by upcountrymen in South Carolina whose grievance was the legislature's failure to provide the western settlements with any local government whatsoever. In the mid-sixties it was borrowed by North Carolina upcountrymen determined to regularize the procedures of the kind of local government they had been given. Its "notorious and intolerable abuses" were denounced in June 1765 by a schoolmaster of Nutbush community, in *An Address to the People*. In August 1766, a group of Regulators was organized in Orange County. *Regulator Advertisement Number 1* called for a meeting to ascertain the extent of the abuses and to select delegates to the November meeting of the colony's general court, where their representative read a statement of their grievances and urged its consideration.

Various other formal complaints were prepared. Simultaneously circulated was a parable written by Hermon Husband. Husband started life in Maryland and ended it in Pennsylvania, but during the Regulator activity he owned one of the better farms in the Carolina upcountry. Spiritually as well as physically he was a wanderer: raised an Anglican, he became first a Presbyterian and

209

then a Quaker—during his Carolina days, he was a Quaker. For that reason he took no part in Regulator violence, but he was privy to their inmost councils, and his homely pen, over a period of years, expressed the illiterate, inchoate emotion of men who used a fist more easily than quill.

His parable on the present discontents announced:

A poor man gives his judgment bond for five Pounds; which bond is by the creditor thrown into Court. The clerk of the county has to enter it on the docket, and issue execution, the work of one long minute, for which the poor man has to pay him the trifling sum of forty-one shillings and five-pence. The clerk, in consideration of his being a poor man, takes it out in work, at eighteen pence a day. The poor man works some more than twenty-seven days to pay for this one minute's writing.

Well, the poor man reflects thus: At this rate, when shall I get to labor for my family! I have a wife and a parcel of small children suffering at home, and here I have lost a whole month, and I don't know for what, for my merchant or creditor is as far from being paid as ever. However, I will go home now and try to do what I can. Stay, neighbor, you have not half done yet, there is a damn'd lawyer's mouth to stop yet, for you empowered him to confess that you owed this five Pounds and you have thirty shillings to pay him for that, or go work nineteen days more; and then you must work as long for the Sheriff for his trouble, and then you may go home and see your horses and cows sold, and all your personal estate, for one tenth of the value to pay off your merchant; and lastly, if the debt is so great that all your personal estate will not do to raise the money, then your lands the same way, to satisfy these accursed catterpillars, that will eat out the very bowels of our commonwealth, if they are not pulled down from their nests in a short time . . . But as these practices are contrary to law, it is our duty to put a stop to them before they quite ruin our country, and before we become willing slaves to these lawless wretches and hug our chains of bondage, and remain contented under these accumulated calamities.

I believe there are few of you who have not felt the weight of these iron fists. And I hope there are none of you but will lend a hand towards bringing about this necessary work, (viz: a reformation) and in order to bring it about effectually, we must proceed with circumspection, not fearful, but careful.

First, let us be careful to keep sober—do nothing rashly—but act with deliberation.

Secondly, let us do nothing against the known established laws of

our land that we appear not as a faction endeavoring to subvert the laws and overturn the system of our government. But let us take care to appear what we really are, free subjects by birth, endeavoring to recover our lost native rights, and to bring them down to the standard of our law.

The social and political gap between rich and poor in the colony, exposed in the vernacular of Husband's parable, was vividly witnessed by the record of the ensuing assembly. Statements of the grievances of the Piedmont lie side by side with a motion, that numbered Edmund Fanning among its sponsors, approving Governor Tryon's project for the erection of a new capital building to overlook the New Bern harbor.

The plans for this edifice were drawn by John Hawks, architect and accountant, who had come with Tryon from England. There, he had been in the service of Stiff Leadbetter of Eton, who designed Nuneham Courtenay for the first Earl Harcourt, became surveyor of St. Paul's in 1756, and constructed Oxford's Radcliffe Infirmary three years later.

Up and down the coast, from Boston to Charleston, imposing public buildings had recently risen. Just to the north, Virginia boasted its governor's palace, repaired and enlarged at midcentury, and its house of burgesses, rebuilt after the fire of 1747. To the south, South Carolina had completed its expensive new state house.

211

Hawks fell in with Governor Tryon's desire to rival these neighbors, producing plans on a scale that raised eyebrows even among the planters of the coast. A three-story brick structure, forming the central unit of the design, provided suitable residence accommodations for the governor and his family on the upper floors and on the ground floor spacious official meeting places for the governor in council and the assembly, a state reception room and dining hall, and quarters for the officers of the guard. On the landward side, the formal entrance was flanked to the right and left by two-story buildings, one housing kitchens and offices, the other stabling for the official coach and horses.

Towards erection of this structure, the Capital Act of 1766 voted £5,000. Initially, the money was to be drawn from an appropriation previously designated for building schoolhouses and purchasing glebes, with repayment to this fund by collection of a new impost of tuppence a gallon on alcoholic beverages imported from any source other than Britain and a poll tax of eightpence, levied on all inhabitants alike during each of the next two years. But the £5,000 proved to be only a third of the sum required. The next assembly voted £10,000 more, to be raised by a further poll tax of two shillings annually for the next three years.

The building was begun in 1766, completed in 1770. Governor Tryon's meticulous inventory shows the similarity of the household effects with which he furnished the palace to those of English country houses such as that of his grandmother, Lady Ferrers, on the Thames at Twickenham—and their contrast to the simple chattels of the man with the hoe in the red hills on whom was levied a pro rata share of the cost of the new magnificence.

In 1768, thirty citizens of Orange and Rowan counties again warned the assembly of the combined effect of increased taxes and abuse of the fee system: "For God's sake Gentlemen be not negligent or unconcerned in an affair of such importance. On your breath depends the Ruin or Prosperity of thousands of Families, & tho' to Gentleman Rowling in affluence, a few shillings per man, may seem triffling yet to Poor people Who must have their Bed and Bed Clothes, yea their Wives Petticoats taken and sold to defray these charges, how Tremendious judge ye must be the consequences . . ."

But officials at the capital dallied while time was running out. By now the Regulators had achieved considerable organization. Their *Advertisement Number 4* advanced a five-point program:

1. pay no taxes unless satisfied they are legal;
2. pay no fees higher than the law allows unless absolutely obliged to do so; and then to "shew a dislike to it & bear open testimony against it";
3. attend meetings;
4. contribute to expenses as able;
5. in the organization, submit to majority rule.

During April, in Hillsborough, the horse and saddle of a Regulator were distrained for nonpayment of taxes. Some seventy armed Regulators rode into town, fired into the roof of Colonel Fanning's house, and took the horse back.

The singing of ballads brought from the old country frequently enlivened upcountry weddings and rural festivities; recently, a schoolmaster named Rednap Howell had begun to set current political words to the old tunes. The Hillsborough incident was shortly described in the form of a dialogue between two county officials, Frank (Francis Nash) and Ned (Edmund Fanning), discussing Hermon Husband and James Hunter:

> Who would have thought Harmon, that hum drum old fox
> Who looks so bemeaning with his towsled locks,
> Would have had resolution to stand to the tack;
> Alas, my dear Ned, our case is quite black.
>
> And who would have thought Hunter, so seemingly mild,
> Would have been so gigantic, mischievous and wile,
> I tho't him a fool, and I took him for one;
> Alas my dear Frank, our cause is undone.
>
> Like Turkish Bashaws they bear absolute sway;
> Alas my dear Frank, we must all run away.

Fanning informed the governor that the country is "the very nest and bosom of rioting and rebellion" and deplored that officers like himself should be "Arraigned at the Bar of their Shallow Understanding and to be punished and regulated at their Will." Tryon issued two proclamations: one ordered the Regulators to disband; the other instructed the militia of seven counties to be ready to march to Fanning's aid.

214

Regulator Advertisement Number 11, of May 21, bearing five hundred signatures, reaffirmed grievances while deploring the firing into Fanning's house. Howell and Hunter went to Brunswick to present this document to the governor in person. Tryon urged them to give up the name of "Regulators," pay their taxes, and cease molesting officers. At the same time he directed the attorney general of the colony to prosecute extortionists and warn officials and lawyers to keep their fees within the law.

Two prosecutions were scheduled for trial at the September term of the superior court at the capital.

At the previous September's session of the superior court at Hillsborough, "Edmund Fanning Register of Orange County duly appointed and qualified, was found guilty of Extortion in his office as Register for taking 6s on ye Deed No. 13." Since this case could become a precedent, advice was sought from London on a series of questions, of which the fourth was: "Whether a Register may be Indicted and punished as an Extortioner for taking more by colour of his office than he is legally entitled to, such taking happening thro' mistake either of the sum taken, or the sum which might lawfully be taken."

The Inner Temple authority to whom the matter was referred thought Fanning entitled to more than one fee on the grounds that the deed itself was one document and the receipt for it another. His suggestion that Fanning move for a new trial had been followed.

Hermon Husband and William Butler, arrested and jailed for "inciting the populace to rebellion," were to stand trial at the same session.

Governor Tryon, after an unsuccessful effort to get twelve Regulator leaders to go bond that no rescue of Husband and Butler would be attempted, called out the militia of four counties near New Bern, at a cost of £4,844 19s. 3d., to protect the court. The presiding judge was Maurice Moore, a man who initially was sympathetic to the Regulators' grievances, then turned against them because of their excesses, but ended the affair outraged at Tryon's conduct.

Husband was acquitted; Butler fined £50 and given six months in jail; two others were each sentenced to a fine of £25 and three months in jail. (At the close of term, the governor released the prisoners and suspended their fines.) On the rehearing of his case, Fanning was found guilty of taking 6s. when his statutory fee was

2*s*. 8*d*. and fined a penny and costs.

Fanning resigned as county clerk, but through the governor's influence the town of Hillsborough was made an independent borough, and at the 1769 elections he was voted its delegate to the assembly. The surrounding countryside (Orange, Granville, Anson, and Halifax counties) chose solidly Regulator slates, with Husband among the delegates. That fall Anson County's petition to the assembly urged that "Dr. Franklin or some other known patriot be appointed Agent, to represent the unhappy state of this Province to His Majesty, and to solicit the several boards in England."

Writing to the Earl of Hillsborough on January 8, 1770, Governor Tryon deplored the turn of events: "Confidence, my lord, that delicate polish in public transactions, has received an ugly scratch, and I fear we have no artists here who can restore it to its original perfection. . . ."

Continuing in a more cheerful vein, he notes that the palace is about completed—he will shortly submit a cost statement. He suggests that he would like to move on to new advancement: "As soon as that business is accomplished I greatly wish to obtain his Majesty's leave of absence from the province (unless my services could be acceptable to his Majesty in the government of New York.) . . ."

Confidence was indeed far gone. During the summer, 174 Orange County citizens petitioned the judges of the superior court to take cognizance of local extortions: "though they attempt to make you believe the charge against them for exacting 4d., 6d., & a shilling extraordinary from ignorant Men Women and in remote neighbourhoods to be a false charge yet it is . . . notoriously known to be the truth by hundreds of people from whom and among whom they exacted it . . ."

Too many people, by this time, believed that words had failed. On Monday and Tuesday, September 24 and 25, a serious riot took place in Hillsborough.

Reporting to Governor Tryon five days later, Judge Richard Henderson called it "The most horrid and audacious insult to Government, perpetrated with such circumstances of cruelty and madness as (I believe) scarcely has been equalled at any time." A Regulator spokesman, Jeremiah Fields, laconically said they thought they couldn't get justice as things were, so would get it their own way.

The riot occurred at the time of the fall meeting of the superior court. The term began uneventfully on Saturday, September 22, Judge Henderson presiding. Adam and Henry Whitsett appeared and took the oaths prescribed for naturalization. Court adjourned until Monday.

Monday morning, some 150 Regulators surged into town, the first wave of a crowd that swelled and seethed for two days. About eleven o'clock, upcountrymen funneled into the courthouse and packed it until not another man and musket could stand. On the Regulators' behalf, Fields accused the court of injustice at its previous term.

Judge Henderson tried to pacify the courtroom. After about half an hour's discussion, the Regulators started to withdraw. As they were filing out of the courthouse, one of the town's attorneys approached it. They set upon him. He escaped into a nearby warehouse.

According to the judge's account, the crowd took Colonel Fanning "off the bench where he had retired for protection and assistance and with hideous shouts of barbarian cruelty dragged him by the heels out of doors," where he, "by a manly exertion miraculously broke holt and fortunately jumped into a door that saved him from immediate dissolution." A number of other members of the courthouse staff, including the clerk, were horsewhipped. Sundry additional gentlemen "timorously made their escape or would have shared the same fate."

Fields then demanded that the judge continue to hold court, trying the cases of indicted Regulator leaders with no lawyers present and with a jury drawn from the Regulators. Sparring for time, Judge Henderson adjourned court until the following morning at ten. After dark, he "took advantage of the night & made his escape, and the Court adjourned . . ."

The crowd spent Tuesday milling around the town, breaking windows. Colonel Fanning's house was ransacked from attic to cellar with a thoroughness that included his personal clothing upstairs, his furniture, papers, and silver downstairs, and the liquor in his cellar.

While this was going on, Regulators got hold of the docket that had been prepared for use of the court. Three of its four columns were already filled, showing the names of the plaintiffs and defendants, the numbers of the cases, the basis of the actions. The fourth column was left blank for entry of judgment.

Isaiah Hogan	Case	Vagant heyn the disease
Norman Howard	21	
Ezekiel Barringfeild		Nonsuit it them by our
James Court	22	for Howell as & me McDowl
Michael Watson		All Haynit's no Rogues
David Harris	23	
John Edward	Case	James Thorne
Philip Edward	24	Non Comonts
Thomas Hammon	Case	Ref Pud is ruled for
William Dunnagan	24	the Med Court

Swarming back into courtroom, document in hand, the crowd held a mock court. They put an effigy on the bench as judge. Fields took the clerk's place. Case after case, they proceeded to clear the docket.

In the empty column, they entered their own judgments.

On December 5, Governor Tryon's state of the province address to the council and assembly contained a recommendation that troops be raised to "march into the settlements of those Insurgents," since if these men "who have broken through all the bounds of human society, and trampled under foot the Laws of their Country, be allowed to shelter themselves under those Laws, the situation of this Country would be deplorable indeed; Social Liberty must then yield to brutal licentiousness . . ."

In the same address, he made his "grateful acknowledgements to the Country" for "A Palace that is a public ornament and credit to the Colony, as well as an honor to British America."

On the twentieth, the assembly expelled Hermon Husband from his seat as representative of Orange County, on the ground that he was a leader of the Regulators, the actual author of a "false Malicious and seditious Libel" in a letter to Judge Moore signed by James Hunter and published in *The North-Carolina Gazette* six days previously, and a man unworthy of a seat in the assembly because of his conduct alike in the house and in the community generally.

Tidewater members, however, feared the result of his return to the back country. So—without a mittimus—he was taken and committed to prison in New Bern to await the next sitting of the superior court.

The terror inspired by the Regulators upcountry, even though the Fanning faction had founded a counter-organization of "Redressors" there, made witnesses for indictment of participants in the September riot hard to come by. None could be found in time for the February court. After the governor sent up a military guard to afford protection, fifteen depositions were assembled and some fifty true bills against insurgents found.

Husband was conspicuously not included. New Bern had become thoroughly uneasy at his continued presence in its jail; a march on the capital to free him was more than half-expected. The Craven County grand jury saw its duty: the prisoner was released.

An intercepted letter from Rednap Howell to James Hunter,

written from Halifax on February 16, substantiated the accuracy of the capital's worry:

> . . . on my arrival here I had certain information that Herman was at liberty; so that I found it needless to raise the Country but I am satisfied it would be easily done in occasion required, however I have animated the people here to join the Regulators; on Saturday come 2 weeks they are to have a meeting for the purpose. If it once takes a start here it will run into the neighboring Counties of Edgecomb, Bute and Northampton, and this will undoubtedly facilitate justice to poor Carolina."

During January, the assembly had transliterated its fears into the Johnstone Riot Act. This statute provided that prosecutions for riots might take place in courts located elsewhere than where the riot occurred. It declared that persons cited who did not surrender within a given time should become outlaws—"it shall be lawful for any one to kill and destroy such offender and his lands and chattels shall be confiscated to the King for the use of Government." And it empowered the governor to suppress the Regulators by military force.

When this law was forwarded to London, British officials in Whitehall found it outrageous. They sent back word that while in view of the current disturbances they would not disallow it, the section on outlawry must not be included in any subsequent enactment: "said clause appears to US to be irreconcilable with the principles of the constitution, full of danger in its operation, and unfit for any part of the British Empire."

The Regulators, likewise outraged, declared Fanning an outlaw to be killed on sight, forbade court sessions, and threatened to kill all lawyers and judges. One deponent, who claimed he was forcibly detained in the Regulator camp, testified to hearing it said that "If they had not made that act, we might have suffered some of them to live. A Riotous Act! There never was any such Act in the laws of England, or any other Country but France, they brought it from France and they'll bring the Inquisition next."

Impressed, officials of county courthouses made arrangements to refund their illegal takings; in Rowan County, headed by Colonel Frohock, they made a collective agreement for "all such . . . sums of money as we or our Deputies have taken through inadvertence or otherwise over and above what we severally ought to have taken."

Writing to inform the governor of their action, Colonel Frohock said, "as the Spirit of sedition has been propagated with much industry among the lower class of Inhabitants here who are loud in their clamors against the officers, We flatter ourselves the Measures we have taken will be approved of and acceptable to your Excellency. . . ."

Governor Tryon's intention to quit the province had been made known to the legislature and was suitably regretted by both houses in their reply to his opening speech in January. His sought-for appointment as governor of New York had actually received royal approval in early December, though the commission did not arrive in Carolina until spring. But before leaving the colony he was determined to settle scores with the Regulators.

He called for a special court session in Hillsborough in May— the March meeting having been omitted because of the unrest— ordered the militia out to protect it, and himself led the approach of the troops. Reporting his plan of operation to Whitehall he declared, "I cheerfully offer my zealous services, relying that the motive of this conduct will be favorably accepted by my most gracious Sovereign."

Though Regulators intercepted a consignment of powder on its way up from Charleston on May 16, Tryon and his militia arrived in good order and camped at Great Alamance Creek (near today's Burlington). The governor had at his disposal some 1,450 men. A mile or so away were the Regulators, numbered—by conflicting accounts—between 2,000 and 4,000.

The Regulators asked for a parley. The governor refused, allowing them an hour in which to lay down their arms.

At the end of that time (one correspondent says sooner), he ordered the cannon fired. The majority of Regulators were unfamiliar with artillery. Overawed, they broke ranks and fled, though some three hundred stood and returned musket fire as long as their ammunition held out.

Two hours later, as the governor subsequently noted in his order book of the campaign, he had achieved "a Signal and Glorious Victory . . . over Obstinate & Infatuated Rebels . . . His Excellency Sympathizes with the Loyalists for the Brave Men that Fell & Suffered in the Action. But when he Reflects that the fate of the Constitution Depended on the Success of the Day & the Important Service thereby Rendered to their King & Country, He considers

221

this Loss tho' at Present the cause of Affliction to their Relations & Friends as a Monument of Lasting Glory & honour to Themselves & Familys."

Next day, Tryon hanged one prisoner in camp without formalities of any kind. He was a man named James Few at whom Fanning pointed the finger as having taken part in the sack of his house. Most of these present regarded him as deranged: a religious fanatic, he declared himself appointed to bring justice to the world, beginning with North Carolina.

The governor offered a reward of £100 and one thousand acres of land for the delivery of Husband, Hunter, Butler, and Howell, dead or alive, at the new camp he had established on Husband's farm. He sent troops to lay waste the holdings of the others who had been declared outlaws. Later, their properties were put up for sale.

Husband and Howell escaped and left the colony. The former, unwilling as a Quaker to take part in bloodshed, is said to have turned his horse's head northward from Alamance when he saw that fighting was unavoidable.

At the same time, Tryon offered pardon to all, except those outlawed or currently held prisoner, who would come into camp, lay down their arms, take an oath of allegiance, and promise to pay all taxes due. The time limit on this offer was extended more than once; over the next months he and his successors pardoned some 6,500 former members of the Regulator organization.

Beginning on May 30, court sat in Hillsborough. On June 20, Tryon announced the arrival of his commission as governor of New York and left. During this interval, twelve Regulators were tried for treason and, on June 19, six of them were hanged.

Conflicting accounts carried the news in all directions. With Husband and Hunter gone, Benjamin Merrill, one of the men hanged, became the Regulators' final hero. Governor Tryon's report of his death, sent to Whitehall from New York whither Fanning followed to become his private secretary, attested that Merrill "died under a thorough conviction of his crime and the justice of his sentence and addressed himself to the spectators to take warning by his suffering."

Other versions of the scene circulated in the colonies. In July, *The Boston Gazette* printed an alleged verbatim transcript of how Merrill was condemned. When the chief justice passed sentence, he concluded in the following manner: "I must now close my afflicting Duty, by pronouncing upon you the awful Sentence of the Law; which is, that you Benjamin Merrill, be carried to the Place from whence you came, that you be drawn from thence to the Place of Execution, where you are to be hanged by the Neck; that you be cut down while yet alive, that your Bowels be taken out and burnt before your Face, that your Head be cut off, your Body divided into Four Quarters, and this to be at his Majesty's Disposal; and the Lord have Mercy on your Soul." In August, it reproduced a long letter from North Carolina and added the information "that Captain Benjamin Merrill, who was lately executed for high Treason in opposing the Career of Governor Tryon, died in the most heroic Manner, his children being around him and animating him at the Place of his Execution."

The Pennsylvania Journal of October 3 carried a sympathetic history of the Regulator movement. *The Virginia Gazette* of November 7 featured a sophisticated open letter to Governor Tryon in New York, possibly by Judge Moore, signed "Atticus," indicting and satirizing his conduct in the affair. The Riot Act, it affirmed, "was equally violative of a sacred right, every British subject is entitled to, of being tried by his neighbors, and a positive law of the province you yourself had ratified." As to the military campaign, "Your active and gallant behaviour, in extinguishing the flame you yourself had kindled, does you great honor . . . It seems difficult to determine, Sir, whether your Excellence is more to be admired for your skill in creating the cause, or your bravery in suppressing the effect." As to the subsequent punishments, "Your conduct to others after your success, whether it respected person or property, was as lawless as it was unnecessarily expensive to the Colony."

The newspaper stories were then supplemented by two consecutive accounts of the entire history of the Regulation. Hermon Husband wrote an *Impartial Relation of the first rise and Cause of the recent difficulties in Publick Affairs in the Province of North Carolina and of the Past Tumults and Riots that lately happened in that province.* It was published in Boston in 1770. The next year, also in Boston, another tract, signed "Regulus" though presumably by him, *A Fan for Fanning and a Touch-stone to Tryon,* was issued serially, with its availability advertised in *The Massachusetts Spy.*

The *Spy* continued to print letters on the Regulators: its issue of June 27, 1771, contained a castigation of Tryon in a letter by

"Leonidas." When a copy made its way south, a public meeting in New Bern adopted a resolution that it be "publicly burnt under the gallows by the common hangman." According to *The Boston Gazette,* an effigy of the *Spy's* printer was burnt at the same time.

So in 1770-71, recent events in the North Carolina upcountry were on men's minds up and down the Atlantic coast.

After Alamance, a large number of Regulator families picked up and moved to Tennessee, putting the mountains between them and Carolina tidewater. Five years later, among those migrants from the upcountry to whom an occasional copy of *The North-Carolina Gazette* found its way westward and among the many more North Carolinians who had lived through these Regulator times without taking direct part in their cause, the Declaration of Rights adopted by the colonial convention at Halifax on December 18, 1776, must have wakened memories. The key word was contained in the phrasing of Article II: "That the People of this State ought to have the sole and exclusive Right of regulating the internal Government and Police thereof."

And Article X repeated: "That excessive Bail should not be required, nor excessive Fines imposed, nor cruel and unusual Punishment inflicted."

NOTE ON SOURCES

NOTE ON SOURCES

U sually, to ask a journalist to name sources is to use fighting words. The mildest of conventional retorts is: "Never you mind how I got it. Here's my story, and I'll stand by it. You'll see."

But this time, my sources are no longer living. They cannot deny me further interviews because I reveal that we have been in touch. And though few reporters will give sources on demand, voluntary name-dropping is perhaps their most common occupational disease. I shall enjoy it.

Pursuit of data for the stories here presented afforded a further unusual pleasure. Most reporters, when writing about living characters, feel it necessary to engage in blandishment well beyond the bounds of sincerity when approaching the hard-bitten guardians of outer offices. But on this assignment, librarian after librarian, in manuscript collections, rare-book rooms, law divisions, print sections, general reference rooms, and in headquarters of historical associations, has given me entree with courtesy, alacrity, and enthusiasm. They have even left me unattended beside the personal files of the man whose views I was seeking. My appreciation, hereby expressed, has the genuineness of surprise.

In many ways, however, the working conditions of reporting on other centuries proved extraordinarily familiar. With the *Dictionary of American Biography* at my elbow, I had compact, quick references comparable to those in *Who's Who* or the *Congressional Directory* and with the advantage of bibliography in case of need to go further.

As to morgues, however, the picture files of the eighteenth century are regrettably selective. The pre-Revolutionary establishment sat for its portrait in satisfying numbers—though some households had unfortunate fires. But the remaining evidence of those whom they regarded as trouble-makers is largely confined to the men who became the post-Revolutionary establishment. The cartoons and caricatures that appeared in increasing numbers as the Revolution came nearer provide some redress of the balance; it is on these that I have placed chief reliance for illustrations. Much of the best of

228

both is assembled in the earlier sections of James Truslow Adams, *Album of American History*; Dumas Malone, *Story of the Declaration of Independence*; Marshall Davidson, *Life in America*; and in *American Processional, 1492-1900,* the book made from the exhibition at the Corcoran Gallery, Washington, D. C., under the auspices of the U.S. National Capital Sesquicentennial Commission. Further material is contained in Charles K. Bolton, *Portraits of the Founders*; the catalogue of the loan exhibition of *One Hundred Colonial Portraits* at the Boston Museum of Fine Arts in 1930; and the catalogue of *Portraits of the Signers and Deputies to the Convention of 1787 and Signers of the Declaration of Independence* at the Corcoran Gallery in 1937-38.

GENERAL REFERENCES

Beginning early in the nineteenth century, and intensively in recent years, historians, political scientists, and lawyers have assembled collections of public and private documents of the pre-Revolutionary period: among earlier works, Peter Force, *Tracts and Other Papers Relating Principally to the Origin, Settlement and Progress of the Colonies in North America,* and Hezekiah Niles, *Principles and Acts of the Revolution in America.* Among more recent books are: Charles McLean Andrews, *Narratives of the Insurrections, 1675-1690*; Andrew C. McLaughlin, William E. Dodd, Marcus N. Jernegan, and Arthur P. Scott, *Source Problems in United States History;* Samuel E. Morison, *Sources and Documents Illustrating the American Revolution, 1764-1788*; William MacDonald, *Select Charters and Other Documents Illustrative of American History 1606-1775*; and Henry Steele Commager, *Documents of American History.*

The *Calendar of State Papers, Colonial, America and West Indies, 1675-76* of the British Record Office and *American Colonial Documents to 1776,* edited by Merrill Jensen as Vol. IX of *English Historical Documents* are indispensable. Thomas Bayly Howell, *A Complete Collection of State Trials and Proceedings for High Treason and Other Crimes and Misdemeanors from the Earliest Period to the Year 1783* reports English cases of pertinence; Sir William Blackstone, *Commentaries on the Laws of England* present British legal philosophy of the mid-eighteenth century; William S. Holdsworth, *History of English Law* is a comprehensive review; Roscoe

Pound, *The Development of Constitutional Guarantees of Liberty* develops the relation between British background and American assertions of right. For a combination of British legal developments and texts and American bills of rights, resolutions of colonial congresses, and state constitutions, most helpful of all is the American Bar Foundation's *Sources of Our Liberties,* prepared by Richard L. Perry and John C. Cooper.

General discussion of the events of the period, with many citations, include Charles H. Van Tyne, *Causes of the War of Independence*; Richard R. Morris, *Era of the American Revolution*; Herbert L. Osgood, *American Colonies in the 18th Century*; and John C. Miller, *Origins of the American Revolution.*

First-hand quotes are available from the papers of the major colonial statesmen, whose definitive publication is in most cases well along; quotes transmitted by second persons are contained in the biographies written by the first post-Revolutionary generation, whose authors frequently based their texts on eyewitness accounts set down by their elders at their request, and modern lives prepared with the advantage of greater documentation and perspective.

The broadsides of political ballads that were pasted up on walls, the cartoons sold in bookshops, and above all the dispatches, editorials, and communications to the editor published in the weekly press of the several colonies indicate the news that induced a mutual sense of urgency by communication from capital to capital. Nuggets await the prospector in the Library of Congress, both in the newspaper files of the Rare Book Room, with its catalogue of surviving copies of colonial papers, and in the boxes of the Prints Division, from which many of the illustrations of this book are taken. The print collections of the New York Public Library are likewise highly rewarding.

Beyond these general sources, a particular bibliography clusters around each of the cases that constitute the chapters of this book. For convenience, these references are presented in groups directly related to the text that they support.

CHAPTER I

GENERAL REFERENCES

Burk, John Daly. *The History of Virginia from its first Settlement to the Commencement of the Revolution.* Petersburg, 1804-5.

Foote, William Henry. *Sketches of Virginia, Historical and Biographical.* Philadelphia, 1850-55.

Gewehr, Wesley M. *The Great Awakening in Virginia, 1740-90.* Durham, 1930.

James, Charles F. *Documentary History of the Struggle for Religious Liberty in Virginia.* Lynchburg, 1900.

Johnson, Thomas Cary. *Virginia Presbyterianism and Religious Liberty in Colonial and Revolutionary Times.* Richmond, 1907.

Little, Lewis Peyton. *Imprisoned Preachers and Religious Liberty in Virginia.* Lynchburg, 1938.

Mecklin, John M. *The Story of American Dissent.* New York, 1934.

Semple, Robert Baylor. *A History of the Rise and Progress of the Baptists in Virginia.* Richmond, 1894.

Thom, William Taylor. *The Struggle for Religious Freedom in Virginia: the Baptists.* ("The Johns Hopkins University Studies," Vol. XVIII, Nos. 10-12.) Baltimore, 1900.

The paragraph on toleration is from Andrew Hamilton's speech on retirement from the Pennsylvania speakership, reproduced in the *Pennsylvania Magazine of History,* Vol. 16, pp. 1-27. *Memoirs of the Life of the Rev. George Whitefield, M.A.,* compiled by the Reverend John Gillies, New York, 1774, and his own collected *Discourses,* London, 1739, preserve the Churchillian periods of his sermons; *The Works of the Rev. George Whitefield,* London, 1771-72, contains a sketch of his plan for an orphanage, not dissimilar to Jefferson's plans for the University of Virginia. *A Continuation of the Reverend Mr. Whitefield's Journal from his Embarking after the Embargo to His Arrival at Savannah in Georgia,* London, 1740, contains the diary of his trip through Virginia in 1739. Luke Tyerman, *Life of the Rev. George Whitefield,* London, 1876-77, contains the quote from David Garrick; the *Dictionary of American Biography,* the account of Whitefield's reception in Charleston; Joseph Belcher, *George Whitefield, a Biography,* New York, 1857, his estimate of his own effectiveness. Benjamin Franklin, on the same subject, is found in his *Autobiography,* New York, 1849.

The bishop of London's comment on Virginia's pastors is in James (listed above); Commissary Dawson's letter to the bishop of July 27, 1750, expressing concern for the state of Virginia, may be found in the Fulham Papers in the Manuscript Division of the Library of Congress.

The Virginia laws governing the practice of religion are reproduced in the first two volumes of William Waller Hening, ed., *Statutes at Large* . . . , Richmond, 1809-23, the third volume of Force's *Tracts* (see p. 229, above), and Foote's *Sketches*. Semple and Mecklin discuss the Roan case.

William Wirt, *Sketches of the Life and Character of Patrick Henry*, 3rd ed. Philadelphia, 1818, and Robert Douthatt Meade, *Patrick Henry: Patriot in the Making*, Vol. I, Philadelphia, 1957, report Mrs. Henry's training of the young Patrick; his Uncle Patrick's letters on the Hanover Dissenters are reproduced in the *William and Mary Quarterly*, second series, Vol. I, p. 261 *et passim*. The story of soil erosion and dissent comes from Robert Beverly, *The History and Present State of Virginia*, ed. by Louis B. Wright, Chapel Hill, 1947.

Shubal Stearns's missionary project is described in Thom; the beginning of Baptist activities in Spotsylvania and nearby Virginia counties is found in Little and Semple and in Morgan Edwards MSS "Notes" and "Materials Toward a History of the Baptists in the Province of Virginia," transcribed by the Virginia Baptist Historical Society in 1941. *The Virginia Gazette's* recipe for an Anabaptist preacher was in its issue of October 31, 1771.

The Spotsylvania *Order Book, 1768-1771* notes the disposition of Waller and Craig's first trial. James Ireland, *Life of the Rev. James Ireland*, Winchester, 1819, dictated when he was an old man, colorfully details the indignities to which religious prisoners were subjected.

The Middlesex County case of 1771 is described in the general sources above, but the originals of the court records, the petitions to the court, and the letter of Waller from prison in Urbanna are preserved in the library of the Virginia Baptist Historical Society in Richmond, Virginia; the open letter of "Timoleon" to the prisoners was published in *The Virginia Gazette* of August 22, 1771.

The Chesterfield wall is described by Morgan Edwards and in James Barnett Taylor, *Virginia Baptist Ministers*, New York, 1860, Vol. I, p. 52. William Cabell Rives, *History of the Life and Times of James Madison*, Boston, 1858-68, Vol. I, pp. 43 and 53, contains Madison's letters to Bradford of January 24 and April 1, 1774; John Leland, *Virginia Chronicle*, Fredericksburg, 1790, records his relations with Madison.

The petitions of the various religious bodies to the Virginia Assembly are collected in the *Virginia Magazine of History and*

Biography, Vol. 18, pp. 140-43 and 255-70; the *Journal* of the Richmond Convention for August 16, 1775, records the exception granted dissenting denominations for conducting services for their members in the army. The mittimus of Jeremiah Moore is cited in Thom.

Mason's and Madison's texts for the article on religious liberty in the Virginia Bill of Rights are quoted in James, Semple, and Thom. James cites the Church of England clergy's petition; that of the Augusta County Scotch-Irish is in the *Virginia Magazine,* Vol. 8, p. 149.

The Report of the Committee of Law Revisors was published by Order of the General Assembly, June 1, 1784; Jefferson's proposed Statute of Religious Freedom is recorded in Hening, Vol. XII, p. 84. Madison's thoughts on "Ecclesiastical Endowments" are part of his "Essay on Monopolies" in his *Detached Memoranda,* in the *William and Mary Quarterly,* third series, Vol. III, pp. 551-62, and his biographer Irving Brant summarizes them in Vol. VIII, pp. 3-24. Madison's letter to George Mason's grandson is in *The Writings of James Madison,* Gaillard Hunt, ed., New York, 1900-10.

CHAPTER II

For this chapter, as for Chapters VII and IX, the essential documentation has been collected in a small number of sources. At the turn of the century, Livingston Rutherford, in his *John Peter Zenger, His Press, His Trial, and a Bibliography of Zenger Imprints, also a Reprint of the First Edition of His Trial,* New York, 1904, assembled practically all relevant material, including the political ballads that were indicted along with Zenger's paper. This book is out of print, but Vincent Buranelli, ed., *The Trial of Peter Zenger,* New York, 1957, and Stanley N. Katz's new edition of the trial, with commentary, *John Peter Zenger, Printer of the New-York Weekly Journal, by James Alexander,* Cambridge, 1963, makes the material easily accessible again.

A near-contemporary account of the case and the incidents that formed its background are in William Smith, Jr., *History of the Late Province of New-York from Its Discovery to the Appointment of Governor Colden in 1762,* New York, 1830; Smith's father was one of Zenger's original lawyers. Chief Justice Mr. Lewis Morris' opinion that occasioned his dismissal by the governor is in his *The Opinion and Argument of the Chief Justice of the Province of New-York, Concerning the Jurisdiction of the Supream Court of the Said*

Province, to Determine Causes in a Course of Equity, New York, 1733. Later accounts of the trial and its surrounding circumstances are in James Grant Wilson, *Memorial History of the City of New-York,* New York, 1891-92, and I. N. Phelps Stokes, *Iconography of Manhattan Island,* Vol. IV, New York, 1922; Peleg Whitman Chandler, *American Criminal Trials,* Boston, 1841, likewise covers the trial. A brief summary of the background and the subsequent influence of this trial is in Richard L. Perry, ed., *Sources of Our Liberties,* New York, 1959, pp. 306-9; the slow rate at which opinion changed is demonstrated in Leonard W. Levy, "Did the Zenger Case Really Matter?" *William and Mary Quarterly,* third series, Vol. XVII, pp. 35-50.

The Bradford case is equally well documented but in less accessible form. The Rare Book Room of the Library of Congress has copies of *The Plea of the Innocent against the False Judgment of the Guilty, a Justification of George Keith and His Friends,* Philadelphia, 1692, the record of his trial that Bradford published in New York in 1693; *New England's Spirit of Persecution Transmitted to Pennsilvania; And the Pretended Quaker Found Persecuting the True Christian Quaker in the Tryal of Peter Boss, George Keith, Thomas Budd & William Bradford; At the Sessions Held at Philadelphia the Nineth, Tenth and Twelfth Days of December, 1692;* and Daniel Leeds, *News of a Trumpet Sounding in the Wilderness,* New York, 1697. *The Tryals of Peter Boss, George Keith, Thomas Budd and William Bradford, Quakers* was published in London, 1693.

In addition to the textual quotations taken from Rutherford, Smith, and *The Tryals of Peter Boss . . .* , the following are specific references:

Berkeley's dictum is in William Waller Hening, ed., *Statutes at Large . . .* , Richmond, 1809-1923, Vol. II, p. 517; that of the Continental Congress, in *Sources of Our Liberties,* p. 285. Milton's plea is in Bartlett's *Familiar Quotations,* 12th ed., Boston, 1948, p. 163. The Licensing Act is 13 and 14 Charles II, c. 33.

Bradford's apologia is in Stokes, Vol. IV, p. 546. Sir William Blackstone's interpretation of freedom of the press occurs in his *Commentaries,* 9th ed., Vol. IV, pp. 151-52.

William Penn's account of the Bushell case is in his *People's Antient and Just Liberties Asserted,* London, 1682, and in Howell, *State Trials,* Vol. VI, p. 999 *et passim.*

Later publications of the records of the Zenger case, with commentary, is covered in Katz; Fox's Libel Act is 32 Geo. III, c. 60. The American Alien and Sedition Acts, I US Statutes at Large, 597, are considered in James Morton Smith, *Freedom's Fetters: The Alien and Sedition Laws and American Civil Liberties*, Ithaca, 1956. The Croswell case, containing Alexander Hamilton's argument, is in 3 Johnson's Reports, New York Supreme Court, pp. 337-59.

Files of the two rival papers, *The New-York Gazette* and *The New-York Weekly Journal*, exist in a fair degree of completeness. The subjects and dates of excerpts quoted are: *The New-York Gazette* on the governor's installation, July 31, 1732; human nature, February 8, 1731/2; the swearing-in ceremony, October 14, 1733; calumny, October 29, 1733; the address to His Excellency, June 3, 1734; and *The New-York Weekly Journal* on Francis Harrison, November 26, 1733; the Van Dam case, December 3, 1773; names of royal governors, December 24, 1733.

Among other sources, reference should be made to George Dana Boardman, *Early Printing in the Middle Colonies*, Philadelphia, 1885 (?); James A. Gallagher, *William Bradford, Printer to the King*, New York, 1930; Charles R. Hildeburn, *A Century of Printing: the Issues of the Press in Pennsylvania*, New York, 1885, Vol. I.

The Grolier Club issued a *Catalogue of Books Printed by William Bradford, and Other Printers of the Middle Colonies*, New York, 1893. John William Wallace's *Address*, May 20, 1863, Albany, 1863, on the occasion of the bicentennary of Bradford's birth gives biographical data; John Peter Zenger's life is covered in the *Pennsylvania Magazine of History and Biography*, Vol. X, p. 385 *et passim*; Andrew Hamilton's early years have recently been reworked by Foster C. Nix in the *William and Mary Quarterly*, third series, Vol. XXI, pp. 390-407.

CHAPTER III

Partisanship is a standard feature of the reporting of civil wars. It permeates all contemporary accounts of Bacon's Rebellion, and persists in modern reassessments. Wilcomb E. Washburn, *The Governor and the Rebel: A History of Bacon's Rebellion in Virginia*, Chapel Hill, 1957, does very well by Berkeley; Thomas Jefferson Wertenbaker, *Torchbearer of the Revolution: The Story of Bacon's*

Rebellion and Its Leader, Princeton, 1940, does equally well by Bacon. Both, especially the former, provide excellent documentation of the entire episode.

H. R. McElwaine, ed., *Journals of the House of Burgesses of Virginia 1659/60-1693,* Richmond, 1914, and *Minutes of the Council and General Court of Colonial Virginia, 1622-32, 1670-1676, with Notes Excerpts from the Original Council and General Court Records, into 1683, Now Lost,* Richmond, 1924, and William Waller Hening, ed., *Statutes at Large . . . ,* Vol. II (1660-1682), Richmond, 1809-1923, provide the essential records. (Hening teases the reader with one tantalizing item. After both husbands were dead, Mrs. Drummond brought suit against Lady Berkeley for having sent her servants to strip Mrs. Drummond's land. Of this case, Hening, Vol. II, p. 558, writes: "The evidence is not confined to the mere action of trespass, but goes fully into the character of Sir William Berkeley, of Drummond and his wife, during the rebellion, and discloses many curious facts in relation to those times. It is to be regretted that want of room prevents its insertion entire." And no one else's transcript has yet been located.)

Other data on the rebellion is copious but scattered. Charles McLean Andrews, *Narratives of the Insurrections, 1675-1690,* New York, 1952, reproduces documents on all the seventeenth-century insurrections up and down the coast. The Charleston revolt of 1719 is covered in Edward McCrady, *History of South Carolina Under the Royal Government, 1719-1776,* New York, 1899, beginning on p. 624. The Albemarle incident, which collaterally involved Sir William Berkeley, is reviewed in *Colonial Records of North Carolina,* Vol. I, beginning on p. 228.

The documents on Bacon's Rebellion included in Andrews are: His Majesty's Commissioners, *A True Narrative of the Rise, Progresse, and Cessation of the Late Rebellion in Virginia,* 1677 (also reproduced in the *Virginia Magazine,* Vol. 4, pp. 117-54); T. M. (Thomas Mathew), *The Beginning, Progress, and Conclusion of Bacons Rebellion in Virginia in the Years 1675 and 1676,* 1705; (the Burwell MSS) *The History of Bacon's and Ingram's Rebellion,* 1676.

Earl Gregg Swem, *Virginia Historical Index,* Roanoke, 1934-36, permits quick access to the multitude of articles and transcripts from both London and Virginia sources contained in the major Virginia historical magazines. Philip Alexander Bruce, author of Volume I of the *History of Virginia* published by the American Historical

Society, Chicago and New York, 1924, covers the period, as does Burk (see p. 230). Force, *Tracts,* Vol. I, gives *The Indians Proseedings, Bacon's Proseedings, and Bacon's Epitaph.* Harry Firestone, ed., *Bacon's Rebellion: The Contemporary News Sheets,* Charlottesville, 1956, contains *Strange News from Virginia* and *More News from Virginia,* two pamphlets published in London in 1676.

The Jefferson quote on the tree of liberty is from a letter to Colonel William S. Smith, reproduced in *The Writings of Thomas Jefferson,* ed. by Paul Leicester Ford, New York, 1892-99, Vol. IV, p. 467. The Hen incident is described in Mathew's account, Andrews (listed above), p. 16. The twin odes are also in Andrews, pp. 75-76. The commissioners' description of Bacon is in the *Virginia Magazine,* Vol. 4, p. 122, and his oath is on p. 124. Berkeley's letter to Ludwell is cited in Washburn, p. 187; the frontiersmen's comment on him in Andrews, p. 20. The commissioners' conclusion on the beaver trade is in the *Virginia Magazine,* Vol. 4, p. 121; the governor's castigation of the slaughter of the Susquehannocks is found in Andrews, p. 23. The popular reaction to the new taxes is in the *Virginia Magazine,* Vol. 4, p. 121; the reaction to confiscation, in Andrews, p. 20.

The Ludwell estimate of the power of the governor is in Bruce, p. 192; Berkeley's mood of 1651, in the *Virginia Magazine,* Vol. 1, p. 77; and his 1671 report in Hening, Vol. II, p. 517. The charge against his appointments to the council is in the *Virginia Magazine,* Vol. 2, pp. 134-35; it was part of the Charles City County attack on the Edward Hills, reproduced on pp. 132-47. The defense of Colonel Edward Hill, Jr., is in Vol. 3, 239-52.

Bacon's enrollment ceremony is described in the *Virginia Magazine,* Vol. 4, p. 125; his "Humble Appeal," in Vol. 1, p. 58; his exchange with the governor and his action at the Occaneechee's trading center, in the *William and Mary Quarterly,* first series, Vol. IX, pp. 1-4. The Smith and Ludwell letter is in the *Virginia Magazine,* Vol. 1, p. 134.

The commissioners' report on the spring election may be found in the *Virginia Magazine,* Vol. 4, p. 127. Andrews, p. 27, describes Lawrence and Drummond; Bacon's interview with his cousin is given in the *Virginia Magazine,* Vol. 5, pp. 64-65; his apology to the governor, in the *William and Mary Quarterly,* first series, Vol. IX, p. 8, and Hening, Vol. II, pp. 534-44. The appearance of the Queen of the Pamunkeys before the assembly is recounted in Andrews, pp. 25-26; the confrontation of Bacon and Berkeley, in Andrews, pp. 29-30, and in the *Virginia Magazine,* Vol. 4, p. 130.

Thomas Mathew's notes on the June assembly are in the appendix of his account. They are supported by the Burwell MSS; William Sherwood, *Virginia's Deploured Condition,* 1676, Massachusetts Historical Society Collections, fourth series, Vol. IX, beginning on p. 162; and *Virginia Magazine,* Vol. 1, p. 59. (Sherwood succeeded in writing on both sides of the Rebellion; the *Deploured Condition* is strongly pro-Berkeley, but after a trip to London, he returned to write against him in the spring of 1677, in correspondence with Secretary of State Williamson. Hening, Vol. II, p. 341 *et passim,* reproduces the laws passed by the June assembly. William Sherwood's comment on them is in the *Virginia Magazine,* Vol. 1, p. 168.

The letters of Mrs. Bacon to her sister are in the *Virginia Magazine,* Vol. 5, pp. 219-20; his father's petition to the King, in Vol. 1, pp. 430-31.

Berkeley's reply to the Gloucester County complaints is in the Massachusetts Historical Society Collections, fourth series, Vol. IX, p. 183; the commissioners' account of the incident, in Andrews, p. 121.

Bacon's "Declaration of the People" is in the *Virginia Magazine,* Vol. 4, pp. 59-61; the oath prescribed thereafter is on p. 135; his exhortations to his men are reproduced on pp. 139-42; Berkeley's decision to leave Jamestown, on p. 148. Bacon's denunciation of the governor is in Andrews, p. 137; the incident of the kidnapped wives, in the *William and Mary Quarterly,* first series, Vol. XVIII, pp. 115-29.

The death of Bacon is reported in the *Virginia Magazine,* Vol. 4, pp. 148 and 153; Berkeley's comment on it, in the *William and Mary Quarterly,* third series, Vol. XIV, p. 412.

Bacon's request for an audit by Whitehall is in the *William and Mary Quarterly,* first series, Vol. IX, p. 9. The rebels' condemnations are listed in the *Minutes of the Council,* p. 454 *et passim,* and in Hening, Vol. II, pp. 545-48. Berkeley's interchange with Drummond is in *Tyler's Historical Magazine,* Vol. I, p. 249; Mathew's warning to him and the Burwell MSS account of his death, in Andrews. Other trials are reported in *Tyler's Historical Magazine,* Vol. I, pp. 248-54.

Ludwell's remark on Moryson is in the *Virginia Magazine,* Vol. 1, p. 176.

The acts passed by the Virginia Assembly of February, 1777, are reproduced in Hening, Vol. II, pp. 366-401; the incident at Rappahannock is in the *Minutes of the Council,* p. 534.

Lady Berkeley's last letter to her husband is in the *Virginia Magazine,* Vol. 33, p. 352; Mathew's account of the governor's death, in Andrews, pp. 39-40. The Virginia Assembly's resolution for a fast day is in Hening, Vol. II, p. 400.

The comet mentioned by Mathew—his recollection was a year early—is substantiated in Fernand Baldet and G. de Obaldia, *Catalogue Général des Orbites de Comètes de l'an 466 à 1952,* Paris, 1952; it was Halley who recorded the bright passage of May 6, 1677.

CHAPTER IV

GENERAL REFERENCES

Becker, Carl L. *History of the Political Parties in the Province of New York, 1760-1776.* Madison, 1909.

Calendar of Council Minutes, 1668-1783 (New York State Library Bulletin No. 58). Albany, 1902.

Collections on the History of Albany, from Its Discovery to the Present Time, ed. by Joel Munsell. 4 vols. Albany, 1865-71.

The Colonial Laws of New York from the Year 1664 to the Revolution. Albany, 1894-96.

The Documentary History of the State of New York, comp. by Edmund Bailey O'Callaghan. Albany, 1849-51.

Jones, Thomas. *History of New York during the Revolutionary War,* ed. by Edward Floyd de Lancey. New York, 1879.

Journal of the Votes and Proceedings of the General Assembly of the Colony of New York from 1766 to 1776 Inclusive. Albany, 1820.

Journal of the Legislative Council of the Colony of New-York, 1691-1775, comp. by Edmund Bailey O'Callaghan. Albany, 1861.

Pargellis, Stanley McC. *Lord Loudoun in North America.* New Haven, 1933.

Smith, William, Jr. *The History of the Late Province of New-York, from Its Discovery to the Appointment of Governor Colden, in 1762.* New York, 1830.

Wilson, James Grant, ed. *Memorial History of the City of New-York.* New York, 1892-93.

239

Braddock's last words are quoted in the *Dictionary of American Biography*. The Petition of Right of 1628 is reproduced in Richard L. Perry, ed., *Sources of Our Liberties*, New York, 1959, pp. 73-75; the Bill of Rights of 1689, pp. 245-50. Lord Loudoun's billeting problems are fully reviewed in Pargellis (listed above); the official action of the New York Assembly, in *New York Colonial Documents*, Vol. VII, p. 204, and *The Colonial Laws*, Vol. VI, p. 123. The provisions of the Quartering Act of 1765 are noted in *Sources of Our Liberties*, p. 72. The *Journal of the Votes* for January 20, 1769, reports the results of the assembly election; the events of the session on December 5 are recorded beginning on p. 37.

The broadside addressed "To the betrayed inhabitants" is reproduced in *Documentary History* (listed above), pp. 317-21; the house action on it, in its *Journal*, p. 37.

Alexander MacDougall's account of his exchange with Chief Justice Horsmanden was printed in *The New-York Journal; or, The General Advertiser* for February 15, 1770, and reprinted in *The Massachusetts Gazette; and the Boston Weekly News-letter* for February 22.

Colden's letters to Hillsborough are given in Jones, pp. 431-32, along with his own version of MacDougall's imprisonment; it is likewise discussed in I. N. Phelps Stokes, *Iconography of Manhattan Island*, New York, 1922, Vol. III, p. 864. The *Calendar of Council Minutes*, p. 481, reports the opening of MacDougall's trial and Cummins collection of his reward.

MacDougall's appearance before the bar of the house is minuted in the assembly's *Journal* for December 13; the house action on the writ of habeas corpus served by the supreme court on the sheriff, its appointment of a committee to search the House of Commons records on prerogative imprisonment, and the report of this committee are in the *Journal* for January 19 and 22 and February 16. The precedent quoted is from the *Journal of the House of Commons*, Vol. XII, p. 565. The November resolution of the New York Sons of Liberty is reproduced in *Sources of Our Liberties*, p. 277.

The public assemblies in New York beginning on May 16, 1774, are reported in Jones, pp. 442-43; Gouverneur Morris' letter to Governor Penn, on p. 445; and Colden's letter to Dartmouth, on pp. 468-69. The resolves of the First Continental Congress are reproduced in *Sources of Our Liberties*, pp. 286-89. Wilson gives a full general account of this entire period.

CHAPTER V

GENERAL REFERENCES

Adams, John. *The Works of John Adams . . .*, ed. by Charles Francis Adams. Boston, 1850-56. Vol. II contains his Diary and Autobiography. Appendix A, pp. 521-25, gives his Notes on the Argument of Counsel, in the Cause of Writs of Assistance, and of the Speech of James Otis, 1761. Vol. X, Boston, 1856, presents his correspondence with William Tudor regarding Otis, pp. 244-53.

Dickerson, Oliver Morton. *The Navigation Acts and the American Revolution*. Philadelphia, 1951.

Hickman, Emily. "Colonial Writs of Assistance," *New England Quarterly*, Vol. V, pp. 83-104.

Hutchinson, Thomas. *History of Massachusetts Bay*, Vol. III. Boston, 1828.

Minot, George Richards. *Continuation of the History of the Province of Massachusetts from the year 1748*. Boston, 1798-1803.

Otis, James. *A Vindication of the Conduct of the House of Representatives of the Province of Massachusetts Bay*. Boston, 1762.

———. *The Rights of the British Colonies Asserted and Proved*. Boston, 1764.

———. *A Vindication of the British Colonies*. Boston, 1765.

Paine, Charles Cushing. "Memoranda of the Cushing Family," MSS in the Massachusetts Historical Society. Boston, Mass.

Quincy, Josiah, Jr. *Reports of Cases Argued and Adjudged in the Superior Court of Judicature of the Province of Massachusetts Bay between 1761 and 1772*. Boston, 1865.

Ridpath, John Clark. *James Otis the Pre-revolutionist*. Chicago, 1888.

Tudor, William. *Life of James Otis of Massachusetts*. Boston, 1823.

Winslow, Warren. "The Colonial Customs Service in Massachusetts and Its Relation to the American Revolution." *Proceedings*, Massachusetts Historical Society, Vol. XLVI, pp. 440-74.

Wolkins, George G. "Writs of Assistance in England." *Proceedings*, Massachusetts Historical Society, Vol. LVIII, pp. 5-84.

Tudor's assessment of the early New England economy is in his 1823 edition, p. 50. The strictures of *The Virginia Gazette* on customs officials appeared May 27, 1773. The estimate of the cost of customs' collections and their yields is in Edward Channing, *History of the United States,* New York, 1929, Vol. III, p. 36.

William Pitt's charge of trading with the enemy is in Quincy (listed above), p. 411; the wording of Charles Paxton's writ, on p. 402. Minot, Vol. II, pp. 87-99, reviews the issuance of writs in Massachusetts.

Hutchinson, Vol. III, p. 86, discusses the Otis family's disappointment at his nomination to the court; the "Memoranda" of the Cushing family suggests the social cleavages that exacerbated it. Quincy, pp. 412-14, cites Lechmere's request to be heard at the same time as the merchants on the propriety of issuance of writs of assistance.

In addition to the *Dictionary of American Biography,* John Sibley, *Biographical Sketches of Graduates of Harvard University,* Cambridge, 1873-1942, is useful for information concerning the individuals participating in the hearing. The various versions of Adams' description of the scene are discussed by Samuel Abbott Green in *Proceedings,* Massachussetts Historical Society, second series, Vol. 59; the version quoted is from Adams, *Works,* Vol. X, 244-45. Quincy gives Keith's and Adams' notes, cites the points made in the argument, and gives a sample writ.

Hutchinson, Vol. III, p. 54, tells of his ruling at the end of the hearing; Hickman reports the court's November decision. Minot quotes Chief Justice Ruggles on the May, 1761, election.

The letter to Bollan on the actions of the new assembly is in *Proceedings,* Massachusetts Historical Society, Vol. 59, p. 415. The governor's correspondence with Lord Egremont is given by Quincy, p. 395 *et passim*; the customs house comedy is reported in Dickerson and in Massachusetts Historical Society Collections, sixth series, Vol. IX, pp. 29-39. The chief justice's willingness to limit individual rights is cited in Quincy, pp. 446-47. Wolkins reviews the Malcolm case; the quotes from Malcolm are in the *Dictionary of American Biography.* Dickerson analyzes the results of the establishment of the American Board of Customs and the *Liberty* incident, pp. 211-31; Hutchinson reports it, Vol. III, pp. 189-91.

The quote from Otis' *Vindication* is from p. 17 of the 1762 edition.

The attack on the writs by the Committee of Twenty-One is recorded in Quincy, pp. 446-47; Adams, *Works,* Vol. IV, p. 219 *et passim* reports the action of the Massachusetts Provincial Congress in May, 1775, and the circumstances of his drafting of the Declaration of Rights accepted by the Commonwealth of Massachusetts in 1780.

CHAPTER VI

GENERAL REFERENCES

Carpenter, A. H. "Habeas Corpus in the Colonies," *American Historical Review,* Vol. VIII, pp. 18-27.

Drayton, John. *Memoirs of the American Revolution from Its Commencement to the Year 1776, Inclusive; as Relating to the State of South-Carolina.* Charleston, 1821.

(Drayton, William Henry.) A letter from Freeman of South Carolina. Charleston, 1774.

Gibbes, Robert Wilson. *Documentary History of the American Revolution.* Columbia, S. C., 1853.

Guess, William Francis. *South Carolina: Annals of Pride and Protest.* New York, 1960.

Hening, Helen Kohn. *Great South Carolinians.* Chapel Hill, 1940.

Hewatt, Alexander. *An Historical Account of the Rise and Progress of the Colonies of South Carolina and Georgia.* London, 1779.

Journals of the Colonial Council of South Carolina.

(Milligen, George.) *A Short Description of the Province of South Carolina, with an Account of the Air, Weather, and Diseases, at Charlestown, Written in the Year 1763.* London, 1770.

McCrady, Edward. *The History of South Carolina under the Royal Government, 1719-1776.* New York, 1899.

O'Neall, John Belton. *Bench and Bar of South Carolina.* Charleston, 1859.

Quincy, Josiah, ed. *Memoirs of Josiah Quincy, Jr., 1744-75.* Boston, 1875.

Ramsay, David. *History of South Carolina.* Charleston, 1809.

Salley, Alexander Samuel, Jr. *Delegates to the Continental Congress from South Carolina* (South Carolina Year Book). Charleston, 1895.

Snowden, Yates. *History of South Carolina.* Chicago, 1920.

Magna Carta's 39th article is quoted in Richard L. Perry, ed., *Sources of Our Liberties,* New York, 1959, p. 17; the entire document, pp. 11-22. The circumstances leading to the adoption of the

Petition of Right in 1628 are considered, and the petition cited, on pp. 62-75; its Article V is on p. 74.

Americans reading law at Middle Temple are listed in McCrady (listed above), p. 475. The Charlestonians deported to St. Augustine are named in Edward McCrady, *History of South Carolina in the Revolution, 1775-1780,* New York, 1901, pp. 715-30; the roster of the post-Revolutionary act of attainder, in South Carolina's *Statutes at Large,* Vol. VI, pp. 629-35.

The correspondence in *The South Carolina Gazette* during 1769, including William Henry Drayton's insult to Christopher Gadsden, Gadsden's retort to it, and Drayton's scorn for Gadsden's constituency are discussed and reproduced in McCrady, *S. C. under Royal Government,* pp. 644-58; the assembly's contribution to Wilkes, pp. 662-64.

Biographical detail on the Draytons, Gadsden, the Rutledges, and William Wragge is available in Helen Kohn Hening, O'Neall, and Salley.

The exchange between the governor and the assembly over the Beaufort session is in McCrady, *S. C. Under Royal Government,* pp. 695-704; Alexander Samuel Salley, Jr., *The State Houses of South Carolina, 1751-1936,* Columbia, S. C., 1937, describes Charleston's mid-eighteenth-century building. Josiah Quincy, Jr.'s impression of the St. Cecilia concert is on p. 70 of his *Memoirs.*

The disagreement within the council, ending in Powell's citation for contempt, is covered in McCrady, *S. C. Under Royal Government,* pp. 713-716.

O'Neall's sketches of Edward and John Rutledge include John's letter to Edward when abroad. Edward's argument against the council's power to commit for contempt is quoted in Snowden, pp. 301-2, and McCrady, *S. C. Under Royal Government,* pp. 718-20. Justice Lowndes' ruling on Powell's commitment is in McCrady, *S. C. Under Royal Government,* pp. 720-21.

Drayton's memorial to the Continental Congress is in Gibbes, p. 11; his charges to the upcountry grand juries, in Snowden, pp. 306-7; and the response of the Cheraws grand jury in McCrady, *S. C. Under Royal Government,* p. 751.

The exchange between Drayton and the other justices, his suspension from the council, and his emergence as head of the Committees of Intelligence are covered in Gibbes, pp. 39-55.

CHAPTER VII

The essential information for this chapter is assembled in *The Records of the Colony of Rhode Island and Providence Plantations, 1770-1776,* ed. by John Russell Bartlett, Providence, 1862, Vol. VII. Earlier, William R. Staples had prepared his *Documentary History of the Destruction of the Gaspee,* compiled for the *Providence Journal,* Providence, 1845, and Samuel Greene Arnold had published his *History of the State of Rhode Island and Providence Plantations,* New York, 1860, of which Vol. II treats of the *Gaspee* affair. Collateral sources include: Antoinette Forrester Downing and Vincent Scully, *The Architectural Heritage of Newport, Rhode Island, 1640-1915,* Cambridge, 1952; David Fisher, "Commodore Abraham Whipple," *Ohio Archaeological and Historical Quarterly,* Vol. II, pp. 180-86; James Blaine Hedges, *The Browns of Providence Plantations,* Cambridge, 1952; Arthur M. Schlesinger, *The Colonial Merchants and the American Revolution, 1763-1776,* New York, 1918; and William B. Weeden, *Early Rhode Island: A Social History of the People,* New York, 1910.

John Adams' *Instructions* are reproduced in Henry Steele Commager, ed., *Documents of American History,* New York, 6th ed. 1958, Vol. I, pp. 56-57. Governor Wanton's letter to Admiral Montagu is found in *Records,* p. 63; Chief Justice Hopkins' ruling on the duties of navy commanders, on p. 60. The business interests of the Browns are analyzed in Hedges.

Arnold describes the departures from Fenner's wharf. The dialogues at the time of boarding *Gaspee* and the following morning are in *Records,* pp. 68-76, as are the letters from Wanton to Hillsborough, pp. 90-92, and Dartmouth to Wanton, pp. 103-4.

The King's proclamation of rewards is on p. 107 of the *Records;* the judges commissions are on p. 108, their instructions, pp. 110-12; the depositions from the ship's company are on pp. 82-84, and that from Aaron Briggs, on pp. 93-94.

The Stephen Gulley episode is covered on pp. 133-35 of the *Records;* Briggs's testimony to the tribunal, on p. 136.

The excuses of the Providence inn-keeper, captain, judge, and lawyers whom Montagu asked to have summoned to Newport fill pp. 154-58 of the *Records;* the court finding on the Briggs deposition is on p. 175; and the tribunal's letter to Dartmouth and final report to the King are on pp. 177-82.

The aftermath of the hearing, in newspapers and private letters, follows the account of the above events; the quoted ballad is on p. 191.

The events which led to the appointment of committees of correspondence are discussed in Schlesinger; the Declaration and Resolves of the First Continental Congress are given in full in Richard L. Perry, *Sources of Our Liberties,* New York, 1959, pp. 286-89, and the Declaration of the Causes and Necessity of Taking Up Arms of the following year on pp. 295-300.

Chief Justice Horsmanden's letter to Dartmouth on the Rhode Island Constitution is in *Records,* pp. 182-85.

CHAPTER VIII

GENERAL REFERENCES

Calendar of Council Minutes, 1668-1783 (New York State Library Bulletin No. 58). Albany, 1902.

Colden, Cadwallader. "The Colden Letter Books," *New-York Historical Society Collections,* Vols. I and II.

———. "Letters and Papers of Cadwallader Colden . . . ," *New-York Historical Society Collections,* Vols. VI, VII, and IX.

The Colonial Laws of New York from the Year 1664 to the Revolution. Albany, 1894-96.

Documents Relative to the Colonial History of the State of New York. Albany, 1853-87.

Dunlap, William. *History of the New Netherlands . . . to the Adoption of the Federal Constitution.* New York, 1839-40.

Goebel, Julius, and Naughton, T. Raymond. *Law Enforcement in Colonial New York*: A Study in Criminal Procedure, 1664-1776. New York, 1944.

Jones, Thomas. *History of New York during the Revolutionary War,* ed. by Edward Floyd de Lancey. New York, 1879.

Journal of the Legislative Council of the Colony of New-York, 1691-1775, comp. by Edmund Bailey O'Callaghan. Albany, 1861.

Journal of the Votes and Proceedings of the General Assembly of the Colony of New York from 1766 to 1776 Inclusive. Albany, 1820.

Keys, Alice Maplesden. *Cadwallader Colden: A Representative Eighteenth Century Official.* New York, 1906.

246

Stokes, I. N. Phelps. *Iconography of Manhattan Island.* New York, 1915-28.

Wilson, James Grant. *The Memorial History of the City of New York.* New York, 1892.

King Charles II's grant to the Duke of York is in *Colonial Laws* (listed above), pp. 22-23.

The incident that initiated the *Forsey v. Cunningham* case is described in the Colden "Papers" (listed above), Vol. VI, p. 236, in Lord Halifax's letter dated September 3, 1763, instructing Colden what to do if Forsey died. Cunningham's other legal difficulties are detailed in the *Calendar of Council Minutes* and the *Report of an Action of Assault, Battery & Wounding, Tried in the Supreme Court of New York,* New York, 1764. Goebel and Naughton deal with his problems in depth.

The difference between Monckton's instructions and those of preceding governors is noted in Keys, p. 305.

The *Dictionary of American Biography* should be consulted for Colden, the "triumvirate," and others connected with the case. Chief Justice Pratt's letter to Pownall is in Colden, "Papers," Vol. VI, p. 115. The attorney general's report to Colden is on pp. 368-69; Smith's comment on Colden in William Smith Manuscripts, Vol. 4, under date of November 24, 1761. The quoted "Sentinel" column is from *The New-York Gazette* of August 23, 1765.

Chief Justice Horsmanden's presentation of the supreme court's view was published in the *Gazette* of January 17, 1765, and is in Colden, "Papers," Vol. VI, pp. 379-96; Harrison's report on the conversation at the Fort is on pp. 387-88. Justice Livingston's position was published in the *Gazette* for December 12, 1764.

The council's January 11, 1765, meeting is reported in Colden, "Papers," Vol. IX, pp. 205-6; Colden's memorandum, in Vol. VII, pp. 1-6. The council's decision is in the *Calendar of Council Minutes.*

Colden's comment on the *Gazette* is in Colden, "Papers," Vol. VII, p. 29. The New York Assembly's resolution on the case is in its *Journal.*

The pertinent articles from the Declaration of Rights of the Stamp Act Congress are given in Richard L. Perry, ed., *Sources of Our Liberties,* New York, 1959, p. 270.

Evers' resignation is in Colden, "Papers," Vol. VIII, p. 60.

Whitehall's work on the request for an appeal and on the instructions to the new governor of New York is reproduced in Colden, "Letter Books," Vol. II, pp. 39-42. His communication to Chief Justice Horsmanden is in Goebel and Naughton, p. 235, n. 47; the supreme court's reply is in *Manuscript Minutes of the Supreme Court of Judicature, 1764-67* (New York County Hall of Records), p. 125.

Stokes, Vol. IV, p. 750, quotes Montresor's description of the effigy of Colden. The *Gazette* of December 5, 1765, cites the New York City Council's welcome to the new governor, and Colden, "Papers," Vol. VII, p. 95, gives his new instructions.

CHAPTER IX

Volume VII-X (1762-1776) of the *Colonial Records of North Carolina,* ed. by William L. Saunders, Raleigh, 1886-1890, contain practically all of the requisite documents on the Regulators.

GENERAL REFERENCES

Boyd, William Kenneth. *Some Eighteenth Century Tracts concerning North Carolina.* Raleigh, 1927.

Dill, Alonzo Thomas. *Governor Tryon and His Palace.* Chapel Hill, 1955.

Fitch, William Edward. *Some Neglected History of North Carolina.* New York, 1905.

Foote, William Henry. *Sketches of North Carolina, Historical and Biographical.* New York, 1846.

Hawks, Rev. Francis L. *History of North Carolina,* ed. by William D. Cooke. New York, 1853.

Haywood, Marshall deLancey. *Governor Tryon and His Administration in the Province of North Carolina, 1765-1771.* Raleigh, 1903.

Henderson, Archibald. *The Origin of the Regulation in North Carolina.* New York, 1916.

Hooker, Richard J., ed. *The Carolina Backcountry on the Eve of the Revolution: The Journal and Other Writings of Charles Woodmason, Anglican Itinerant.* Chapel Hill, 1953.

Hudson, Arthur Palmer. "Songs of the Regulators," *William and Mary Quarterly,* third series, Vol. IV, pp. 470-85.

(Husband, Hermon?). *A Fan for Fanning and a Touch-stone to Tryon by Regulus.* Boston, 1771.

———. *Impartial Relation of the First Rise and Cause of the Recent Difficulties in Public Affairs in the Province of North Carolina and of the Past Tumults and Riots That Lately Happened in That Province.* Boston, 1770.

Lazenby, Mary E. *Herman Husband: A Story of his Life.* Washington, 1940.

Lefler, Hugh T., and Paul Wager. *Orange County, 1752-1952.* Chapel Hill, 1953.

Powell, William S. *The War of the Regulation and the Battle of Alamance, May 16, 1771.* Raleigh, 1949.

Williamson, Hugh. *History of North Carolina.* Philadelphia, 1812.

Thomas Bayly Howell, ed., *A Complete Collection of State Trials and Proceedings for High Treason and Other Crimes and Misdemeanors from the Earliest Period to the Year 1783,* London, 1816, Vols. VI and VIII, reproduces the charges brought against Clarendon and Scroggs. Lefler (listed above), Vol. I, pp. 191-99, cites the complaint against Frohock; *Colonial Records,* Vol. VII, p. 294, quotes Tryon's report on the sheriff's embezzlements. Hudson's song collection includes the ballad on Fanning, whose biography is in E. W. Caruthers, *Revolutionary Incidents and Sketches of Character, Chiefly in the "Old North State,"* Philadelphia, 1854. Husband's parable is in *Colonial Records,* Vol. VII, pp. 89-90.

The story of the construction of Tryon's palace is given in full in Dill.

The petition of Orange and Rowan counties is in Fitch, pp. 126-28; the Ned and Frank ballad, in Hudson. Fanning's complaint to the governor is in *Colonial Records,* Vol. VII, pp. 713-16; Regulator Advertisement No. 11, in Fitch, pp. 145-55. The legal advice given Fanning is in *Colonial Records,* Vol. VIII, pp. 33-36; Tryon's journal describing the calling out of troops is quoted in Vol. VII, pp. 819-38. Anson County's suggestion that Franklin be called in is in Fitch, p. 133.

Tryon's letter to Hillsborough is in *Colonial Records,* Vol. VIII, pp. 169-70; the Orange County petition of 1770, on pp. 231-34; Judge

Henderson's report of the riot, on pp. 241-44; the trials by the mock court, on pp. 236-40; Tryon's address to the legislature in December, on pp. 282-86; the expulsion of Husband, on pp. 330-31; the court session of March, 1771, on pp. 531-32; and Howell's letter, on pp. 536-37.

Williamson, Vol. II, p. 516, discusses the Riot Act. The refunds by local officials are noted in *Colonial Records,* Vol. VIII, pp. 533-36; Tryon's Order Book on the preparations for and the conduct of the Battle of Alamance, on pp. 574-600; the immediate aftermath of the battle is recorded in Vol. VIII, p. 617 *et passim*; Merrill's death as described in Tryon's Letter Book, on pp. 648-51; Merrill's death in other versions, on pp. 639-40 and 643-48; and the open letter to Tryon by "Atticus," on pp. 718-27.

The North Carolina Declaration of Rights adopted in 1776 is reprinted in *Colonial Records,* Vol. X, pp. 1003-4.

INDEX

Adams, John, 128, 129, 140, 144, 165
Adams, John Quincy, 169
Adams, Samuel, 140, 141, 179, 180
Alexander, James, 38, 41-43, 45-47, 63, 197
Alsop, John, 119
Andrews, John, 177
Andros, Governor Sir Edmund, 70, 166
Auchmuty, Robert, 128, 173
Aylesbury, Thomas, 175

Bacon, Elizabeth, 74, 83, 89
Bacon, Nathaniel, Sr., 74, 85, 95
Bacon, Nathaniel, Jr., xiv, 71, 74-76, 82-100
Bacon, Thomas, 89
Berkeley, Lady Frances Culpeper, 74, 81
Berkeley, Sir William, 30, 73, 76-87, 89-91, 93-100
Bernard, Francis, 125, 126, 129, 134-35, 136, 137, 140, 141
Berry, Captain Sir John, 95
Blackstone, Sir William, 32
Blair, Commissary John, 8, 16
Bland, Giles, 90, 92, 96
Blanton, Thomas, 88
Bollan, William, 133
Boone, Governor Thomas, 149
Borden, Joseph, 175-76
Bowdoin, James, 144
Bowen, Ephriam, 171
Braddock, Major General Edward, 102, 103
Bradford, William, Sr., 31, 40, 41, 48-57, 71
Bradford, William, Jr., 20
Bradley, Richard, 57, 58, 63
Brent, Colonel George, 73
Brent, Colonel Giles, 92, 93
Briggs, Aaron, 174, 176-77, 178
Brown, Chad, 168
Brown, George, 177
Brown, James, 168
Brown, John, 168, 175
Brown, Joseph, 168, 175
Brown, Moses, 168, 179, 182
Brown, Nicholas, 168
Brown, Obediah, 168
Brown family, 168, 175, 176

Bucklin, Joseph, 171
Bull, William, 152, 160, 162
Burke, Edmund, 165
Burnet, Governor William, 38
Butler, William, 215, 223
Byrd, Colonel William I, 74

Carver, Captain John, 90, 92
Chambers, John, 46, 57, 63, 192
Charles I, 78, 80, 102, 146, 157
Charles II, 48, 78, 80, 129, 158, 186, 204
Chisman, Edmund, 96, 97
Chisman, Lydia, 97
Clarendon, Earl of, 204
Clinton, Governor George, 192
Cockle, James, 124, 127, 130, 135
Coke, Sir Edward, 146
Colden, Cadwallader, xvi, 108, 110, 112, 114, 119, 189, 190-202
Cole, John, 178, 179, 182
Cook, Justice Arthur, 51-55
Cosby, Governor William, 35, 36-38, 44, 48
Craig, Lewis, 14-17, 20
Crewes, Captain James, 84, 96
Cruger, John, 107, 117
Cummins, Michael, 111
Cunningham, Waddell, xvi, 187-96, 198-202
Curtis, Jane, 205
Cushing, John, 125
Cushing, Thomas, 140
Custis, Colonel John, 90

Dale, Sir Thomas, 9
Dartmouth, Earl of, 119, 159, 172, 178, 183
Davies, Samuel, 11
DeLancey, James, Sr., 35, 38, 39, 42, 46, 57, 60, 61, 107, 108, 191
DeLancey, James, Jr., 108, 109, 110, 117, 197
DeLancey, John, 108
DeLancey family, 106-7, 108, 110
Dickenson, Midshipman William, 171, 174
Dobbs, Governor Arthur, 207
Dongan, Governor Thomas, 187
Drayton, Charlotte Bull, 152
Drayton, Dorothy Golightly, 150

251

Drayton, Eliza Bull, 152
Drayton, John, 152, 155
Drayton, Thomas, 152
Drayton, William Henry, 148-55, 159-62
Drayton family, 152
Drummond, William, 84-85, 92, 93, 94, 95-96
Duane, James, 119
Dudingston, Lieutenant William, 166, 167, 171-72, 175, 179
Dudley, Charles, 172
Duke, Sir Edward, 74
Dunmore, John Murray, Earl of (Governor of New York), 117

Earle, Patrick, 177
Edward III, 164
Edwards, Jonathan, 2
Egremont, Earl of, 134
Ellery, William, 169
Erving, John, 126

Fanning, Colonel Edmund, 209, 211, 214-16, 217, 220, 223, 224
Fenner, Arthur, 177, 178
Few, James, 223
Fields, Jeremiah, 216-17
Fletcher, Governor Benjamin, 56-57
Forsey, Thomas, xvi, 187-92, 199
Fox, Charles James, 33, 64
Fox, George, 48
Franklin, Benjamin, 5, 38, 40, 63, 168, 216
Frohock, Colonel John, 207, 221

Gadsden, Christopher, 148, 149, 156, 159, 160, 199
Gage, General Thomas, 105, 106, 115, 141
Gardner, Captain Thomas, 85-86
Garrick, David, 5, 150
George II, 124, 192
George III, xv, 69, 150, 173, 179
Gooch, Governor Sir William, 3, 10
Gordon, Thomas Knox, 152, 160
Gridley, Jeremiah, 128-30
Gulley, Stephen, 175

Hallowell, Ben, 140
Hallowell, Robert, 140
Halifax, Earl of, 36, 189
Hamilton, Alexander, 64, 66
Hamilton, Andrew, 2, 33, 38, 46-48, 57-63, 66
Hancock, John, 136-42, 165

Hansford, Thomas, 97
Hardy, Governor Sir Charles, 104, 105, 108
Harrison, Francis, 41-42, 43
Harrison, George, 193, 196
Hawks, John, 211
Hen, Robert, 73
Henderson, Judge Richard, 216, 217
Henry VIII, 164, 165, 182
Henry, John, 12, 13
Henry, Mrs. John, 12
Henry, Patrick, 12, 13, 20, 26
Henry, Reverend Patrick, 11, 13
Hill, Edward, Sr., 81, 86
Hill, Edward, Jr., 81-82
Hillsborough, Earl of, 112, 137, 140, 141, 165, 167, 172, 216
Hitchcock, Daniel, 178
Hopkins, John B., 169
Hopkins, Stephen, 169, 179, 180
Hopkinson, Francis, 38
Horsmanden, Chief Justice Daniel, 111, 173, 183, 192, 194-96, 198, 200
Howe, General George, 120
Howell, Rednap, 214, 219, 223
Hunt, Thomas, 57, 62
Hunter, James, 214-15, 219, 223
Hunter, Governor Robert, 41, 108
Husband, Hermon, 209, 211, 214, 215, 219, 220, 223, 224
Hutchinson, Thomas, 125-26, 129-30, 133, 135, 140, 180

James II, 56, 103, 129, 186, 204
Jauncey, James, 107
Jay, John, 64, 119, 159
Jefferson, Thomas, 3, 25-26, 66, 68-69
Jeffreys, George Jeffreys, 1st Baron, 204
Jeffreys, Colonel Herbert, 95, 97, 100
Jenkes, Francis, 204
Jennings, Justice Samuel, 51-56, 61
Jones, Thomas, 114, 192

Kearsley, John, 46
Keith, George, 50, 52, 57
Keith, Israel, 128
Kempe, John Tabor, 114, 193, 196, 198
Kempe, William, 84
Kirk, Thomas, 138, 140

Lamb, John, 111
Larrimore, Captain Thomas, 92
Lawrence, Richard, 84, 85, 87-88, 92, 93
Lechmere, Thomas, 123, 124, 127

Lee, Richard Henry, 182
Lee, Thomas Ludwell, 25
Leigh, Sir Edgerton, 152
Lilburne, John, 30
Lindsey, Captain Benjamin, 169
Linzee, Captain, 174-78
Livingston, Philip, 119
Livingston, Robert R., 192, 197, 198
Livingston, William, 190, 193
Livingston faction, 106-8, 117
Lloyd, David, 52-54
Locke, John, xi
Loudoun, Earl of, 103-4, 114
Low, Isaac, 107, 118, 119
Lowndes, Rawlins, 153, 157-59
Ludwell, Philip, 78, 92, 97
Ludwell, Thomas, 76, 83
Lynch, Thomas, 159
Lynde, Benjamin, Jr., 125

McComb, John, 50-52
MacDougall, Alexander, 63, 107, 111-18
McEvers, James, 199
Mackan, James, 17
Madison, James, xiii, 3, 4, 20-21, 24, 26-28
Malcolm, Daniel, 136-40
Manigault, Peter, 150, 154
Mary II, 10, 56, 57, 103, 204
Mason, George, xi, 3, 22, 25, 28
Mason, Colonel George, 73, 86
Mather, Cotton, 50
Mathew, Thomas, 73, 86-88, 95, 100
Maury, Reverend James, 13, 14
Mawney, John, 171
Merrill, Captain Benjamin, 223-24
Middleton, Henry, 159
Milton, John, 30
Mingo, James, 88
Monckton, Governor Sir Robert, 187, 190, 196, 202
Montagu, Governor Charles Greville, 152, 154, 155
Montagu, Admiral John, 166, 167, 171, 173, 176, 177, 179
Montgomerie, Governor John, 37, 38
Moore, Governor Sir Henry, 202
Moore, Jeremiah, 22
Moore, Judge Maurice, 215, 219, 224
Morris, Gouverneur, 119
Morris, Lewis, Sr., 38, 39, 41, 62-63, 106
Morris, Lewis, Jr., 38, 39, 41, 108, 197
Morris, Richard H., 192

Morris, Samuel, 9, 10
Moryson, Colonel Francis, 94
Munday, Richard, 167

Nash, Francis, 214
Newcastle, Duke of, 36
Nicholas, Colonel George, 28
North, Lord Frederick, 118

Oliver, Peter, 125, 126, 173
Otis, Colonel James, 125
Otis, James, Jr., 125-37, 140-42
Owen, William, 63

Pamunkeys, Queen of, 86, 92
Parker, James, 111, 115
Paxton, Charles, 123-24, 126-27, 134, 137
Pendleton, Edmund, 25, 26
Penn, Governor John, 119
Penn, William, 5, 33, 46, 47, 48, 49
Philipse, Frederick, 38, 39, 57, 106
Pinckney, Charles, 150
Pinckney, Charles Cotesworth, 150
Pinckney, Eliza Lucas, 150
Pinckney, Harriott, 150
Pinckney, Roger, 156
Pinckney, Thomas, 150
Pitt, William, 123
Powell, George Gabriel, 157, 159
Powell, Thomas, 147, 155-59, 162
Pownall, Thomas, 192
Pratt, Benjamin, 128, 129, 192

Quincy, Josiah, Jr., 148, 154
Quincy, Samuel, 128

Ramsdale, Saul, 175
Randolph, Attorney General John, 16
Ray, John, 74
Richards, Owen, 138
Rivera, Jacob Rodriguez, 168
Roan, John, 10
Robinson, John, 137, 142
Ruggles, Chief Justice Timothy, 134
Russell, Chambers, 125
Rutledge, Edward, 156-57, 159, 162
Rutledge, John, 156-57, 159

Sabin, James, 169, 177
Scott, John Morin, 107, 115, 117, 190, 193, 198
Scroggs, Sir William, 204-5

Sears, Isaac, 107, 114
Sessions, Darius, 171-72, 176, 179
Sewall, Jonothan, 138
Sewall, Stephen, 124, 126, 140
Shelburne, Earl of, 136
Sherwood, William, 88
Shirley, Governor William, 102, 133
Smith, Francis, 205
Smith, Robert, 83
Smith, William, Sr., 38, 45-46, 192-93
Smith, William, Jr., 107, 115, 190, 193, 194, 198
Smythe, Frederick, 173
Spencer, George, 188

Temple, John, 135, 137
Ten Broeck, Abraham, 108
Thacher, Oxenbridge, 128-29, 130
Thayer, Captain William, 175-76
Toovey, Sampson, 135
Tryon, Governor William, 207, 211-16, 219, 221-24
Tudor, William, 122, 129

Van Dam, Rip, 37-43, 57

Waddell, Robert, 193, 196, 200
Wafford, Thomas, 18
Waller, John, 14-15, 17-20
Wanton, Gideon, 167
Wanton, John, 167
Wanton, Governor Joseph, 167-68, 172-75, 179
Wanton, William, 167
Ward, Samuel, 169
Ware, Robert, 17, 18, 20
Washington, George, 22
Washington, Colonel John, 73
Weatherford, John, 20
Webber, William, 17-19
Wentworth, Sir Thomas, 146
Wesley, the brothers, 2, 5
Whipple, Captain Abraham, 169-71
Whitefield, George, 2, 5-9, 11, 13, 136
Wilkes, John, 112-14, 119, 149, 154
William III, 10, 56, 103, 130, 204
Wragge, William, 148
Wythe, George, 25

Zenger, John Peter, xii, 31-33, 35-36, 41, 45-48, 57-58, 61-64, 107, 112, 190

8. That in all capital or criminal prosecutions, a man hath a right to demand the cause and nature of his accusation, to be confronted with the accusers and witnesses, to call for evidence in his favour, and to a speedy trial by an impartial jury of his vicinage, without whose unanimous consent he cannot be found guilty, nor can he be compelled to give evidence against himself; and that no man be deprived of his liberty, except by the law of the land, or the judgment of his peers.

9. That excessive bail ought not to be required, nor excessive fines imposed, nor cruel and unusual punishments inflicted.

10. That in controversies respecting property, and in suits between man & man, the ancient trial by jury is preferable to any other, & ought to be held sacred.

11. That the freedom of the press is one of the great bulwarks of Liberty, and can never be restrained but by despotic governments.

12. That a well regulated Militia, composed of the Body of the people trained to arms, is the proper, natural, & safe Defence of a free State; that standing armies, in Time of Peace, should be avoided, as dangerous to Liberty; and that, in all cases, the Military should be under strict Subordination to, & governed by the civil power.

13. That no free Government, or the Blessing of Liberty can be preserved to any people but by a firm Adherence to Justice